Business Networks in Syria

Stanford Studies in Middle Eastern and Islamic Societies and Cultures

Business Networks in Syria

THE POLITICAL ECONOMY
OF AUTHORITARIAN RESILIENCE

Bassam Haddad

Stanford University Press
Stanford, California

Stanford University Press
Stanford, California

© 2012 by the Board of Trustees of the Leland Stanford Junior University. All rights reserved.

No part of this book may be reproduced or transmitted in any form or by any means, electronic or mechanical, including photocopying and recording, or in any information storage or retrieval system without the prior written permission of Stanford University Press.

Printed in the United States of America on acid-free, archival-quality paper

Library of Congress Cataloging-in-Publication Data

Haddad, Bassam, author.
  Business networks in Syria : the political economy of authoritarian resilience / Bassam S. A. Haddad.
     pages cm. — (Stanford studies in Middle Eastern and Islamic societies and cultures)
  Includes bibliographical references and index.
  ISBN 978-0-8047-7332-4 (cloth : alk. cloth)
  ISBN 978-0-8047-8506-8 (pbk. : alk. cloth)
  1. Syria—Economic policy. 2. Business networks—Syria. 3. Industrial policy—Syria.
  4. Syria—Economic conditions. 5. Syria—Politics and government—1971–2000. 6. Syria—Politics and government—2000– I. Title. II. Series: Stanford studies in Middle Eastern and Islamic societies and cultures.
  HC415.23.H33 2012
  338.8'7—dc22
                         2011012228

Typeset by Bruce Lundquist in 10/14 Minion

For Asmahan, the endless fountain and a rock for so many

"They say 'no one sleeps hungry in Syria.'
This is true, but we can do better than that."

—Young Syrian cab driver
January 2011

CONTENTS

ILLUSTRATIONS

FIGURES

TABLES

PREAMBLE

An Arab Spring for Syria?

AS I WRITE THESE LINES, Syria is engulfed in antiregime protests, spanning nearly its entire territory; the two largest cities, Damascus and Aleppo, have experienced the least turmoil. Hundreds of protesters have been killed, and thousands have been injured or detained.

Though the protests are ongoing, it is difficult to assume or even imagine they would result in a scenario similar to that of Egypt and Tunisia, where the head of the regime departs or resigns in favor of an outcome that, by and large, sustains the institutions of the regime. An all-out civil war similar to that in Libya is possible only if external factors become increasingly involved. At this point, in May 2011, it seems the regime is gaining the upper hand by violently crushing the uprisings, knowing full well that many if not most Syrians have refrained from taking to the streets largely because of fear of the unknown: for many, the regime's departure or fall may result in a vacuum of sorts that might be filled by a more undesirable alternative, including sectarian strife, external intervention, or an all-out war of reprisal. Thus, the question for most Syrians is not whether they would like to see a less repressive regime but whether they think such a change is likely under these local and regional circumstances. The complexity of the Syrian situation is evident, but can be overestimated by those who favor the status quo for one reason or another.

In this book, these recent and ongoing events will not figure explicitly except when certain facts have been altered, such as the literal elimination of the hitherto pivotal post of deputy prime minister for economic affairs, which was occupied before March 2011 by Abdallah al-Dardari (this is a sign of a reversion to more public-sector-friendly policies). Completed in January 2011, the analysis herein comports with the unfolding events by way of a number of warnings against the perils of "continuity without change" in the political sphere. More pertinent is the analysis of how elite economic networks, combining political and economic actors, have for decades undermined even the semblance of equality and productivity in the Syrian economy in favor of the few. The delete-rious outcome of this largely informal nexus of economic power came increas-ingly at the expense of the largest segments of Syrian society, which continue to be disenfranchised both politically and economically. Thus, the reservoir of discontent in Syria runs much deeper than one might think on the basis of the modest number of protesters we have witnessed, for there are always other con-siderations made by citizens before taking to the streets, as suggested above. Fortunately for the regime, unsavory actors regionally and globally have once again played an unintentional role in keeping it afloat.

I will leave the reader with no scenarios or predictions, as this is not my role. Suffice it to say that structural factors dealing with the relationship of state, society, and market will outlive any social force, or regime, that remains stand-ing. It is these factors to which this book has been devoted over its fifteen years of research and preparation, and with which researchers will grapple endlessly, irrespective of the political form of rule.

PREFACE

DAMASCUS IN JANUARY 2011, where I wrote these lines, is a different city from its earlier incarnation in 1991. It is brighter, taller, and sprinkled with ostentatious displays of consumerism. There are far fewer portraits of the president adorning buildings and billboards and far more portraits of parliamentarians, entrepreneurs, and entertainers. The economic reforms of the father, Hafiz al-Asad, and his son and successor in 2000, Bashar al-Asad (henceforth Bashar), have certainly changed the face of Syria, not least since 2005 when Bashar introduced the notion of the Social Market Economy, in which market arrangements are officially tacked on to older quasi-socialist arrangements.

Under the surface, these transitions have been in process since the mid-1980s when Syria's state-centered economy nearly collapsed. The officially sanctioned private sector moguls have since replaced the state and public sector strongmen of yesterday in the storefront of Syria's polity. These moguls publicly and proudly boast of their private investments in a country where holding a dollar bill in public was a daring act just a few years ago. Newly acquired wealth is ubiquitous, in restaurants and cafés, on the street, and in village villas that line mountaintops and tower over earlier twentieth-century structures. Real estate in Damascus is now among the most expensive in the world, certainly making the top-ten list. Yet, various internet sites (for example, Facebook and Amazon) are still banned; independent parties are prohibited; and parliaments continue to act as rubber-stamp institutions—albeit in a more polished manner than their counterparts in the 1970s and 1980s. More urgently still, most Syrians are finding it harder to make do with just one job. The juxtaposition of the new face of Syria for the few with the realities of economic and political marginalization for the many is not lost on visitors who choose to wander out of the compelling shine of Damascene consumerism.

This book chronicles the state-business networks that have dominated economic policy changes since the late 1980s and diminished the country's economic productivity and developmental potential. As state-centered economies faltered in the 1970s and 1980s, the Syrian leadership along with a host of other developing countries started to shift alliances from labor to business. This alliance building began informally and was gradual. Initially, networks of bureaucrats and capitalists consolidated around public sector patronage. Subsequently, these networks embraced private business initiative in the late 1980s, 1990s, and early 2000s. Maturing privileged ties combining state officials and business actors represented themselves (not the state qua state nor the larger business community) and exercised a disproportional influence on policies of economic change, shaping the parameters of reform and development. In presenting the Syrian case, this book argues for the analytical imperative of examining networks as a method for understanding political-economic outcomes that cannot be reduced to state or class power.

The post-2005 changes underwritten by Bashar's consolidation of power in that year might hold conditional promise. For the first time in decades, Syrians have a unique opportunity to fix the economy, strengthen and democratize Syria's polity, and stave off unprincipled external actors seeking an emasculation of its power. The question is whether the Syrian leadership has the administrative capacity and the political will to take the necessary risks that accompany the expansion of political freedoms and the inclusion of all local stakeholders in economic decision-making. Admittedly, Syria's tough neighborhood may simultaneously make it potentially costly to take such risks and provides excuses for maintaining the status quo. Before the ongoing uprisings (at the time of writing), the current leadership was sufficiently consolidated and popular to take such risks. This moment might well have passed, and it remains to be seen to what extent the regime will be able to pull itself together if indeed it weathers the protesters' storm. In any case, if economic fortunes continue to decline in the coming years as a result of growing unemployment, dwindling oil production, or devastating drought, the discontent that sparked the uprisings will deepen. For the time being, the undying dictum "change within continuity" is the order of the day, with varied doses of change or continuity depending on the time, place, and issue. One discernible outcome of the current uprisings is that the regime's leadership is now able to see the cost of more continuity and less change. What the regime might do with this realization remains to be seen; it would be a fool's errand to try and second-guess its preferences—these preferences were sufficiently obscure under almost three decades of "stability" before the uprisings.

As the grimmer end of the "new face" confronts Syria, for many—some say most—the more things change, the more they stay the same. Some have seen their fortunes diminish alongside the gradual but persistent attenuation of public welfare provisions since 1991, the year that heralded the policy of "economic pluralism," *al-ta'addudiyya al-iqtisaadiyya*. Economic pluralism officially recognized the legitimate role of the private sector alongside the stalwart public sector that had dominated Syria's economy since 1963. The slashing of subsidies continued until December 2010, interrupted only by the Tunisian and Egyptian revolts, prior to the eruption of protests in Syria in March 2011. Cuts in subsidies were coupled with an undying hope that neoliberal trickle-down economics will carry the day while the private sector takes care of business. Yet, even with renewed investment initiatives, all statistics point to the inability of the private sector to absorb the more than 250,000 new job seekers per year. This is especially true given that the drought of recent years has produced an equal number of forced urbanizations per year. The trend is not likely to subside, as rainfall has steadily decreased. Any political economist with intellectual integrity and a desire to see Syria prosper is troubled by this predicament, irrespective of political context or personal political views. I am certain that the top leadership is deeply troubled by this environmental state as well—though other deeper and perhaps existential concerns occupy Syria's strongmen at the time of writing. But this is all the more reason to understand the patterns of the past and open the door for sustainable development from which everyone benefits. I do not offer solutions herein but rather their prerequisite: a diagnosis of a pattern of development that fell considerably short of meeting Syria's potential.

Finally, though most analysts hope that Syrian decision-makers will spend more time focusing on how to create a better future for all Syrians and less time sanctioning critics, they are not naïve about the broader political context. Writing critically about Syria is tricky, but not because it is difficult to criticize the Syrian regime—for it has come a long way in tolerating criticism over the past decade, notwithstanding its responses to the uprisings. Rather, while Syria's domestic politics legitimately attract ample critique, and more so today than ever, there are various political actors in the region and internationally who will exploit such criticism to problematic ends. A band of unsavory neoconservative actors in and around the United States' administration, for instance, lobbied to strike or invade Syria in 2005 on grounds as faulty and deceptive as those that led to the invasion and devastation of Iraq and Iraqi society. An entire think-tank industry promotes similar ends for reasons that have nothing to do with the well-being of Syria and Syrians. In stark contrast, all analysis of Syria's domestic political economy in this book proceeds from an independent political-economic perspective and not from the perspective of any external actor, not least the United States' foreign policy or its supporters and allies. I hope that the contributions of this book, notwithstanding its imperfections, will be of some use to those who have the best interest of Syrians, and sound political-economic analysis, in mind.

ACKNOWLEDGMENTS

THE RESEARCH FOR THIS BOOK lasted nearly fourteen years. It is therefore near impossible to acknowledge all who contributed to it. In any case, I am indebted to more people than I can list. There are those who helped me devise a framework of study, those who helped me conduct the field research, those who granted me interviews, and those who contributed to the production process, either directly or indirectly. And certainly, there were those who were in the vicinity during some or all of these processes, and had to hear about this project for years on end, until this very minute. I sincerely apologize if I have missed anyone in my acknowledgments below. Also, there are those who do not wish to be acknowledged, and for understandable reasons. Generally, I must say that I have not encountered another people as helpful and pleasant as Syrians have been.

First, I would like to thank Stanford University Press editor Kate Wahl for making the entire process smooth and productive at every turn. This process would have been treacherous without her support. The same goes for Stanford's able editors, including Carolyn Brown and others who labored over these hundreds of pages. I would also like to thank those who contributed to the early framing and review of the research endeavor, including my former advisors and colleagues: Michael Hudson, Robert Vitalis, Daniel Brumberg, and Stephen King. I am also indebted to Mark Warren for ample intellectual inspiration from unrelated subfields that have nonetheless shaped my critical thinking. Many of the valuable comments of Timothy Mitchell on an earlier incarnation of my work have seen their way to the final manuscript. Through my research, Steven Heydemann was a constant source of inspiration and support in the field of political economy. I am indebted mostly to him for encouraging me, and many others, to consider and develop the concept of networks in understanding complex patterns of economic policy change. His 1994 edited book, *Networks of Privilege*, in which I have a chapter, is a critical cornerstone of the current volume. I would also like to thank Palgrave and the London Middle East Institute for granting copyright permission for portions of chapters appearing in this volume.

My field research in Syria would have been impossible without the support and trust of many individuals who share a commitment to the enhancement of Syria's political-economic potential. I have learned much more from economists and writers like Nabil Sukkar, Nabil Marzouq, Rizqallah Hilan, Jamal Barout, Nasir Nasir, and Khalid Abdulnour and others than I have in several books on Syria. I have also had the pleasure of sitting down for extended periods with businessmen who were both candid and supportive, irrespective of any differences regarding the matters at hand. I would like to thank Muhammad al-Qalla' for a firsthand introduction to the historical context of state-business relations, and also the fearless industrialist Riad Seif and the outspoken parliamentarian and businessman Dr. Ihsan Sanqar for sharing with me the troubles and tribulations involved in doing business in the 1990s. I must also say that the articles of the prolific Ibrahim Hamidi in the daily *al-Hayat* newspaper constituted remarkable signposts for any observer of Syria. I would also like to thank Dr. Rateb Shallah, the head of Syria's Union of Chambers of Commerce, and prominent businessman Haitham Joud for their candidness and generosity with their time. I am grateful to the able Abdallah al-Dardari, Syria's former deputy prime minister for economic affairs, for the long, open, and insightful discussion we had. Most of all, I am indebted infinitely to the critical mind and unparalleled courage and integrity of Dr. 'Arif Dalila, who guided more than a generation of economists and inspired friends and foes alike—and he had many foes. Dalila's work and contributions will one day have their unique moment. I would certainly like to thank friends and family who made my work in Syria smooth and enjoyable, though any visitor to this truly beautiful country will find it remarkably easy to feel at home and to experience unforgettable moments.

A number of research assistants, editors, and readers provided me with ample support, in the field and beyond. These include Liz Kepferle, who edited the earlier versions of this work; Chris Toensing, from whose godlike editorial skills I've benefited greatly; and more recently, Rhea Myerscough, who kept my data updated and in check. I thank them and also Samer Hamati, John Warner, and Toufiq al-Thaqn. Most of all, I would like to thank my competent and diligent right-hand assistant, Lindsey Stephenson, who kept me in check, on time, and on point throughout the final writing and rewriting stages. I couldn't have completed this work without her continued support. And I must thank Nadya Sbaiti and Lisa Hajjar for last-minute edits and revisions.

I cannot assume that a writing and research process this long could have taken place without unknown soldiers whose support and belief in my work made my journey possible; these include Sinan Antoon, Dirar Hakeem, Nadya Sbaiti, and Sherene Seikaly. Also, As'ad AbuKhalil, despite his inconsistency, has been a tremendous moral force behind my academic and public pursuits. I thank him and everyone for their undying faith in me—even when I did not deserve it. Closer to home is the support of my wife, Noura Erakat, who had to deal with all the odds, ends, and idiosyncrasies associated with finishing a manuscript while juggling (too) many projects. Finally, over the years in which I worked on this project, what made all or any of it possible in more ways than I can count or ever fully appreciate are the gems Elie Haddad, my brother, and my sister and brother-in-law, Carole Haddad and Khalid Namez. I dedicate this book to my mother, Asmahan Richeh, without whose strength and belief in me I would not have been able to do much.

I would *not* like to thank Elie Abuzeid, because he had nothing to do, in any way, shape, or form, with any aspect of the production of this book.

Business Networks in Syria

INTRODUCTION
Economic Reform and Network Analysis

AFTER A TWO-HOUR INTERVIEW on the Syrian private sector's relations with the state, the interviewee—a well-informed manager at the Ministry of Industry in Damascus—gets up, walks around his mahogany office desk, sits directly opposite me, leans forward, glances toward the office door to make certain it is firmly shut, and says: "It's true; this regime helped the private sector grow, but it will never tolerate a strong private sector. *I am under your control when I am a twig in your hand, but not when I become a palm tree.*"[1]

The government official was referring to the growth of the private sector in the early 1990s. For the first time in three decades, its share of new net investments was nearly double that of the public sector.[2] In Damascus, then and now, the operative thinking is that the state needs the urban-Sunni-dominated private sector but is wary of its potential strength. In 1961, the then-ousted urban-based liberal parties were able to mount a coup and recapture power, ending three years of state-centered economic planning under the United Arab Republic, which had united Syria and Egypt in 1958. When the rejuvenated Ba'th reversed what it called the liberal "Separatist Coup" after an even shorter stint in power, in 1963, it did so under the more radicalized rural-minoritarian leadership, which vowed never again to allow for such reversals. This episode was preceded by several others that colored urban-rural relations of conflict and exploitation. For several decades, if not centuries, the dominance of urban-Sunni society had not been challenged in that manner. With the 1963 coup of the Arab Socialist Ba'th Party, urban-Sunni dominance of the Syrian polity ended, ushering in a new era in which the political helm was to be dominated by rural-minoritarian social forces. The antagonism was now reversed, but the mutual mistrust persisted.

Given this political antagonism and social mistrust between the political and economic elites, the Syrian regime strove to find ways to make business relevant without allowing it to convert its material wealth into political power. Thus the Hafiz al-Asad regime, representing the more pragmatist wing of the Ba'th party,

1

brought parts of the private sector "back in" beginning in the early 1970s, albeit initially through the back door and informally. Informal and crony-like state-business networks mushroomed henceforth, giving rise to what is called the "new rentier bourgeoisie" in Syria, and to a pattern of economic change that left developmental imprints on Syrian society that show to this day. Misallocation of resources and the proliferation of nonproductive, non-labor-intensive, but lucrative business ventures and practices ultimately dominated Syria's economy for decades on. Syria's promising resource-based potential (human and material) became official rhetoric for public consumption, or a story that is told by dissidents, former exploiters, and emerging nationalist critics alike.

In the process, the Syrian regime maintained its security, but at a high economic and developmental cost that was passed down (along with the leadership of the Ba'th party and the country) to Asad's son, Bashar. This inheritance landed on Bashar's shoulders at a time when the Middle East was sinking into intensified conflict and war, complicating what was already a very late reentry into the global economic system.[3] The legacy of entrenched state-business networks poses a tremendous challenge for the new leadership's proclaimed desire for economic progress and modernization, though the horizon is not as bleak as it had been under Bashar's father. This legacy of entrenched economic networks—its nature, dynamics, impact, and unintended consequences—is the analytical narrative that this book addresses.

This study of the Syrian case seeks to explain prolonged economic stagnation marked by costly developmental outcomes in one of the most durable authoritarian regimes in the Middle East and the developing world. The "winner" in Syria, and much of the rest of the Middle East, has been a set of exclusionary state-business networks that have been able to skew the benefits of economic change in their favor. The "loser" is the average consumer (especially workers in the public and informal sectors) and, indeed, the health of the overall economy, as state officials and their business cronies misallocated resources and mismanaged policy change by subordinating a semblance of economic rationality to a political logic of regime security.

From Egypt to the former Soviet republics, socialist and socialist-leaning states have brought business back into the political-economic equation. The broader historical context in many postcolonial settings such as Syria and Egypt is the social conflict that shaped the consolidation of populist rule.[4] Nearly everywhere, this transformation has been highly politicized, for it has fostered a new business class growing in the shadow of the state. The Syrian case displays a similar pattern but with a twist: the relationship between politicians and capitalists is scarred by deep-seated historical antagonism and mistrust. The division in the 1960s between the rural-minoritarian political leadership and the Sunni-majoritarian business community persisted through patterns of promotion and (s)election that, with few exceptions, preserved the social homogeneity of those in power. This was not carried out as an affirmation of sectarianism, as will be discussed in Chapter 2. Rather, it was a regime's response to security concerns where the overlap of sect, region, community, and class intensified the modal political antagonism between a populist regime and the putatively exploitative business class in postcolonial societies. Hence, in the Syrian case, bringing business back in to rejuvenate or propel the economy was viewed in zero-sum terms, whereby empowering business was viewed as empowering the urban-Sunni community over and against the rural-minoritarian leadership. Alternatives to official or formal (re)incorporation of the business community had to be sought. In countries largely enjoying social-communal homogeneity between politicians and capitalists, such as Egypt in 1974, the regime faced far less of an impediment as it brought business back into the political-economic equation.[5]

Syria's legacy of state-business mistrust produced a particular form of state-business cooperation—that is, selective and informal economic ties (networks) between state officials and private actors—that spawned its own exclusionary economic institutions and tailored policies.[6] Buttressed by a constant flow of external rents (from oil and aid), these economic institutions had a significant influence on patterns of economic change beginning in the late 1980s. Lacking an alternative to the vision of a centrally planned economy, the state's day-to-day intervention in the Syrian economy was highly influenced by a narrowly defined set of interests.

The import of the Syrian case for the study of the politics of economic reform is considerable, if only because state-business relations have not been at the forefront of this field of inquiry. The analysis here proceeds from a comparatively informed perspective of similar cases and also sheds light on a broad range of topics, including questions of agency (for example, what kinds of actors influence policy outcomes?), the relationship between economic and political change (does private sector expansion really have a political impact?), the impact of (mis)trust on institutional development (as opposed to the other way around), and the merits of adopting the analytical tools of economic sociology (networks) in explaining political-economic outcomes, especially in contexts where a substantial portion of transactions occurs in the informal realm.

Though the case of Syria is not unique, it has important specificities, as the data reveal throughout this book. The time period under study stretches back to the 1960s but begins formally in 1970, when the pragmatist wing of the Ba'th party captured power, and ends in 2005. However, it wasn't until 1986 that the top leadership internalized the need for reform as a result of a severe foreign exchange crisis. The year 2005 ends the period under study because it denotes two developments: first, it refers to the year when Bashar al-Asad consolidated his power at the helm, a process that started after his father's death in 2000 when the legacy of Hafiz al-Asad's leadership remained apparent in theory and in practice. Second, and as a result, the year 2005 represents the first official and public expression in four decades of a desire to move away from a state-centered economy and *toward* a mixed economy where market forces play a more significant role. Proceeding from a more solid base of leadership and control, President Bashar al-Asad announced the adoption of a Social Market Economy during the Ba'th's tenth Regional Command Conference in June 2005. Henceforth, more genuinely representative business institutions began to emerge, signaling a break in the economic governance structure in Syria. Economic networks persisted, albeit in a more narrow yet effective form.

THE CHANGING FACE OF SYRIA'S ECONOMY
AFTER PROTRACTED STAGNATION
Opportunities, Constraints, and Legacies

For the period between 1986 and 2000, most analysts of Syria's political economy have lamented the absence of any real movement away from the stagnant state-centered economy, established and institutionalized with the rise of the Ba'th in 1963. After the death of President Hafiz al-Asad in 2000, however, developments in the financial sector have given analysts something to write about. Between the emergence of the first private banks (in 2004), the establishment of holding companies (in 2007), the launch of the Damascus Stock Exchange (in 2009), and the establishment of new joint business associations in 2010, a new reality seems to be setting in. Alongside these changes, the regime also made a bold rhetorical commitment in 2005 regarding the adoption of a Social Market Economy,[7] an odd combination of central planning and market forces. The question, however, is whether these developments are the start of an earnest reform trend or merely a regime security measure or are simply a new storefront for existing networks of privilege. Though new opportunities loom on the horizon, the historical legacy of economic change and development poses serious constraints.

Since 1986, when Syria began gradually to dismantle its command economy, the pattern of economic change has been erratic, producing severe economic and developmental costs, notwithstanding spikes in economic growth. The culprit for the most part has been unbridled and unproductive rent-seeking that produced egregious misallocation of resources. Though these costs were largely offset at the time by external rents from oil and Syria's geostrategic role, they became too high for an economy with an increasingly inefficient public sector and a largely stunted private sector. Moreover, both the public and private sectors were incapable of producing added value commensurate with population growth.

As laid out in the tenth Five-Year Plan drafted in 2005, Syria must achieve 5 percent GDP (gross domestic product) growth during the 2006–2009 period and 7 percent by the start of 2010, with population growth kept under 2.1 percent, in order to meet its basic economic goals.[8] While the Central Bureau of Statistics has announced that Syria achieved 7 percent growth in 2008, external organizations such as the Oxford Business Group and the IMF estimate growth in 2008 at roughly 5 percent, while population growth remains between 2.5 and 2.7 percent.[9] In fact, real GDP growth continued its decline from 2005 until the time of writing.[10] Though the global economic downturn had much to do with this decline after 2008—which Syria weathered better than most of its neighbors—it does not fully explain the general trend.

The reasons for such uphill economic struggles lie in the period of prolonged economic stagnation between 1994 and 2005. During the last half of the 1990s, the Syrian economy took a steep downturn, both in terms of GDP growth and, more so, in per capita income.[11] And though GDP growth resumed slowly and erratically after the lowest point in 1999, per capita income growth actually slumped to unprecedented and sustained negative levels until 2004, reflecting not just economic but developmental woes.[12] It is these developmental reversals that distinguish Syria's prolonged economic stagnation and the outcome to be explained in this book. Unless the pitfalls of that period are avoided in the emerging political economic equation since 2005, the future of economic growth and development in Syria will remain grim. Historically, analysts addressed such developmental problems and solutions in various ways. The more refined perspectives eschewed the question of whether states should or should not intervene and focused instead on "getting state intervention right."

Getting State Intervention "Right" for Whom?

Peter Evans's work *Embedded Autonomy: States and Industrial Transformation*[13] examines how states successfully promote industrial transformation: how they intervene and manage the economy, what kinds of ties they develop with the private sector, what kinds of policies are formulated, and how they are implemented. The Syrian regime has managed to avoid all such lessons. Unlike in East Asian countries, the web of public-private ties that obtains in Syria has resulted in a dismal outcome for development in general and state intervention in particular: it has led to the penetration of state bureaucracy, to the erosion of the state's administrative capacity, and to a serious drop in economic productivity. So far, it is the consumer who has paid the price. For the Syrian regime, the criterion for the "right" state intervention was not economic rationality, or growth. Rather, it was regime security: its maintenance and decisional autonomy vis-à-vis broader strategic issues. But not all political rationalities, including that of regime security, produce homogeneous outcomes. Regime maintenance in countries like Egypt, Tunisia, Jordan, Morocco, and Algeria produced some variation in economic and developmental outcomes, despite some structural similarities. Thus, the focus on state intervention and the response of the business community bypasses the more effective locus of economic decision-making, namely, the informal web of relations between the political and economic elites, that is, economic networks.

In virtually all developing countries,[14] and perhaps beyond,[15] relations between the state and business have taken the form of what can be called economic or policy networks that may or may not operate through formal institutions. The impact of such networks on economic growth and development can be more or less detrimental or positive depending on the conditions of their emergence, their internal dynamics, and their relation to the broader institutional and social context.[16]

Notwithstanding the potential for reductionism,[17] the stress in political-economy literature on the resilience and policy impact of economic networks in developing countries is well founded and well documented.[18] I posit that the effects of the maturing economic networks—combining capitalists and bureaucrats/politicians—in Syria in the late 1980s became evident in the economic, regulatory, and fiscal policy reforms of the late 1980s and 1990s, and after the presidential succession in 2000. The foreign exchange crisis of 1986 marks the acceleration of economic networks' consolidation and influence, albeit at an informal level until 1991, when these networks came to dominate the official institutional expression of the "private sector" under the rubric of the government's reform policy, *al-ta'addudiyya al-iqtisadiyya* (economic pluralism). The role of privileged economic networks[19] in bringing about economic and fiscal change henceforth can be analyzed through the examination of the institutional and social contexts within which these networks emerge and on which their sustenance rests. Although such networks have influenced primarily middle- and lower-range policies,[20] their ability to bypass or manipulate laws and regulations has significantly widened their reach and allowed them, intentionally or inadvertently, to shape general developmental change in idiosyncratic ways that have been detrimental to economic efficiency and productivity.[21] What is peculiar here is that these economic downturns were neither desired nor intended by the state, the business community, or the participants in these networks who represent the primary beneficiaries of the reform process. Economic decline was largely a result of a preoccupation with regime security, on the one hand, and the related rampant rent-seeking that was misdirected by a widely penetrated and incoherent bureaucracy, on the other.[22] The proximity of these networks to decision-making bodies, and the participation of decision-makers and top officials in the networks, made rent-seeking and rent allocation an extremely efficient process during the past quarter century. This book does not assume that state-business relations or networks have not been treated before. However, a review of the literature on the political economy of reform reveals a dearth of focus on agents of change that are not part of a traditional research canon. State-business relations in general, and networks in particular, are such agents that for the most part escaped both state-centered and society-centered approaches dominating the discussion on reform outcomes.

STATE-BUSINESS RELATIONS AND ECONOMIC REFORM: A CONVERSATION WITH THE LITERATURE

Despite an increase in published research on the topic, literature on state-business relations in late-developing countries, and certainly in the Middle East, remains scattered and so far not sufficiently cumulative to develop an identifiable discourse and a series of shared propositions. Moreover, a substantial portion of the literature for the most part cuts off the dominant political logic that pervades such regimes from the ensuing economic reform processes. Thus, we witness excessive attention to details regarding changes in economic policy as an indication of progress, rather than an indication of these regimes' adaptation to a changing world,[23] domestically and internationally. Some way lies ahead, empirically and analytically, before research on state-business relations in populist-authoritarian regimes catches up with its counterpart in newly industrialized countries (such as Japan, South Korea, Singapore, Taiwan) as well as some developing countries (Brazil, Argentina, Chile). Reviewing the general literature on state intervention and the politics of economic reform and their correlates is a good starting point.

Getting State Intervention Right

The literature on development in the 1980s and 1990s emphasized the variable of state intervention in explaining developmental successes (for example, East Asian tigers) or developmental failures (some Latin American and sub-Saharan countries) of all sorts. Getting state intervention right emerged as the key to a productive management of developing economies. This statist emphasis is premised on the contention that the state in such countries is the institution most capable of collective action and collective mobilization of resources to shoulder the project of development.[24]

However, getting state intervention in the economy right has proved a formidable task in countries wracked by social struggles and institutional incapacities such as postcolonial nationalist constraints, class struggles, or penetrated bureaucracies. Nonetheless, not all developing states fared similarly or failed miserably: Zaire, a classic predatory state, fared much worse than Turkey; and Argentina fared better than both Egypt and Syria. Taiwan and South Korea fared better than all the above, despite recurring economic boom-and-bust cycles among the others.

Developmental state theorists delved into the middle levels of analysis to explain the state's ability to intervene effectively in the economy. Robert Wade and Chalmers Johnson emphasized the insulation of decision-makers from other social forces and, in some cases, the suppression of representative institutions.[25] Theda Skocpol and Peter Evans emphasized the importance of a coherent and competent bureaucracy that is able to formulate policies independently of particularist pressure groups.[26] Louis Putterman and Dietrich Rueschemeyer warned of excessive state power where there is a dearth of state capacity, for "if a state's capacity to act coherently and effectively is very limited, it is a prescription for disaster to assign major policy tasks to it."[27] Furthermore, if this situation occurs in an authoritarian context, it results in grave developmental consequences for which the state cannot be held accountable. Yet most developing states are or were authoritarian and have possessed a weak capacity for coherent action.

Although these arguments seem to point to necessary preconditions for proper state intervention anywhere, they seem to involve a hidden tautology or, alternatively, lack explanatory power. From where does state capacity come? From where does its ability to mobilize social sectors, gather appropriate information, and provide a hospitable and lucrative investment environment come? Moreover, why would the state elite be interested in collective goals as opposed to their narrow self-interest, and conversely, why should the business community make risky, long-term productive investments or cooperate with a largely insulated bureaucratic system run by an unaccountable or uncontested executive? Ultimately, under what conditions would reciprocal cooperation between the state and the business community—a cornerstone for long-term development—be perceived to be too costly for the political elite? These are the sorts of questions I shall try to answer using the Syrian case.

Politics of Economic Reform

Systematic research on the politics of economic reform typically focuses on one of the following themes and topics: (1) reform strategies,[28] (2) reform politics/dynamics,[29] (3) reform outcomes,[30] and (4) developmental implications/consequences. As the available literature suggests, a large number of factors must be investigated to understand the causes and consequences of what is called economic reform. Perhaps the most notable of such factors is the relationship between power and capital, or state and business. This nexus speaks to all four themes: it addresses the impact of capital on reform strategy; the relational dynamics between state, capital, labor, and community; the readiness of capital holders to invest, as well as the choice and target of investment; and finally, the alternative or latent strategies of capitalists and other social forces related to them.

The principal problem, however, remains that state-business collaboration has not been taken up vigorously as an object of study. It is usually considered a residual category that is referred to or implied in discussing broader processes or strategic contexts.[31] Thus, the explanatory import of state-business collaboration has not been sufficiently tapped into, notwithstanding some research on newly industrialized countries. Even that literature did not consider state-business collaboration an object of study: it regressively pointed to this relationship by way of explaining successful industrial transformation.[32] A particular type of state-business collaboration was considered conducive to industrial transformation. Nonetheless, the relations between state and business—how do they form and develop? what structures such relations?—broadly remained an implicit, not an explicit, object of study.

State-Business Relations

At the turn of the century, when putative linkages between economic and political restructuring did not materialize, the focus began to shift to more deep-seated investigation into histories, legacies, cultural traits, and globalization factors that explain the absence of such links. It became clear that labor did not, and remains unlikely to, pose a serious threat to reforms that continue to gore its interests, largely because of its weak organizational capacity and lack of autonomy.[33] The research focus began to shift from the subversive potential of losers in the process of reform to the tendencies of winners (business and the political elite) to hijack such processes in the pursuit of noncollective goals.[34] With this empirical and research development, the preoccupation with linkage gave way to a more specific and focused emphasis on different types of economic reform patterns, their institutional and coalitional basis, and their likelihood of success in stabilizing economies and making them more productive.[35] State-business collaboration emerged as a key factor, not only in explaining the success of reform, transition, and transformation but also as a probable site of rent-seeking and corruption, an area that harbored a potential path to economic failure.

Rent-Seeking and Corruption

From the rational and public choice literature came progress on issues such as corruption and rent-seeking. The dominant postulate was that, when they can, capitalists and bureaucrats collaborate and/or collude to form distributive networks that shift the allocation of resources away from collective—that is, socially efficient/optimal—targets to themselves.[36] Maxfield and Schneider assert that healthy government-business relationships should be collaborative, but not so much that they degenerate into unproductive rent-seeking activity.[37] Such formulae led to the Washington Consensus type of antidote: cut off rent from the root, that is, from government, by encouraging the breakdown of centralized economies and the establishment of market-oriented economies. However, problems persisted for a variety of reasons, including the narrow and depoliticized neoliberal conception that the government is the sole source of economic rent. As the experience of most developing countries has shown in the 1980s, the 1990s, and the 2000s, the process of economic reform itself has often generated far larger opportunities for rent.[38] Indeed, Lucas explains that "government officials support public-private partnerships in order to enhance the capacity of the state."[39] In Syria the gain is twofold, as *many* of these political elites are part of the economic networks of rent-seekers, and thus have no motivation to create a fair playing field for the private sector proper. More analytically rich is the literature that reconceptualizes the process of economic reform as one where rent-seeking patterns are simply restructured and where reform is more about "reregulation" than about deregulation of market relations.[40]

Despite the marked improvement that recent literature on state-business relations[41] exhibits over the older indirect treatment, there still seems to be a missing component: how do we account for agency? The question of agency has not been tackled adequately in much of the reform literature, including some of the literature that examines state-business relations as an explanatory variable. What has been lacking is a conceptualization of agency, or actors, that helps us explain the contradictory outcomes of reform processes and the messy split between overdetermined categories of winners and losers.[42] The fact that winners sometimes cut across traditional class, sectoral, and/or ethnic categories compels us, at least in the Syrian case, to reexamine what we take to be the unit of analysis vis-à-vis the actors involved. The move from rigid categories like incumbents, bourgeoisie, and bureaucrats to distributive coalitions in the mid- and late 1990s in Latin America is a positive step in that direction.[43] However, more needs to be done to hone our conception of such coalitions and whether they are indeed "coalitions" rather than more loosely related, cross-cutting economic networks.

Economic Networks: Early Analysis

The question remains as to whether and when state-business collaboration, a seemingly inevitable outcome in the era of globalization, will degenerate into unproductive collusion or, alternatively, the kind of rent-seeking arrangements that are detrimental to economic productivity and efficiency. Despite the partial neoliberal influence on the early literature on economic networks, the focus on this topic and dynamics therein is a significant step toward a more empirically accurate conceptualization of state-business relations. This literature suggests that types of economic networks are correlated with particular performance outcomes. Those state-business networks that enjoy higher levels of trust, transparency, information exchange, credibility, and reciprocity promote a positive case of collective collaboration and outcomes. Conversely, state-business networks that lack trust between capitalists and bureaucrats degenerate into collusive networks that undercut the possibility of collectively productive outcomes by promoting particularist interests.[44]

Most studies in this subfield draw on cases from Latin America and East Asia.[45] Less represented even in political-economic literature on developing countries are late-developing countries (LDCs), such as Syria, which ostensibly represent cases of state-business collusion marked by collectively costly outcomes. What needs to be researched further are the institutional, legal, and social conditions that give rise to, and sustain, collusive relations between "bureaucrats" and "capitalists" in such cases and how, under such conditions, economic networks influence patterns of economic change in unintended ways.

Institutional Context

This book is concerned primarily with reform processes in populist-authoritarian regimes that are typically found among postcolonial late-developing countries. Notably, the institutional context of populist-authoritarian rule, with its attendant coalitional arrangements, presented another caveat for research on economic reform as well as on state-business relations in such reforming economies. To be sure, systemic constraints forced "populist" elites to launch reform processes that were invariably informed by the growing neoliberal hegemony. Certainly "modernization and its contemporary incarnation as neoliberalism, has enjoyed long-standing dominance on account of the power of its institutional advocates and the discrediting of interventionist strategies."[46] Therefore, reformers had to reconcile the neoliberal content of reforms with populist— and often socialist—political economies or find a way to camouflage it.[47] With some exceptions, the literature did not sufficiently specify the linkages between the political logic of populist-authoritarian elites and the dynamics of the reform process. This study addresses such linkages at various levels, with a focus on the relationship between state-business collaboration and the institutional context during different periods.

Trust and Institutions

Lucas theorizes that in developing nations "[business] associations will use their leverage to challenge specific ineffective or exploitative policies."[48] Business associations are able to accomplish these kinds of feats because they are unified and transparent. However, because Syria's regime is highly suspicious of the traditional bourgeoisie, or a strong private sector in general, what might have been a powerful coalition of business actors/interests has disseminated into many smaller independent groups with little political power. The lack of trust that often characterizes the relationship between the regime and the business community in most postcolonial societies has manifested itself not only in the type of informal state-business networks that arose but also in the institutions and associations that emerged.[49]

The dominant literature on institutions and trust addresses the effects of institutions on trust among actors that must operate within those institutions in a strategic context.[50] This book addresses the question of how mistrust among actors that find it in their interest to cooperate impacts the kinds of institutions that they develop, and how, in turn, intra-network dynamics affects both trust and institutional change. In other words, mistrust between the regime and the business community as a whole is itself largely responsible for producing a particular kind of exclusionary institution that ends up exacerbating mistrust. Deepening or prolonging mistrust, however, does not occur automatically. The unintended consequence of internal network dynamics is crucial in understanding why mistrust does not subside, as this research indicates. Furthermore, exclusionary elite recruitment and promotion patterns at the macro level also speak volumes regarding the lack of trust that continues to plague the Syrian polity today.

The contribution of new institutionalist and network literature is most useful. This book adopts these approaches to grasp how a crucial part of informal state-society relations that develops alongside the formal institutional structure ends up subverting both the structure itself as well as the initial intentions of the state elite who promoted such relations. This occurs primarily, but not exclusively, through the impact of informal state-business networks on economic and fiscal policy reform and, more generally, on patterns of political-economic development. To explain how such relationships evolve and unfold, I focus on the impact of state-business networks on the course of economic liberalization in Syria in the years 1986–2005.

NETWORK ANALYSIS: A COMPLEMENTARY APPROACH
Networks and Institutions

To examine state-business relations by focusing exclusively on official organizations and relations in any context is to assume that formal institution building is the actors' preference for maximizing their interests. Often, the "institutions" one is looking for—either those that represent business or those that link the state with business—do not exist. More importantly, to assume that such institutions serve the functions for which they are created, irrespective of the contexts in which they are lodged, is to look for answers in the wrong place. This is not a dismissal of institutions, and neither is it a call for "Middle East exceptionalism." It is simply an affirmation of the need to prioritize how power works, whether or not through formal institutions. Analysts often try to squeeze interests and worldviews into formal "representative" institutions (for example, parliaments and associations) or institutions that are marked by corporatist interests (for example, the state). Even in the presence of well-functioning formal institutions, there is a residue of preferences and, potentially, behavior that is not accounted for through reference to formal institutional characteristics. And when such institutions are in short supply, irrespective of the reasons, it would be folly to insist on prioritizing them as objects of study for inferring preferences and understanding behavior. Network analysis helps us capture the fuller scale of such preferences, including the residue that accounts for behavior not always squarely attributable to formal institutional interests and factors. Capturing the interplay between formal institutional and network analysis is one challenge that is taken up in this book.

The concept of economic networks[51] is at the center of this research. I define *economic network* as an informal institutional agency with limited autonomy. The relationship between networks and the larger social and institutional context is considered recursive or dialectical, where networks are both formed and reformed by the context in which they are embedded and, as with other forms of agency, they in turn impact their environment (in this case, economic and developmental processes). Network analysis is not a panacea, however. In the Syrian case economic networks help us explain the exacerbation of economic decline and its developmental correlates, but they do not as an agency cause the decline single-handedly. Other factors are at play, including the regime's broader political logic, which subordinates economic rationality. The historical legacy that has shaped both the regime's political logic and its interaction with the business community is addressed in Chapter 2.

Networks and Class

The analytical utility of networks resides in the argument that networks cut across classes, identities, and various corporate interests, bringing together strange bedfellows who might be united by particular short- or long-term goals. It is a concept that allows us to rethink forms of political and social agency and identify the potential for explanatory analysis in the types of *relations between* individuals, not just in the class, cultural, or positional attributes of individuals. Instead of having a rigid conception of class or community as our starting point and "[i]nstead of analyzing individual behaviors, attitudes, and beliefs, social network analysis focuses its attention on social entities or actors *in interaction with one another* and on how those interactions constitute a framework or structure that can be studied and analyzed in its own right."[52]

Though this study emphasizes network analysis as a dominant explanatory variable, it is not mutually exclusive with other approaches, including class. In fact, network analysis can complement them. According to Knoke and Yang, "[a]lthough attributes and relations are conceptually distinct approaches to investigating social behavior, they should not be viewed as mutually exclusive options. Instead, many actor attributes can be reconceptualized as relations among dyads,"[53] or a pair of actors. In this book, the tension is resolved by recognizing the distinction between objective attributes (for example, one's class position) and the relational frameworks that mediate them. Network analysis constitutes a relational framework that both structures interaction between individuals and influences subsequent economic behavior. As Granovetter and Swedberg assert, "[e]conomic action is socially situated and cannot be explained by reference to individual motives alone. It is embedded in ongoing networks of personal relationships rather than being carried out by atomized actors."[54]

Class refers to a social-structural stratification to which individuals objectively belong and to which observers may actually ascribe objective interests that may or may not be pursued. However, examining the actual recurring relations between individuals in particular contexts is to elucidate how the interaction itself mediates a variety of positional and structural interests in practice. In other words, network analysis tells us *how* interests—all kinds of interests—were mediated. The *why* is inferred by examining the framework of interaction that characterizes different types of networks.

Thus, even if networks are embedded in a social structure with antagonistic class or communal categories, the framework of interaction among individuals constitutes an independent effect on behavior. Broader strategic or class and communal concerns may initially be the raison d'être of the emergence of particular types of networks, but the dynamics and interactions within the networks acquire some autonomy in time, and thus merit our attention as objects of study. This is why this book emphasizes state-business networks: neither state nor class interests alone sufficiently explain economic and developmental outcomes. Network relations based in constant and continuing interaction between individuals breed their own rationality, which is embedded in the dynamics of a given network. A network, in this sense, can be understood as

> a regular set of contacts of similar social connections among individuals or groups. An action by a member of a network is *embedded*, because it is expressed in interaction with other people. The network approach helps avoid not only the conceptual trap of atomized actors but also theories that point to technology, the structure of ownership, or culture as the exclusive explanation of economic events.[55]

Networks and Trust

In an important study by Lomnitz and Sheinbaum titled "Trust, Social Networks and the Informal Economy,"[56] the authors discuss a case of trust within social networks made up of individuals whose interests were harmed by postcommunist transitions. We can think of these networks as positive instances where trust was a bottom-up conduit for coping, one that produced informal networks of social cooperation and even solidarity. In the Syrian case, we have a different model: the legacy of mistrust between the political and economic elite led the regime to encourage the formation of top-down informal economic networks, combining state officials and private business actors. The purpose in this case was to preserve the regime's economic security by safely bringing business back into the political economic equation. In the former case, the conduit was trust; in the latter, it was mistrust.

Lomnitz and Sheinbaum defined trust as "the real or effective psychosocial distance between individuals. It is associated with social closeness in the sense of sharing the same categories of expected rights and duties, plus shared values and interests."[57] The absence of these attributes characterizes the legacy of social antagonism and mistrust in Syria between the rural-minoritarian holders of state power and the historically dominant urban-Sunni business community. Here trust is not understood in a broad cultural sense, as used by Francis Fukuyama or, to a lesser extent, by Robert Putnam, both of whom use trust as a ubiquitous cultural variable that exists to various degrees *in* society.[58] Rather, this research uses trust in the more restrictive sociopolitical or strategic sense, that is, trust *between* social forces or groups, which may be present or absent as a result of historical interaction. The crux of the difference between the cultural and the sociopolitical understandings is simple. The cultural sense of the word refers to the trustworthiness of *all* individuals within a particular context. In the sociopolitical sense, trust refers to the trustworthiness of a particular group of people vis-à-vis another particular group of people: for instance, between black and white people, or between Sunnis and 'Alawis. In this latter sense, historical factors come into play to create or further a divide, an antagonism, between two (or more) groups or social forces.

Though this mistrust was a principal factor in determining courses of action for the Syrian regime, it was not reflected fully in the interaction between individuals within the emerging economic networks, precisely because of the independent dynamics that developed within. By the same token, mistrust was not completely absent within the networks, nor was it simply confined to communal sentiments. It was also political in nature and figured in other cases, such as Egypt, even in the absence of a sociocommunal divide between the political and economic elite there. The broader sociocommunal and sociopolitical mistrust in Syria permeated not the form of relations within the networks but the content of deals and ventures made. In short, it manifested itself in shortening the time horizons of investors within the networks, revealing a cautionary business behavior and affirming the dialectical relationship between networks and the broader social and institutional context. In any case, the independent effect of networks was evident in the nature and direction of economic change, which was marked by a distinct emphasis on short-term, nonproductive investments.

As the Syrian, Egyptian, and other late-developing countries illustrate, we often find unlikely partners with putatively opposing interests working within the very same networks, side by side.[59] According to Heydemann,

> [n]etworks disrupt, undermine, and cut across the categories that appear regularly in the research literature as the principal agents of reform. Networks permit the formation of unexpected coalitions of actors. They promote patterns of bargaining and interaction that appear counterintuitive based on a less flexible reading of the categories that actors are presumed to occupy. Networks, in other words, contribute to environments in which policy reforms take shape as regulatory hybrids, compromise formulas, half-measures, and unwieldy amalgams of seemingly conflicting interests.[60]

This disrupting effect of networks is not always easy to discern. The manner in which networks affect the policy environment depends on the particulars of a given case. The fact that networks can serve as both constraint and opportunity for actors is the source of their utility at the analytical level and the difficulty in tracing processes of cause and effect. This volume has benefited from exceptional access that illuminated how network relations pose as both an opportunity to cooperate and serve mutual interests (of the political and economic elite), and a constraint on the sort of cooperation that takes place between actors in a context of deep historical mistrust.

PLAN OF THE BOOK

The causal narrative discussed at the outset of this introduction informs the basic structure of this book. Chapter 1 is an introduction to the intertwined topics of state, business, and reform. I introduce three important variables that have shaped the context of Syria's political economy: (1) state-business mistrust, (2) the importance of external rent, and (3) the absence of checks on the power of the Syrian regime, a negative variable that is conspicuous by its absence. I situate the explanatory concern within a two-step framework: first, I treat state-business relations as an outcome to be explained, and then as an intervening variable that gives rise to particular economic and developmental outcomes. Chapter 2 grounds the book historically by addressing the roots of state-business mistrust. It is concerned primarily with the coincidence of populist consolidation and attendant social struggles, notably that between the increasingly rural-minoritarian regime and the Sunni-dominated urban business community. The Hafiz al-Asad regime of 1970, its institutional trade-offs and attempts at establishing a cross-class coalition, is more than colored by the preceding legacy of mistrust. Chapter 3 addresses the ensuing state–private sector relations, primarily for the purpose of distinguishing between the corporate interests of a private sector "proper" and the interests of the new economic elite who dominate the economic networks. The institutional context within which the private sector operates is presented as an arena that reflects the interest of privileged networks.

The pivotal climax of this book's argument is presented in Chapter 4, which examines the emergence of state-business networks by tracing the economic windfalls and opportunities that gave rise to the new economic elite between 1973 and the early 1990s. Each period of state-business interaction was characterized by a particular weaving of economic ties between state officials and individuals in the private sector. The entry of "bureaucrats" into the business world in the second stage, and their offspring in the third, changed the face of Syria's business community and anchored economic networks firmly at the center of Syria's political economy. The characteristics and internal dynamics of these networks as well as their interaction with, and impact on, the institutional context are examined and analyzed. Chapter 5 traces the impact of economic networks on Syria's pattern of economic change since 1986, with particular emphasis on the distinction between official and unofficial liberalization measures. Finally, I examine the developmental consequences of Syria's homegrown liberalization policies, with emphasis on how the nonproductive economic activities of rent-seeking "entrepreneurs" have gravely influenced the economy, the state's administrative capacity, and most importantly, the labor market. In Chapter 6, I trace the impact of economic networks on fiscal change, a case study delineating the influence of privileged economic networks. Once more, the distinction between official fiscal measures and actual fiscal realities is highlighted to demonstrate the ability of well-connected businesspeople to sidestep laws and regulations and enjoy tax exemptions and holidays that far exceed the state's total revenue from taxation. I identify the policy mechanisms and the institutional sites through which a bottom-up redistribution of wealth took place through 2005. In the Conclusion of this book I discuss of its empirical and conceptual findings and contributions, and their relevance to similar cases. I close with an analysis of potential breaking points in reference to regimes such as Syria's, where the dispersion of resources and capital accumulation proceed beyond the regime's ability to contain all the consequences.

TERMINOLOGY, ANONYMITY, AND DATA
Terminology

A note on the terms *regime, economic elite,* and *reform/liberalization* is in order. Regime is usually defined as the rules that govern the relationship between the ruler and the ruled; state is usually defined as the legal authority over a population in a given territory, and comprises a set of institutions and the personnel that run them. *Regime* and *state* have been largely collapsed into one another in Syria, and can be used interchangeably, because of the absence of separation of powers and the weakness, if not absence, of an independent judiciary. In this book, the word *regime* refers to the broader, fixed rules set by those in power at three levels: top regime leadership (which usually includes the president and his closest aides and family members); top security apparatuses chiefs (including heads of the Republican Guard); and top army chiefs and the most senior party officials sitting on the Ba'th Regional Command Council. That does not mean that statesmanship is not exercised in certain arenas and junctures, especially in foreign policy. Even domestically, in times of crisis, the regime leaders may snap back into their statesman roles and make difficult decisions that address systemic imbalances. Also important is the category of paraofficials, that is, close relatives of regime officials, who are recognized in Syria as part of the regime, unless there has been a fundamental break with it, as is the case with Rif'at al-Asad, the late president's brother.

Because of the massive influx of state officials into private business, a further clarification of terms is necessary. In discussing economic actors, I will use the following breakdown: the *new economic elite* refers to all those who, after 1970, possess considerable economic assets, whether they are state officials or private businesspeople. The word *new* here is intended to distinguish new wealth from the old wealth associated with the now-nostalgic category of "old bourgeoisie" in Syria. The *state's economic elite* or the *regime's economic elite* refers to those segments that have an official or paraofficial (close relative) position within the state, government, or ruling party. In the literature on Syria, this segment is sometimes referred to as the "state bourgeoisie." The *private economic elite* or *business elite* refers to the new business elite who are not formally connected with the state. In the literature on Syria, this segment is sometimes referred to as "crony capitalists" or the "new rentier bourgeoisie."

The terms *reform* and *liberalization* are often used interchangeably in the literature, though the term *economic liberalization* describes more accurately Syria's experience until 2005. *Reform* often carries meanings and referents that are more open-ended and that might not obtain in Syria. *Liberalization*, as it will be used in this book, refers more specifically to degrees of retreat by the state from the economic sphere, a movement that might or might not result in what is called structural reform. Another layer that complicates matters is the meaning and usages of these words in Arabic. *Reform* (*islaah*), as opposed to "to form anew," literally means "to fix" or "to make better," which implies that something was initially wrong, thus causing the creation of a "politically correct" vocabulary in the dominant discourse in Syria, at least throughout the 1990s. "Modernizing the economy" has become the preferred usage after 2000. Nevertheless, "reform" and "liberalization" will be used in this book depending on context.

Anonymity

The research in this study is based on numerous field interviews conducted over the past fourteen years, predominantly in Syria. All interviews were conducted by the author, and a considerable number were conducted on the condition of full anonymity, which is understandable considering the subject matter at hand. Some were conducted on the condition of selective anonymity, in which statements could be disclosed without attribution. Whereas it is preferable to disclose specific names at times, I have honored my assurance to protect the anonymity of these individuals, considering their relationships and the contexts in which they find themselves. And though such anonymity raises the level of abstraction in some sections of the book, and admittedly in regard to the networks themselves, it is precisely in those contexts where these individuals wish to remain anonymous. This disclaimer does not preclude disclosure of certain claims and statements by individuals who were generous and perhaps courageous enough to speak out without regard to their own safety. Some of these individuals, who do not happen to be part of the economic networks discussed in this book, have lingered in prison for years and have been released only recently, these including Professor 'Arif Dalila and industrialist Riad Saif.

Data in Syria: Beyond Numbers and Statements

This research is based on public and private accounts and statistics obtained from the Central Bureau of Statistics in Damascus and from private studies and interviews over a period of nearly two years—including ten months of continuous field research in various Syrian cities in 1998–99.[61] I engaged in some events as participant-observer after having established some connections. Data are primarily drawn from interviews, the national press, official records and statistics released by the various ministries and the Damascus-based Central Bureau of Statistics, university dissertations in the Faculty of Economics, and various public lectures held throughout Syria (primarily Damascus and Aleppo). The data required unpacking, decoding, and sometimes discarding. Although I arrived in Syria at a time when public discourse on economic issues became more pervasive and more open,[62] the tightly controlled political environment meant relying heavily on indirect inference and cross-referencing in order to verify various parts of the data. The data accumulated were of a substantive quality and highly consequential in allowing me to draw conclusions based on inductive methods.

Those who have conducted field research in Syria have been sufficiently prudent not to take data (from statistics, interviews, and speeches) at face value. This caution has led to treating such data with extreme "care," and using them as an indicator that reflects "trends" rather than "realities."[63] I shall discuss the reliability of numerical and nonnumerical data and the difficulties in obtaining expressive and sincere information.

Careful researchers would take into consideration that the methods themselves of obtaining the available official statistics lack accuracy and rigor: the Central Bureau of Statistics itself does not have the "real" information. Added to that is the government's control of the bureau, which translates into various attempts at skewing, distorting, and eliminating obtained information (let alone not attempting to obtain certain potentially controversial data in the first place). Official statistics are therefore both obtained and presented by the bureau in a highly politicized manner.

On the other hand, most numbers given by members of the private sector are inaccurate as well. This is, of course, for fear of revealing wealth that is subject to taxes, or to avoid empowering employees who must be provided for or supported in one way or another. Added to that are the numerous and contradictory laws and regulations that reward or punish on the basis of proclaimed data from the private sector. Private statistics are therefore presented in a highly politicized manner as well. There is no antidote-formula, and there is no substitution for cross-referencing when dealing with data of sorts in similar contexts.

1 STATE, BUSINESS, AND REFORM

METHODOLOGICALLY SPEAKING, state-business relations as an object of study can be approached as both a cause and an effect. Although it is difficult to separate the two in practice, they can and should be distinguished analytically if we are to operationalize state-business collaboration. As an effect, or an outcome, the study of state-business relations involves the examination of the interactions of various macrolevel variables. This kind of examination can be carried out by drawing primarily on historical-institutional analysis and structural variables that shape the creation of networks. As a cause, the study of state-business relations aims to operationalize the nexus between state and business in order to determine its impact on economic change and developmental outcomes. Here the outcome to be explained is prolonged economic stagnation with costly developmental outcomes. The analysis proceeds by conceptualizing the category of "business" (for example, business as capital, network, sector, association) in respective contexts, in both time and space. In the Syrian case during the period under study, as in many developing countries with a similar level of development, "business" can be conceptualized as network, for it exhibits network-like structures rather than those of sectors, firms, or meaningful associations.[1]

As a causal factor, the study of state-business collaboration draws on more microlevel strategic analysis and choice theories that are bound up with rational choice and historical institutionalism. A fruitful explanatory *and* interpretive analysis would be one that dynamically integrates the study of state-business collaboration as both a cause and an effect; that is, it would examine the origins or causes of the interaction between the state and the business community, and then examine the effects of those interactions. This causal chain represents both the argument and the analytical map of this book, and explains the transformation of the business community in general across time. The starting point is the state of the Syrian economy, followed by the factors that help shape it.

THE STATE OF THE SYRIAN POLITICAL ECONOMY: A BRIEF OVERVIEW

After a brief period of nominal economic growth in the early 1990s—financed largely by a consumption boom and erratic debt-for-commodities substitution schemes with the former Soviet Union and its immediate inheritors—signs of Syria's decrepit economy began to surface. After peaking in 1992 and 1993, economic growth continued to decline until 2005 (see Figure 1.1). The available data from virtually all sources also denote a considerable decrease in GDP per capita, signaling not just economic trouble but also increasing socioeconomic disparity.[2] After its decline in 1994, "GDP per capita growth" through 2005 never again reached 1994 levels (see Figure 1.2). Notwithstanding variables such as rain seasons and oil production, the dominance of privileged rent-seeking networks has contributed immensely to the direction and type of economic and developmental outcomes that obtained in Syria between 1986 and 2005.

The cracks in the façade spread after 1993 as the result of an inhospitable investment climate and tailored policies that marginalized competitive and production-oriented businesses in favor of protection for well-connected and service-oriented private ones. Invariably, the primary beneficiaries of protection and tailored policies were the same individuals and groups—in both the private and public sectors—who were benefiting from prior state-centered economic arrangements. What changed was the formalization of previously in-

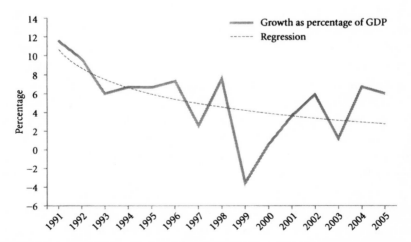

Figure 1.1. Economic growth in Syria, 1991–2005. Data from Economist Intelligence Unit, "Syria Country Report," 1991–2009.

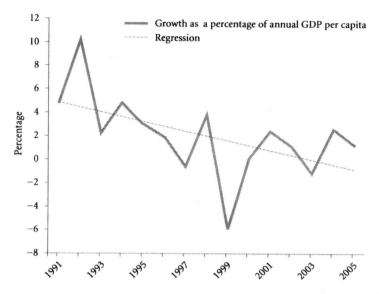

Figure 1.2. GDP per capita growth, 1991–2005. Data from World Bank, World Development Indicators Database.

formal partnerships and relations between state officials and private business actors. In some cases, this involved the entry of numerous businessmen into public life through parliament and "subsidized"[3] election onto the boards of Chambers of Commerce and Industry. More conspicuous was the formal entry of the regime elite and their offspring into the private sector on a large scale. These new "entrepreneurs" began to crowd out traditional businesses and businessmen, especially in the commercial and transportation sectors, in the mid- and late 1990s.[4]

In the late 1990s, economic downturns persisted and collided with the broader political logic of the regime,[5] one that subordinates economic rationality to security concerns, although not to the point where economic decline serves neither. It is as though the Syrian regime, by virtue of its exclusionary relations and practices, had hit an institutional dead end: it had lost much of its already modest ability to mobilize collectivities or discipline social sectors[6] for the purpose of producing collective gains.[7] Instead, the regime could exercise control only by limiting and constraining certain economic activities or, alternatively, by providing rent opportunities for allies—opportunities that did not bode well for the health of the economy as a whole.

The limits of economic change in Syria coincided with the limits of state-business collusion (that is, cronyism) as manifested by networks of capitalists and "bureaucrats." After half a dozen years of stagnation, it took a succession crisis in June 2000 to shake the stalemate: immediately after the death of President Hafiz al-Asad, several prominent members of these networks were cast aside and many others were arrested or hassled under charges of corruption, such as the businessman and former parliamentarian Ma'moun al-Homsi.[8] But such reshuffling had limited effects as it was also intended to consolidate the rule of the new leadership under Bashar al-Asad, a challenge that was accomplished in 2005 with the holding of the tenth Ba'th Regional Command Conference. By 2001, the Syrian economy began to witness some change in the cornerstones of central economic planning at the macroeconomic level, including the financial sector. Bashar's first ministerial shuffle brought new faces into key economic posts, and this new team undertook such tasks as overhauling the outdated state banking system, creating new, highly lucrative opportunities in the telecommunications sector, and expanding free trade zones around the country.[9] The finance and banking sector in particular has seen a slew of ostensible liberalizations, beginning with the process of legalizing private banking in 2001—the first private banks opened in 2004, and the private banking sector has claimed 20 percent of the financial services market share in four short years.[10] In 2005, the regime established the Syrian Stocks and Financial Markets Authority to oversee the Damascus Securities Exchange, which opened in March 2009. The first years of Bashar's rule also saw the legalization of private currency exchange, lowering the financial barriers to trade. Midway into the first decade of Bashar's rule, these developments mobilized the upper echelons of the private sector irrespective of their membership in privileged networks. In 2007, private sector interests banded together to form two holding companies—Cham Holding and Syria Holding[11]—which have since invested in a new domestic airline and pursued development projects alongside Gulf investors. During the same year, some of the same investors formed the Syrian Business Council, a new and self-proclaimed "modern" business association that looks after their interests while addressing the needs of a new, information- and communication-driven economy.[12] Though such developments are beyond the confines of this study, they indicate the decline of privileged networks as the dominant route to economic "success" after 2005, and for good reason.

Regime-Business Mistrust

I argue that public-private networks emerged as a result of the state elite's security concerns shortly after the 1970 coup, launched by the more pragmatic wing of the Ba'th party, and led by then defense minister Hafiz al-Asad. By 1970, the helm of the Ba'th regime was dominated by an increasingly rural-minoritarian leadership. This social stratum was embattled by the social and political struggles of the 1950s and 1960s, and was seeking both to moderate the politically unsustainable radicalism of the Ba'th and to establish détente with the weakened but potentially destabilizing traditional sectors (primarily urban-Sunni sectors). Not lacking social historical roots, this adversarial legacy between a radicalized rural-minoritarian regime and a conservative urban-Sunni business community bred mistrust and antagonism between those who held power and those who held capital.[13] At the same time, however, the two parties needed each other: state intervention in the economy required the cooperation of the private sector, or parts of it; and the disempowered business community was looking to rejuvenate itself. From the perspective of a quasi-socialist regime that places a premium on statist development and decisional autonomy, a formal incorporation of the entire business community was politically risky and untenable. Alternative forms of incorporation had to be sought.

On the eve of the 1970 coup, state-business antagonism and mistrust were already a deep-seated legacy. Initially, this legacy prevented Hafiz al-Asad's regime from dealing formally with the business community as a whole, and from legitimizing the role of the private sector. Unable to discipline the private sector as a whole, the Syrian regime resorted to the creation of informal ties with particular members of the existing business community, some of whom acted as the unofficial partners of state elites (later called the "state bourgeoisie"). Thus, in contrast to the post-Nasir Egyptian regime, the Syrian regime opted for maintaining its principal cornerstone, a weakened Ba'th party, and replacing a politicized army with a massively refurbished security apparatus that constituted a strong backbone for public-private ties. Emerging state-business networks served as an alternative agency for capital accumulation and, in the late 1970s and early 1980s, as an alternative support base during times of political crisis—particularly when the Muslim Brotherhood sought to undermine the authority of the regime.[14]

Over time, these informal webs of state-business ties formed and reformed rent-seeking networks that developed a life of their own, as demonstrated by their impact on economic change after 1986, as the regime attempted to handle a major economic crisis. This was even more evident after 1991, when these networks became the basis of the official institutional expression of the private sector. Nonetheless, most changes in economic policy after 1986, including the active resistance to change in some economic policy areas, can be traced back to the influence of these economic networks rather than to either the aspirations of the business community as a whole or the statist logic that guided economic policy until 1986.

Oil and Strategic Rents

At the macroeconomic level, the policies promoted by state-business networks involved massive misallocation of resources and a lack of comprehensive vision for reform and constituted a drain on the state budget. Nevertheless, the networks' sustenance was secured by substantial oil and strategic rents that the Syrian regime has been able to extract since 1973, notwithstanding a temporary downturn in rents in the mid-1980s. This source of "external" or "rent" income (income that derives from ownership of natural resources or directly unproductive profit-seeking) is the principal reason the Syrian regime was able to maintain (and not forced to substantially downsize) the public sector and public spending. Oil proceeds are handled directly by the political elite within the Syrian regime. How much of this revenue is incorporated into the yearly budget and where it is incorporated are still obscure matters.[15] It is safe to assume, however, that the regime disposes of this revenue in a manner that sustains its ability to make high-policy decisions independent of any other social forces. The key to its decisional autonomy is its financing of the patronage around the public sector, particularly that which relates to public-private networks.

The public sector serves crucial political purposes for the regime: employment generation, benefits for the urban working classes and the families it employs,[16] and the dominance of the largest sectors of the economy. Without the kind of dependency, albeit decreasing, that the public sector fosters in Syrian society, the regime would become far more vulnerable vis-à-vis social unrest. The regime has hitherto unwaveringly refused any form of official privatization of state-owned enterprises and has repeatedly rejected proposals to downsize the public sector in any significant way, insisting on preserving it as the "leading economic sector," to be complemented by the private and mixed sectors.[17]

Thus, economic liberalization occurred alongside a bolstering of the public sector, notwithstanding the decreasing output of the latter. This two-pronged strategy of economic "reform" (expanding both the public and the private sectors) has been costly and irrational from an economic point of view. However, political logic alone was not sufficient to sustain the economy: thus far, it is external rent income that has allowed the regime to subordinate economic rationality to its own security concerns, at least until 2005.

Strategic rents in the form of "aid" or "assistance" from rich Arab states in the Gulf reached their peak in the late 1970s at approximately $1.6 billion per year. This external assistance reached some 10 percent of gross national product (GNP) in the late 1970s and early 1980s and was resumed in the 1990s to reach some 5 percent of GNP.[18] Meanwhile, oil rents—also crucial to the regime's rentier survival strategy—grew steadily from 1975 onwards, peaking in the mid-1990s and slowly declining thereafter (see Table 1.1).[19] On average, since 1975 oil rents alone constituted at least 60 percent of Syria's foreign exchange earnings and a similar proportion of its total exports, allowing the regime to finance its patronage relations, cover more than 50 percent of total imports, and substitute for the necessity of industrial deepening or diversification.[20] In 1995, at Syria's peak oil production, oil constituted 65 percent of exports, 35 percent of fiscal revenue, and 34 percent of GDP.[21] However, even after oil production began to decline in 2000, oil rents on average continued to constitute 60 percent of export earnings, between 40 and 50 percent of total revenue, and between 15 and 20 percent of GDP (see Figure 1.3).

Table 1.1. Syrian oil production, 1970–2005

Year	Barrels per day (in thousands)	Year	Barrels per day (in thousands)	Year	Barrels per day (in thousands)
1970	85	1982	155	1994	563
1971	106	1983	161	1995	596
1972	117	1984	162	1996	586
1973	111	1985	159	1997	577
1974	129	1986	201	1998	576
1975	192	1987	231	1999	579
1976	201	1988	268	2000	548
1977	183	1989	341	2001	581
1978	179	1990	407	2002	548
1979	167	1991	472	2003	527
1980	158	1992	514	2004	495
1981	164	1993	566	2005	450

SOURCE: British Petroleum, "Statistical Review of World Energy."

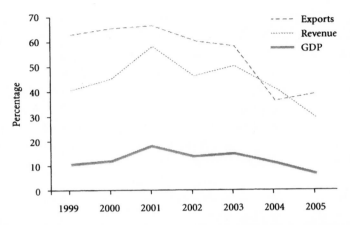

Figure 1.3. Oil as a percentage of exports, GDP, and revenue. Data from IMF and World Bank Development Indicators Database.

Nonetheless, rent income is not without its perils. It can fluctuate and even disappear. In recent years, foreign aid and oil have become less dependable sources of rent income for the regime. A variety of data sources indicate that oil production in Syria has been slowly scaled back since reaching its production peak in the mid-1990s at nearly 600,000 barrels per day. Between 2000 and 2005, production averages decreased to 525,000 barrels per day, and by 2008 production had dropped to just under 400,000 barrels per day—a 30 percent decrease in just over a decade.[22] In 2007 Syria became a net importer of oil for the first time in thirty years.[23] It is indisputable that Syrian oil is a finite resource, although estimates vary on when exactly Syrian oil will run out, and the Syrian government did not publicly acknowledge the reality of finite oil resources until 2002.[24] In 2003 an optimistic (or politically shrewd) minister of petroleum and mineral resources predicted a 50 percent increase in oil production in successive years, and to that end, the government has attempted to entice oil companies into renewed exploration.[25] There have been some new discoveries and increased output at smaller oilfields; however, no new large discoveries are expected to be on the horizon, and nongovernment estimates place the end of oil somewhere near 2030.[26] All such studies, and facts, influenced how the regime relied on nonstate economic actors, which until 2005 were dominated by privileged networks.

It would be a mistake to look to the "new leadership" of Bashar as the only reason for a more serious desire to liberalize the Syrian economy. In an interview with Abdallah al-Dardari, the former deputy prime minister for economic affairs and the star of a new economic policy cohort, he was forthcoming about Syria "running out of alternative sources" of revenue after the late 1990s, and the fact that Syria "can no longer depend on oil revenues as we once did."[27] The speeding up of Syria's economic reform policies after 2005, however meager they might be viewed by observers, is also a function of this seemingly continuing drop in rent income, including foreign assistance. Since the 1990s, foreign assistance has decreased consistently, to 0.9 percent of GNP in 2000 and 0.3 percent of GNP in 2005.[28] And although foreign direct investment (FDI) has begun to increase in its stead, the increase has been far from dramatic, as such inflows remain quite low compared with similar economies in the region (see Figure 1.4).[29]

Embeddedness and Linkage: The Global Economy

The relatively unfettered operation of these networks was facilitated by the absence of checks and scrutiny from either inside or outside the country. On the global front, the rampant rent-seeking that pervades the Syrian economy was not obstructed by any international actors (for example, international financial institutions) throughout the past three decades. Perthes rightly points out that

in contrast to countries like Egypt, whose development path is seen by many a Syrian observer as the model Syria is following with something like a decade's

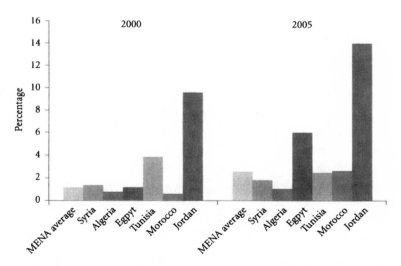

Figure 1.4. Private foreign direct investment as a percentage of GDP. Data from World Bank, World Development Indicators Database.

time lag, and unlike most other adjusting countries in the Arab world, Syria has never, to date, allowed bilateral donors or international financial institutions to interfere in any substantial way with its economic policies, nor negotiated aid for economic reform programs.[30]

Moreover, Syria's liberalization experience has been an affair of the regime that has not been determined or guided from abroad, making Syria, in the words of Perthes, a "laboratory case of sorts" because of the relative absence of external interference.[31] This is significant since much of the available literature on reform experiences in developing countries, including the Arab world, emphasizes the leverage of international financial institutions (IFIs) over indebted countries: "Indebtedness has given international actors a stick with which to push these countries toward policies of economic reform."[32] A sample of Arab countries' long-term debts as a percentage of GNP in 1988 is revealing: Yemen AR (41.6%), Algeria (46.6%), Tunisia (64.2%), Sudan (74.8%), Morocco (89.8%), Jordan (94.0%), Egypt (126.7%), and Yemen PDR (199.4%). By contrast, Syria's total long-term debt as a percentage of GNP was the lowest, at 25.0 percent.[33] Although many of these countries have since reduced their debt to levels approximating Syria's as a result of international financial institution programs, Syria has maintained a low level of foreign debt throughout. Russia restructured Syria's outstanding debt in 2005, removing a substantial portion of its burden, and the most recent Five-Year Plan noted that debt constitutes "no burden on the state budget or balance of payments."[34] This partly explains why Syria is excluded from samples that emphasize international factors (primarily indebtedness, the crux of IFIs' leverage) in stimulating economic reforms and guiding policy decisions.[35]

On the domestic front, save a half dozen years of domestic challenges and turbulence between 1976 and 1982, regime-business networks were unchallenged locally because of the absence of institutionalized or legitimate opposition. Furthermore, until recently, with the exception of a brief liberalization in 2000–2001, the media served more as a tool of government interests than as an impartial means for reporting the news and questioning authority.[36] Combined with the continuous variable of lack of trust between the regime and the business community as a whole, the variables of substantial external rent and relatively unchecked power left the regime to its own devices for nearly three decades. State intervention in the economy prioritized security, not efficiency concerns.

EXPLANATORY MAP AND ANALYTICAL FRAMEWORK

In the following chapters, I address two related processes: (1) state intervention in the economic sphere and its attendant outcomes, and (2) the impact
of the resulting state-business networks on economic and fiscal change. My
documented observations so far suggest that such processes have been viewed
as disjointed or addressed as being independent of one another. In this book,
I seek to rejoin them in order to conduct a proper process-tracing: first, from
the Syrian regime's interests and constraints to its interventionist posture and
decisions, which produced certain forms of informal state-business networks
initially; then, to the effects of these networks on economic and fiscal policies
(see Figure 1.5).

Analytically, the Syrian case instructs us that the two processes are not only
related but can be mutually reinforcing, thereby necessitating the adoption
of economic-sociological and historical-institutional perspectives. Empirically, the Syrian case presents a useful beginning for explaining a particular
brand of erratic economic change and stagnation in a number of developing
countries. State intervention without either "dense relations," as Haggard and
Moon classify it, or "embedded autonomy," as Peter Evans puts it, is unlikely
to produce the kind of incentives and institutions necessary for sustained economic growth. Such relations between the state sector and the business community may be scarce or conflictual in many postcolonial countries, requiring
historical analysis of various social categories (class, community, region, sect,
and so on). In the Syrian case, the ruling regime's distrust of the traditional
business community is the precursor for discussing the emerging nexus between state and business. I trace the effects of such conditions—where the
state considers cooperation too costly—on the kind of relations it develops
henceforth with the private sector or the business community as a whole. To
the extent that mutually beneficial cooperation with the business community
as a whole is too costly to the political elite, they will pursue other forms of relations that mitigate the risks of such cooperation. More often than not, state
elites seek to develop selective and informal ties with members and groups
within the business community. These ties can develop a life of their own by
virtue of the unintended informal network structure that emerges between a
risk-averse elite and entrepreneurs or capitalists with a low opportunity cost.
These economic networks of bureaucrats and capitalists, and their historical
background, nature, and dynamics, become the principal object of research as

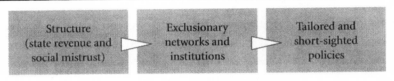

Independent variables

Structure of state revenue
> External oil and strategic rents buttressed the regime's relative autonomy vis-à-vis society

Structure of social mistrust
> Legacy of political-economic and social antagonism led to an emphasis on regime security at any cost

[*Unchecked power of regime (external insulation, internal oppression)*]*

Intervening variable

Exclusionary networks and institutions
Marked by: calculative trust (short time horizons); tailored policy formulation reflecting particularist rather than collective interests; poor information exchange (and thus lack of rational grounding of policies); and lack of conditionality on privileges doled out to business actors

Causal mechanism

Given internal and external regime autonomy, exclusionary institutions exacerbated mistrust and shortened time horizons of investors by undermining information exchange and reciprocal relations. They did so in favor of promoting rent-seeking and risk-averse patterns of economic reform; that is, a "circumscribed liberalization" that served the interests of those who benefited from prereform arrangements (through restrictive fiscal and regulatory policies).

Dependent variable

Prolonged economic stagnation
Marked by poor economic performance and misallocation of resources toward nonproductive sectors (an emphasis on commerce and a neglect of production and development)

*The brackets denote that this variable is conspicuous by its absence.

Figure 1.5. Explanatory map

I trace their impact on economic and fiscal change, along with their attendant developmental distortions.

The lessons learned from the Syrian case are instructive. The analytical, methodological, and empirical findings represent yet another launching pad for investigating the nature of such emerging societies, their elites and institutions, their social and political structures, and potentially, the contingency-framed pattern of their future development. In the explanatory map (Figure 1.5), I unpack the dependent and independent variables, namely, state-business mistrust, strategic rents, and economic stagnation.

2 THE LEGACY OF STATE-BUSINESS ANTAGONISM

THE LEGACY OF SEVERE STATE-BUSINESS ANTAGONISM in Syria has its roots in the turbulent years of the 1960s when radical Ba'th party members assumed power and marginalized the hitherto dominant social forces, spearheaded by the urban-Sunni business community. The political radicalization and social polarization that ensued further exacerbated this antagonism and contributed to the gradual ascendance of rural-minoritarian elements to the helm of the regime. This process also involved internecine conflicts within the Ba'th party, which ended in the capture of power by Hafiz al-Asad in 1970. Asad's regime reformed the institutional context to secure the regime's political gains while reducing social polarization through his famous détente with conservative social forces, both domestically and regionally. Within the rubric of détente, one began to witness the informal reincorporation of parts of the marginalized business community into the political-economic equation. This context, as well as the adversarial state-business legacy of the late 1950s and 1960s, shaped the development and dynamics of the emergent economic networks.

The Syrian case illuminates a particular dimension in the dynamics of state-business relations in authoritarian regimes and their effect on economic change and development. Whereas state and business in some authoritarian countries, notably those of East Asia, have collaborated both to survive and to industrialize the economy, state and business in Syria have colluded primarily to survive, and sent the economy on a downward trend after a short honeymoon burst of consumption in the early 1990s.[1] The debate over whether democratic or authoritarian regimes are better economic liberalizers came and went, and did not end with a clear judgment,[2] precisely because regime type was not the sole determining factor: as some democracies faltered, other authoritarian regimes successfully liberalized and even prospered. Nonetheless, some authoritarian regimes seem to have a more difficult time when they simultaneously attempt to liberalize the economy and promote economic growth.

In his "embedded autonomy" argument, which attempted to explain suc-cessful industrialization in essentially nondemocratic regimes, Peter Evans emphasized both the embeddedness of the bureaucracy in economically func-tional social forces, and its decisional autonomy and coherence.[3] As these states are based on selective exclusion and inclusion, embeddedness becomes a critical factor in heavy-handed populist-authoritarian states that seek to maintain their decisional autonomy amidst pressures for capital accumula-tion and legitimation.[4]

Embracing a broad coalition of social forces that largely represent the masses over and above the interests of the upper classes, populist-authoritarian regimes are risk-averse toward the incorporation of non- or antipopulist forces such as business. Even when embedded networks have developed naturally, as in the case of the Asian Tigers, the trust that collaboration requires between the state and business has had to be carefully cultivated. A high level of trust between state officials and private business facilitates the dynamics of all as-pects of productive collaboration, including information exchange, transpar-ency, and reciprocity.[5] This trust was in severely short supply in the Syrian case.

LOW-TRUST SYSTEMS

In assessing the quality of relations between state and business, the issue of trust occupies center stage. Trust between bureaucrats and businesspeople is said to "reduce transaction and monitoring costs, diminish uncertainty, *lengthen time horizons*, and thereby increase investment (and policy fulfillment generally) above normal levels."[6] Thus, when trust obtains between state and business, in-formation is exchanged more generously; reciprocal relations can develop with minimal monitoring costs; decision-making processes become more transpar-ent; and investors assume the credibility of policies in terms of formulation *and* implementation. Hence, uncertainty decreases; investors' risk-aversion di-minishes; and commitment to both short- and long-term investment becomes more a matter of economic, not political, calculation. In the absence of trust between state and business, a broad safety net is removed and all aspects of the relationship suffer. Individual bureaucrats and capitalists, or networks thereof, are left to their own devices. They can develop a narrower relation of trust, what can be called calculative, strategic, or circumscribed trust.[7] Such strategic trust can be put to the service of various particularistic goals while compro-mising collective ones. Generally, high-trust systems are more competitive and develop positive forms of state-business collaboration, while low-trust systems are noncompetitive and develop forms of state-business collusion that are detrimental to the rest of society.

Historically in Syria, the 'Alawis in power do not trust the Sunni-dominated business community, not because Syrians do not trust each other (this would be the culturalist notion of trust) but because the dominant Sunni community has historically subjugated and denigrated the rural-minoritarian communities from which the 'Alawis hail. In other words, because of the relationship of subordination, both communities qua communities might see their interests as divergent, and this apparent divergence of interests creates mistrust. However, at the individual level, in the context of smaller groups or networks, this mistrust does not necessarily apply. For instance, an 'Alawi member of the regime elite will trust, befriend, and become partners with a Sunni businessman if such a partnership serves both their individual interests—thus debunking the culturalist notion. This is indeed the state of affairs that perpetuates economic networks in Syria: the 'Alawi regime elite invariably have gone into business with Sunni partners they could trust for that defined purpose. However, as a group that could potentially engage in collective action against the regime or its interests, Sunni businessmen were not trusted by the 'Alawi-dominated leadership. Many of the unintended economic consequences discussed in this book flow from this difference between trust at the individual level (which allows Sunnis and 'Alawis to cooperate as serves their individual goals) and trust at the group level (the lack of which hinders cooperation on a broader level).

Thus, to the extent that trust is absent in networks combining state officials and business actors in such authoritarian regimes, they are likely to fall short of developing the kind of embeddedness, let alone the meritocratic bureaucracy, that economic transformation or development requires. The causal mechanism at work is precisely the inverse of what trust inspires between state and business: lack of trust stifles the possibilities of information exchange and transparency that are crucial for productive collaboration. In effect, lack of trust shortens the time horizons of potential investors, usually pushing investments away from businesses that provide added value and toward those with short-term profit, such as trade in consumer goods targeting the middle and upper classes. On the other hand, lack of government trust vis-à-vis the business community as a whole shapes the pattern of institutional and extrainstitutional relations that develop between power holders and capitalists. Two questions suggest themselves: How do we operationalize embeddedness in the Syrian context? And how do we identify sources of trust, or lack thereof, between state and business?

Network analysis is how we operationalize embeddedness, while a historical-institutionalist analysis of state-business relations helps identify sources of trust. Particular state-business legacies give rise to particular types of networks characterized by mutual trust or mutual suspicion. In turn, particular types of networks, marked by variable degrees of collusion or collaboration between capitalists and officials, covary with particular reform policies and agendas.[8] In Syria, the legacy of sharp social and political antagonism between state and business is largely responsible for the kind of institutional and extrainstitutional relations that developed between them, thereby undercutting the possibility of approximating either productive embeddedness or bureaucratic coherence and autonomy. To be sure, there are other factors that impinge on the kind of institutional development that ensues, but the focus of this book is on those institutional and relational forms that influence economic behavior. In particular, we are looking at how this historically rooted and deep-seated suspicion influenced and delimited the general course of both state-business relations and economic change by prejudicing against the formal inclusion of the private sector.

STATE-BUSINESS NETWORKS AS AN EFFECT

The form state-business relations took in Syria (that is, networks) is the first outcome to be explained here, followed later with explaining the impact of these relations on liberalization patterns. Again, state-business networks are themselves an effect of the sociopolitical context at first, but then help us understand economic outcomes.

The social, economic, and political factors and processes that shape the nature and dynamics of state-business relations are numerous but can be condensed—on the basis of the common experiences of development in late-developing countries (LDCs)—into a set of structuring factors that carry differential weight across cases depending on what is to be explained. Each of these factors has implications regarding the nature of the nexus that forms and develops between state and business. This research identifies the legacy of state-business mistrust not only as a factor contributing to emerging state-business networks but also as a factor that characterizes the networks themselves, and thus compromises Syria's developmental potential.

Legacy of State-Business Relations

As discussed above, "state-business relations" can be examined as both a dependent and an independent variable, an effect and a cause. As such, these relations are continuously formed and reformed. This research operationalizes state-business relations as networks that bring together power holders and capitalists. Depending on the kind of interaction between state and business, these networks may assume different forms: as a dependent variable, they could emerge to be exclusionary or inclusive, collusive or collaborative, rentierist or productivity-enhancing, owing largely to historical factors that shape their development. In the process, state-business networks influence patterns of economic change and economic development. I shall discuss the most salient factor that shaped state-business interaction in Syria, namely, the marked lack of trust between power holders and capitalists. This lack of trust, sustained by subsequent patterns of promotion and recruitment, gave rise to an exclusionary institutional context that bred its own economic and developmental outcomes.

Despite variations in the experiences of LDCs, the factor of mutual trust or distrust is important. It bears on the nature and form of relations that develop between power holders and capitalists. At the risk of stating the obvious, one may propose that adversarial legacies of state-business interaction increase the likelihood of state-business collusion,[9] while harmonious legacies increase the likelihood of state-business collaboration.

Collusion Versus Collective Collaboration

Collusion is defined literally as a "conspiracy for fraudulent purposes."[10] But it is a term that is at once more expansive and more precise. Collusion refers to a form of "secret agreement" or "secret cooperation for a fraudulent *or* deceitful purpose." More specifically, it is understood as a "secret agreement between two or more persons to defraud a person of his rights often by the forms of law."[11] Thus, collusion involves a sort of fraudulent collaboration marked by secrecy, a state of affairs that accurately describes the kind of rent-seeking state-business networks that exist in most developing countries, not least those in the Middle East, and Syria in particular.

Successful collaboration—where benefits are more collectively distributed—invariably refers to a positive sum game between state and the entire business community, where the laws, rules, and regulations apply to all members of that community, and where exceptions are rooted in a principle of reciprocity marked by some form of economic rationality—that is, privileges and distinctions are provided selectively according to performative criteria. Collusion, however, implies selective relations rooted primarily in the logic of political rationality and at the expense of economic rationality. Thus, distinctions and privileges are routinely provided in a covert manner to a selective set of beneficiaries according to political criteria. In return, privileged business actors provide capital and relinquish their right to call for (further) reforms. The value of the privileges and distinctions—many of which are naturally packaged in the form of a license for transgressing the law—rises to the extent that the community as a whole is excluded while the opportunity to extract rent is present. Hence, collusive relations between state and business are necessarily exclusionary and tend toward dissolution or reorganization under deteriorating economic circumstances.

In sum, collusive relations are sustained invariably at the expense of pursuing more collective goals, whether we view such goals in terms of sustained economic growth, employment generation, distribution of wealth, or the productivity of the economy. In any event, the initiative to collaborate is that of the state elite: the state and the business community as a whole collaborate when state elites find it in their interest to produce collective benefits.[12] When state elites view collaboration with the business community as a process that empowers antagonistic social forces, they seek alternative forms of interaction. This has been the norm in authoritarian regimes.

The Coincidence of Class, Social Status, and Communal Identity

One of the important factors in shaping the legacy of state-business relations is the relative dissonance and consonance between the holders of state power and the social carriers of capital. Dissonance and consonance refer to socioeconomic, sociopolitical, and sociocultural homogeneity or heterogeneity between these actors. Although most cases are a mixed bag, some are characterized by a well-defined separation between the backgrounds of capitalists and bureaucrats. In Syria, the sociocultural divide between the regime elite and capitalists coincided with the socioeconomic divide: the regime elite were predominantly rural and minoritarian and belonged to the underprivileged classes (some even by rural standards), while members of the business community were predominantly urban and Sunni[13] and belonged to the dominant class. This coincidence of class, social status, and communal identity on either side of the divide further polarized the political context in Syria in the 1960s, when dominant classes were displaced by the historically downtrodden social forces.[14] Longstanding and deep-rooted adversarial relations in Syria—which represent a crucial case—led each party to view the relationship in zero-sum terms: advances on one side are automatically considered to be losses on the other side; increases in private capital diminish state power, and vice versa.

However, the political context of populist-authoritarian consolidation accentuated sociocultural dissonance. It must be noted that this is not a cultural argument: the regime elite were seeking to consolidate populist rule, which invariably involved the marginalization of the dominant classes in favor of a populist coalition dominated by labor and the peasantry, and guaranteed by the army.[15] As will be discussed below in detail, the political and social dimensions combined to privilege "sect" in Syrian politics.

Thus, one can propose that in the context of populist consolidation, to the extent that the societal backgrounds of state power holders and capitalists are dissonant, the probability for collective collaboration between state and business decreases. Collective collaboration here refers to the ability and willingness of the state to deal with the business community as a sector and not as isolated capitalists. There is one caveat: adversarial relations in cases of the aforementioned dissonance are exacerbated when the holders of power belong to a communal minority. In such cases, authoritarian political elites become more risk-averse vis-à-vis political and economic liberalization and with respect to strategies of broadening dictatorship. This situation is not experienced in Egypt, for instance, where by and large bureaucrats and capitalists are not from communally antagonistic backgrounds. Identity and identity construction are both causes and effects in how adversarial dynamics unfold. The ascent of a (regional and sectarian) communal underclass such as the current power holders in Syria is not simply explained by their seeking power and profit: as individuals, they are seeking social legitimacy and retribution vis-à-vis the dominant culture, pursuits that augment the severity of the struggle.

THE HISTORICAL ROOTS OF STATE-BUSINESS ANTAGONISM

The historical causes of state-business antagonism in Syria can be divided into two categories: sociopolitical and sociocultural. While all populist-authoritarian regimes encounter sociopolitical differences with the business community, only a few encounter sharp sociocultural differences. Nonetheless, because of the inclusionary dynamics of populist regimes, the driving force of such antagonism is of the sociopolitical variety. In the Syrian case, the sociocultural differences between the holders of power and capitalists exacerbated this basic source of conflict by creating an exceptionally "low-trust system" that severely constrained the process of "bringing business back in." Not only were the political elite and the business elite divided by their sociopolitical location or position vis-à-vis redistribution; they were also divided by their sociocultural or sociocommunal identities. What then evolved was a keen perception of a zero-sum game between the holders of state power and the holders of capital.

Antagonistic relations between state and business in populist regimes is not a surprising matter, for the harbinger of such regimes is the redistribution of wealth from capitalist to populist sectors in a protracted process by which capitalists—and landlords—are marginalized as a class.[16] Emerging as they do as the vehicle for the winners in a class conflict that pits populist against privileged social sectors, populist regimes embrace a coalition that includes hitherto excluded sectors (for example, workers, peasants, radical intelligentsia) and excludes the largest segments of the business community, apart from what is often called the "nationalist bourgeoisie."[17]

The antagonism between holders of power and holders of capital persists for a number of reasons, chief among them being the sociopolitical variety. Populist leaders harbor an agenda which strikes at the core of the preceding "liberal" social order: it reorganizes the relationship between the state and the economy and creates institutions that oversee and consolidate a transition to a statist economy, in which the state replaces private capital as the engine of economic growth. Keeping capitalists at bay has proven to be a constant occupation of populist regimes in their early years.[18] Recalcitrant capitalists and their institutions first struggle to reverse the status quo, but then, as often happens, they end up struggling simply to stay afloat or—in cases where they neither leave the country nor cooperate with the regime—to survive. In fact, much of the populist rhetoric in the early populist years reflects these regimes' preoccupation with delegitimizing the "liberal" social order and, simultaneously, cushioning the rapid transition into a state-managed social order, though not a socialist order.

BRINGING BUSINESS BACK IN

In virtually all populist-authoritarian regimes, state and business have experienced some form of rapprochement after initial period(s) of mobilization and consolidation. For economic and coalitional reasons, periods of rapprochement usually accompany or follow periods of populist demobilization, as populist regimes seek to broaden their social and economic base by bringing business back in, or to rearrange their corporatist-like system of representation altogether. The severity of economic crisis, the imperative of sustainable capital accumulation, and the necessity of political legitimation play a major part in compelling populist regimes to reconsider the role and participation of the private sector, or parts of it.[19]

The extent and nature of the antagonism between state and business and its attendant consequences in nearly all populist regimes have had a significant impact on the (re)incorporation of business. Thus, it is important to analyze the classification "antagonistic relations" and trace the specific coalitional and institutional consequences to which they give rise, or to discern those options that are eliminated de facto as a result of the regime's pursuing particular paths. If later processes of economic liberalization are said to be influenced by the institutional context from which they are launched, then it becomes just as important to deconstruct these antagonistic relations in order to discern their often enduring links to these processes of liberalization, especially when early institutional configurations have severely constrained subsequent choices. Entangled as it was in communal, class, and subregional conflicts, the Ba'th party in Syria and its development in the 1960s is a case in point. The dynamics of populist consolidation and their attendant dilemmas—mobilization, countermobilization, and state autonomy[20]—exacerbated conflict and in turn radicalized the ruling elite, leading to the polarization of Syrian society by the end of that decade. When the regime was compelled to establish détente with parts of the bourgeoisie in the following decade, after a domestic and regional isolation set in, the legacy and nature of state-business antagonism constricted the process of rapprochement in an unmistakably evident manner. The coincidence of sociopolitical *and* sociocultural differences between state power holders and capitalists, reinforced subsequently by patterns of recruitment and promotion, added a distinctive strategic problematic to the reincorporation of business in the 1970s and 1980s. In retrospect, it may seem that the nature of the antagonism caused the regime to overreact and unnecessarily exclude urban conservative social forces from formal politics. The violent confrontations between the regime and the Muslim Brotherhood in the late 1970s, however, suggest that the regime had much to fear from a business community with firm ties to, and roots in, the traditional *suq* (the traditional market of manufacturers and artisans) from which the rank and file of the Muslim Brotherhood were drawn.[21]

THE RADICALIZATION AND RURALIZATION OF THE BA'TH PARTY

The Rural-Minoritarian Factor

The Ba'th party is best understood as a coalition of social and ideological currents, united by their opposition to the status quo during the preunion period between Syria and Egypt: the formation of the UAR (1958–61) created a split between the old guard (who favored the union) and the rest of the party, and the conservative Separatist Movement (1961–63) created another split between the hard-line regionalists (the rural base) and everyone else. By the time the regionalists (themselves an amalgam of rural minorities) wrested power in 1966, the 'Alawi element dominated that fringe, although it still included some nonminoritarian elements. By the end of the 1960s, the Ba'th leadership was less urban and more rural, less Sunni and more minoritarian, less diversely minoritarian and more 'Alawi. Initially, the radical leadership's drive in the 1960s had been the need for establishing a mechanism of loyalty in the absence of strong institutions and in the presence of a strong urban opposition. Sectarian identity was used to mobilize support for political goals—that is, as a means, not an end—although the coincidence of class, regional, and sectarian divisions made it difficult to isolate the causes.[22] Such communal mechanisms would have to be buttressed by structural and strategic rationality. 'Alawis, though divided among themselves on political as well as personal grounds, and though they did not rule in the name of or for the benefit of that community, were seen by excluded groups as 'Alawis nonetheless, and thus found sectarian-based alliances to be rational. However, "[t]he conflict was, at bottom, over issues—over different views of how radical the Ba'thi revolution should be and how it should deal with the urban opposition."[23] Nonetheless, to rely solely on the rural-minoritarian factor would have spelled political suicide for the regime.[24]

When Asad came to power in 1970, the use of this mechanism of loyalty to further consolidate and insulate the regime internally and externally became more pressing, while at the same time the means to establish firm control became more within reach. Equally important is that Asad knew the history of Syria and the ostensibly unruly nature of its society well, as demonstrated by his recognition of the need for a centrist position in his conflict with the agrarian radicals.[25] He knew he could not both 'Alawize the elite and maintain the exclusion of the urban middle classes, which were predominantly Sunni. His regime had to accommodate parts of the urban-Sunni establishment politically and socially, and harness their economic as well as their disruptive potential in order to step up the capital accumulation needed to build a stronger, more stable state.

By reaching out to segments of urban society through policies of economic rapprochement and controlled liberalization, Asad was at once able partly to legitimize a moderate nationalist-socialist regime, secure capital accumulation, and appease powerful segments of the business community that remained in Syria. The effect of these achievements is immense, and they have played a significant role in keeping the Islamists under ultimate control—as the outcome of the state-Islamist confrontation made evident in and after 1982, when the regime ruthlessly crushed that opposition. Nonetheless, regime-opposition tensions persisted and colored much of the relations between state and society, not least the relationship between state and business, including the subsequent process of business reincorporation.

The Consolidation and Unraveling of Populist-Authoritarian Rule

From a political economic perspective, the consolidation of populist-authoritarian regimes involves collective dilemmas of investment and capital accumulation as these states shoulder the project of industrialization on their own and replace the largely private economic base. Such dilemmas are resolved by instituting waves of nationalizations and land reforms that allow the state to guarantee for itself sources of capital accumulation.[26] The unraveling of populist-authoritarian regimes, on the other hand, involves a collective dilemma of efficiency:[27] as these states' redistributive functions create entrenched entitlement groups and rent-seeking economic networks, economic efficiency becomes elusive.[28] This research generally addresses the difficulties associated with the unraveling of populism: how populist-authoritarian regimes face the challenges of keeping their economies functioning efficiently despite distributive commitments (or burdens, from their perspective), which are nonetheless crucial for the regimes' legitimacy, and often survival. A key factor in understanding these processes of consolidation and unraveling is the relationship between power and capital.

According to Waterbury[29] and Heydemann, the consolidation of populist-authoritarian regimes in dependent developing states involves decisive challenges and trade-offs. These regimes face what Heydemann calls dilemmas of "popular mobilization," "countermobilization," and "limited state autonomy under conditions of dependent development."[30] Each of these dilemmas involves a set of trade-offs, the tenor of which is generally a balance between deepening populism through "radical extractive measures" (the hard-line socialist-state option), and diluting populism by pursuing the kind of "dependent accumulation" that compromises national autonomy (the soft-state option).[31] For Waterbury, Egypt took the soft-state option because the alternative "simply cost[s] too much,"[32] while for Heydemann, Syria took the hard-line option. The analysis herein concurs with Heydemann's characterization of the Syrian path in the 1960s.

In the 1970s, however, Ba'thist moderation did not occur through the dilution of populism but rather through a protracted period of actual societal demobilization. The coincidence of the class, communal, and regional identity of the new Ba'th leadership—the historical rural-minoritarian "underdogs"—and its disproportional proximity to and participation in the military apparatuses, created a relatively more cohesive and potent political bloc. Thus, the same factor of the coincidence of historically exploited identities drove the triumphant faction of the leadership to seek legitimation *and* stability by safely broadening dictatorship. For after the 1967 military defeat at the hands of Israel, the ever-narrowing leadership of the Ba'th, drawn increasingly from traditionally exploited and socially downtrodden rural-minoritarian backgrounds, confronted a largely withdrawn society—yet one with resilient urban-Sunni and commercialized segments standing to lose in the existing political economic status quo. The available alternatives at the time gave credence to a historical compromise, for it seemed the Syrian regime could not pursue the risky hardline option beyond the 1960s. In sum, while a soft-state option was not feasible politically before 1970, the continuation of the 1960s' hard-line position was not sustainable, both politically and economically, for much longer after 1970.

Deepening socialism was viewed as slow political, if not economic, suicide; on the other hand, diluting socialism à la Egypt did not bode well in the medium-to-long run for the largely rural-minoritarian leadership. The post-1970 regime opted for large-scale demobilization domestically, punctuated by extrainstitutional rapprochement with parts of the bourgeoisie, and embarked on a systematic project of boosting its nationalist credentials by shifting conflicts outwards. The conflict with Israel occupied center stage in Syria's foreign policy henceforth, while Syria's involvement in Lebanon rendered that country "a main arena of conflict between Syria and Israel once the post-1973 peace process stalled."[33]

Subsequently, populism was demobilized,[34] what was left of the big bourgeoisie was temporarily contained, and the regional isolation of the Ba'th underwent a speedy, if incomplete, recovery. Nonetheless, the new leadership still could neither officially undermine the role of the socialist-egalitarian Ba'th (which was largely shunted aside by security apparatuses in practice) nor officially incorporate urban business interests as the Egyptian regime had done after Gamal Abdel Nasir. The ever-clearer social dissonance between the holders of power and the carriers of capital—not a significant factor in Egypt—rendered populist unraveling options à la Egypt highly risky, if not politically untenable. On this count, two eventual post-Nasir developments or options were nonoptions in the Syrian case: the dissolution of the Egyptian ASU (Arab Socialist Union Party) and the creation of the NDP (National Democratic Party), which is institutionally and ideologically more amenable to the official incorporation of business interests for the purposes of capital accumulation.

The difficulty the Ba'th encountered subsequently in incorporating urban business interests dates back to its ruralization in the 1960s, which exacerbated rural-urban cleavages:

> The fact that the Ba'th leadership was . . . increasingly minoritarian—'Alawi, Druze, and Isma'ili—and predominantly rural lower middle class and its rivals were chiefly urban, Sunni, and of higher social status represented a major social cleavage underlying political differences and gave the conflict between it and the opposition at this time more of [an] urban-rural than a class character.[35]

Furthermore, the Ba'th's simultaneous radicalization was spurred by failures of the old guard Ba'thists and the brief resurgence of the urban establishment. The manner in which radicalization and ruralization of the Ba'th party unfolded in the 1960s solidified rural-urban and, by association, state-business antagonism.

THE ISOLATION OF THE PARTY AND THE POLARIZATION OF SYRIAN SOCIETY IN THE 1960S

A legacy of deep mistrust between state power holders and capitalists led ultimately to the polarization of Syrian society in the late 1960s, setting the stage for intraregime change.[36] The causal mechanism at work was the actual socialist policies that were adopted at the time to "deepen socialism." These policies were the new Ba'th's means to erode the power base of the urban establishment.

In the eyes of new-generation Ba'thist radicals, the disappointments of the UAR—including its mild socialist measures, the dissolution of the Ba'th, and the compromising of Syrian national autonomy—as well as the resurgence or resilience of the bourgeoisie in its aftermath, confirmed and strengthened their radical convictions and their resolve to erect a hard-line movement that would avoid such pitfalls. According to Heydemann, "the 'counterrevolutionary' episode of Syria's secession from the union taught Ba'thist elites how high the costs of soft authoritarianism could be. . . . These lessons were reinforced by the increasingly hostile opposition of business and landed interests to the Ba'th after 1963."[37] For as a party, "the Ba'th was shattered as a unified movement by the union."[38]

Nonetheless, three Ba'thist factions lingered after the breakup of the UAR. One of these factions was led by Michel Aflaq, the party cofounder, and his primarily student support base. Another was made up of a "large grouping of rural intellectuals who controlled the remnants of many provincial party branches . . . who would come to be called the *Qutriyun* (Regionalists)." Last, and most important, was a group of younger Ba'thist officers, "mostly rural and disproportionately from the minority 'Alawi, Druze, and Isma'ili communities,"[39] and the faction that was perhaps most disenchanted by the dissolution of the Ba'th party. This latter faction "remained loyal to the Ba'th but not to its historic leaders. They violently disputed the dissolution of the party, which seemed to destroy the vehicle of their political and social ambitions."[40] All the militarily well-connected leaders of the latter two factions had lost faith in the traditional leadership, but only the third faction with the junior officers harbored the kind of determination and civil-military networks necessary to launch an enduring coup.

A group of officers, not all of them Ba'thist, staged a coup in 1963 that brought the new radical Ba'th to power. The nucleus of this group included what is now known as the secret Military Committee, formed during the UAR years by a handful of members of the Syrian Officer Corps. It is out of this clique that the effective rulers of Syria were drawn for the next three dozen years. The committee included Salah Jadid (Syria's effective leader from 1966 to 1970) and Hafiz al-Asad (Syria's defense minister until 1970), as well as others who were predominantly from rural backgrounds.[41]

Significantly, "on the eve of the party's seizure of power, the 'Ba'th' had no widely acknowledged leadership and enjoyed no ideological consensus. . . . It was organizationally dispersed and fragmented, its former mass base either alienated or de-mobilized."[42] The rural social origin of the new Ba'thists gave priority to what Hinnebusch termed "agrarian radicalism" at the expense of Pan-Arabism; hence, "the Ba'th would long face the hostility of much of urban society, not only of the landlord elite and Islamic conservatives but of many middle class Nasirites and liberals as well." Ultimately, the new Ba'th would have "bases of power in the army and the village ruling from the heights of state power over an urban milieu which rejected its legitimacy."[43] The ruling strongmen proceeded to recruit and promote intellectuals and officers from the rural masses, a segment of society that had been mobilized by the bourgeois regime in the 1950s as part of the regime's effort to win over the masses in its short-lived rift with the landed notables.[44] Strategically speaking, the 1960s proved most receptive to the kind of semisocialist and nationalist message the Ba'th was sending, irrespective of the social carriers, for "by contrast, its rivals all labored under fatal liabilities"; these rivals included the Muslim Brethren, the SSNP (Syrian Socialist Nationalist Party), and the communists.[45] In fact, it is this context that led the Ba'th to advance a distinct path. The new Ba'th leadership needed a doctrine of revolutionary transformation, which classical Ba'thism did not provide, and at the same time one that would be "distinguishable from Nasirism." Thus, the conflict between the existing political forces shaped and rationalized the Ba'th's political and ideological preferences: pan-Arabism was retained as a distant goal to be preceded by revolutionary transformation heralded by Syria. This politico-ideological stance distinguished the new Ba'th. The new leadership considered the "fusion of Ba'thi nationalism and Marxism . . . to be an ideological alternative to all the things they rejected—traditional Islam, Western liberal capitalism, communist internationalism—and a viable blueprint for a socialist but authentically Arab revolution."[46] Socially and economically, the picture was more complex, as the new regime radicals had to exclude and disempower an economically functional sector of Syrian society, the bourgeoisie, thereby further radicalizing and polarizing Syrian politics. But the disempowerment of the bourgeoisie was inevitable if the new Ba'th was to embark on any social transformation. The resilience of the establishment in fact served as an unintended catalyst in radicalizing and hardening the new Ba'th.

The failed political ventures prior to 1963, namely the UAR and the Separatist Movement, pushed the party further to the left and induced a heavy-handed authoritarian rule.[47] The separatist coup that followed the dissolution of the union was a testimony to the failure of Syria's soft authoritarian rule and compromise on social policy during the UAR. In sum, soft-state options were ruled out in favor of a hard-line view that perceived a zero-sum conflict between progressive reformers and the establishment. Although a hard-line approach was not a smooth ride for the rural-minoritarian leadership, the stakes were too high to avoid it. The years between 1963 and 1966 reflected this concern on the part of the leadership. Internecine Ba'thist conflicts at the time between the old guard and the new guard clouded the rural-minoritarian factor and aided the radical leadership in consolidating its hold on the heights of power behind the scenes.[48] By 1966 this triumphant faction was ready to implement more openly its radical policies of nationalization and land reform—which had effectively started in 1965—that were meant to deal the final blow to the urban establishment and to other rivals and former allies, including the Nasirists.[49] Further nationalization in 1965 stripped the private sector of much of its remaining economic power, while implementing the new agrarian reform law, which "halved the amount of land owners could keep, and going beyond the earlier (1958) attack on the greatest magnates, struck at the power of medium landlords."[50] Clearly put by Hinnebusch, "[t]he effect of these policies was to polarize Syrian society." To contain countermobilization and reprisals, the party had to rely increasingly on the military and on party elements whose loyalty was unquestionable. The cost was both high as well as internally detrimental to the Ba'th party, and would prove decisive in effecting an internal shift, especially after the 1967 war. Institutionally speaking, this securitization marked the beginning of the dominance of security apparatuses after 1970. In the meantime, however, and before the internal Ba'thist disputes were settled, it was the army that served as a life jacket for the triumphant faction.

Because of its heavy reliance on the military, the party could not dominate or subordinate it; rather, the reverse was true. This lack of institutional legitimacy of the party privileged the army and, later, the notorious security apparatuses.[51] The regime was in a perpetual state of precariousness that led to its exploitation of all noninstitutional advantages and cleavages, including "personal, generational, class, regional and, not least, sectarian."[52] Needless to say, such practices further undermined not only the legitimacy and institutionalization but also the cohesion of the Ba'thist regime. Although the radicals had clearly triumphed by 1966, they were rather isolated, not only from their opponents but also from their former allies and from a significant segment of society, from which the regime itself felt far removed because of that segment's antiradical sentiments.[53]

After 1966 the new Ba'th had a scheme to alienate every conservative sentiment, whether social or economic, even pragmatic-nationalist sentiments: Asad, a pragmatic-nationalist himself, was alienated.[54] Serious and active implementation of the new agrarian reforms took place after the radical branch of the party took the helm. Coupled with ideological rigidity,[55] the regime's policies led to the polarization of society into (albeit loose) leftist and rightist divisions. The ruralization of cities, especially Damascus, ensued and was matched by bourgeois exile. Big business, notably merchants and religious groups, was most affected. Antirural and anti-'Alawi attitudes and jokes proliferated in the private popular culture of the cities, signaling the beginning of a shift in the perception of the nature of the conflict—especially from the perspective of hardliners within and outside the regime—from a class-oriented to a social-communal conflict.

The Decisive Impact of the 1967 War

The 1967 war, said to have been invited by the haste of the radical Ba'thists, was the germ for a turning point in the modern history of Syria, even if no actual changes took place until a few years down the road, in 1970. Whereas radical regimes such as Nasir's Egypt moderated their socialist programs after 1967, Syria's regime "was determined to continue the 'revolutionary course,' internally mobilizing the population for national resistance, externally making Syria an obstacle to any political settlement of the Arab-Israeli conflict."[56] In light of Nasir's and the USSR's acquiescence vis-à-vis a political settlement and the moderate-led Ba'th coup in Iraq in 1968, this postwar "lone star" strategy increased the regime's isolation both regionally and domestically and struck at its political legitimacy.

Most important, the ramifications of the 1967 war led to a general ideological vacuum within the Ba'th. Intra-Ba'th recrimination shattered the Ba'th unity once more. Asad led Ba'thist moderates arguing for a détente with conservative forces, locally and regionally, for the purpose of pursuing nationalist aims. In retrospect, it is indubitably evident that Asad saw the long-term survival and unity of the Ba'thist regime as a function of its regional performance. The flip side of this "external" concern was the necessity, minimally, to neutralize external influence, a harbinger of Syrian foreign policy under Asad after 1970. His explicit calls for subordinating class conflict to the goal of national unity and for achieving reconciliation with the conservatives were met with appeasement from the radical wing of the Ba'th.[57] Consequently, Asad tapped into a number of Ba'thist officials, many of whom were opportunity seekers from the lower and middle rungs of the Ba'th's party, military, and bureaucratic apparatuses. The amalgam of careerist Ba'thists that he was able to form exacerbated clientelism and led to the consolidation of the networks that would prevail and run the state after 1970.[58]

Economically, amidst a drainage of resources to the military, Asad wanted to persist with refurbishing the army, while the radicals wanted to resume socialist deepening. Their plans were extended to the countryside, where middle peasants had already benefited from earlier land reforms but now stood to lose from further reforms. However, problems of mismanagement, and often the lack of any management in some remote areas, prevented such socialist deepening from taking place. As a result, Asad had his way and was supported by the middle peasants, who by then knew well which Ba'thist faction would preserve their interests.

The events surrounding Jordan's "Black September" in 1970 precipitated Asad's final blow to the radicals. In several ways, these events were reminiscent of the 1967 debacle, as the radicals were impulsive and Asad was reluctant to intervene on behalf of the Palestinians in their armed conflict against the Jordanian army. After a series of internecine skirmishes, which were incursive and mobilizational, Asad mounted a coup in 1970 against the radicals, capturing the leadership of the Ba'th for three decades to come.

Ba'thist Policies and the Transformation of Syria's Social Structure

Socioeconomically, Ba'thist policies in the 1960s decisively altered Syria's social structure for decades to come in favor of the less privileged (regardless of sect) and at the expense of the landed-mercantile sectors. In sum, "agrarian reform, nationalizations, and the creation of a large state sector demolished rigid class inequalities rooted in monopolistic control of the means of production and more broadly diffused property and opportunity."[59] By 1970, land reform and the expansion of the bureaucracy, military, and the public sector had ameliorated significantly the fortunes of the agricultural proletariat and small peasantry—then forming 47.9 percent of Syria's class structure[60]—creating an organic alliance that the state could draw upon so long as it upheld their interests.[61] According to Hinnebusch, this came at the expense of the shrinking of the bourgeoisie:

> Increased fluidity of opportunity and diffusion of property gave rise to a significant increase in the middle strata while narrowing the top and very bottom of the social structure. . . . There was a decline in the bourgeoisie, not only in its wealth and power, but even in its numbers through downward mobility or exit from Syria. There was a corresponding expansion in the state-dependent salaried middle and working classes, increasing from 32.9% of the economically active population in 1960 to 33.6% in 1970 and 37.8% in 1975. . . . A significant portion of the landless agricultural proletariat was raised up and transformed into a small holding peasantry.[62]

Significantly, because of nuclear and extended family relations in Syria, the various social strata that benefited from the rise of the radical Ba'th formed a sizeable social sector, often termed the petite bourgeoisie; more accurately, this is the *lower* middle class with small land holdings and property.

The Ba'th's policies amounted to what can be seen as a semiegalitarian socioeconomic leveling, very much an intended outcome of its foreseeable socioeconomic and sociopolitical goals. Socioeconomic leveling and egalitarianism at first enhanced state autonomy in the absence of any dominant social power controlling the state. Until the mid-1970s, it also provided a rural and minoritarian elite with a rare political opportunity of ruling with some legitimacy in the name of the majority.

The Origin and Impact of the 'Alawi Factor

While urban-Sunni dominance of the business community is easily discernible from any reading of contemporary Syrian history,[63] the ascendance of rural minorities, especially 'Alawis, to the heights of power and their dominance of commanding state apparatuses require elaboration in light of the state-business antagonism argument advanced herein. The social and economic grievances suffered by rural minorities, primarily the 'Alawis, are one and the same factor largely responsible for their adoption of radical political views and, after 1970, the adoption by the 'Alawi leadership of a less conflictual, cross-class political economic agenda that preserved their dominance and ended their exploitation as a community. To preserve the dominance of a minoritarian leadership, the institutional context had to be modified: the populist Ba'th party was compromised as an authoritative body by the role of the army in the late 1960s. In turn, however, when Asad came to power, the army itself as a locus of actual authority gradually gave way to the dozen security apparatuses that marked Syria's *mukhabarat* (or secret service) state.[64] This gradual shift in the locus of power, if not authority, permitted a small group of people to rule Syria, unencumbered by party politics and competing bureaucratic preferences. Once more, regime security was purchased at a high price. A rural-minoritarian rule was set in place at all costs.

Where did rural minorities, especially 'Alawis, acquire this revolutionary zeal *and* pragmatism?

Although the middle class in Syria in the 1950s was very much opposed to the status quo—that is, the dominance of bourgeois parties and lack of a just redistribution of wealth—their plight as a class could hardly be compared to that of the rural populations, especially the 'Alawis. According to Hinnebusch, the 'Alawis'

> modest origins and closeness to village grievances made them much more antagonistic to the traditional urban establishment and determined to carry out a radical revolution than the party's urban middle class leaders. Their attitudes reflected a long gestating rejection of traditional society and a powerful longing for the overthrow of a social order they blamed both for their lack of personal

opportunities and for all Syria's ills—its backwardness and inequalities, its weakness in face of Israel and the West.[65]

The social mobilization that the middle classes and some of the bourgeois parties undertook, especially in the realm of education and—earlier under the auspices of French colonialism—army recruitment,[66] was the vehicle the rural youth used to enter into the heart of Syrian society. Ideologically,

> Alawi adhesion to the Ba'th and Arabism expressed a natural and powerful drive for acceptance as equals in the dominant Arab culture. . . . The Alawi attraction to Ba'th "socialism" was also natural: a community with limited land resources, a bursting population, and little commercial tradition, could only hope to pull itself out of poverty through state aid and reform. It is perhaps not surprising that of Syria's four minorities, the agrarian radicalism of the Alawis ran the deepest[,] for far more than the others, they were victims of Syria's "feudal" order.[67]

Thus, at each successive stage in confronting the urban establishment and in purging internal elements, it was invariably the 'Alawi officers who sought to press on with more reforms in the economic sphere and more purges at the political level.[68] Indeed, shortly after the Ba'thist seizure of power in 1963, "hundreds of conservative or Nasirite officers, chiefly of the urban Sunni upper-middle and middle classes, were purged. Their places were filled by a wholesale recruitment of Ba'thists of chiefly rural and often minority origin, many, indeed, the kinsmen of leading Ba'th officers."[69] This cycle of revolutionary economic transformations and purges persisted well into the end of the 1960s, when what is called "the duality of power" emerged between Asad and Jadid over the appropriate course of action regarding further domestic reforms and regional politics. All this turmoil occurred within the rubric of a radical party with conflicting leaderships, not within a relatively personalized leadership, as was the case after 1970.

By 1970 the party had been effectively ruralized, if not 'Alawized—the latter did not occur until after 1975—to the point where the imperatives of consolidating populist-authoritarian rule started to conflict with the systemic imperative of legitimation. This is evidenced by the party's isolation even from social forces on the left, such as the Nasirists, socialists, and communists. While the "Ba'th's drive to consolidate its rule began as a matter of turning the institutions of state power into rural strongholds dominating the cities," the end of that process had isolated the party, especially after 1967, both regionally and domestically. According to Hinnebusch, "the Ba'th faced the formidable challenge of a severe crisis of legitimacy."[70] The time had come for a slowing down of the revolutionary course and for the reincorporation of urban society. The question was how and to what extent. Regardless of the Asad regime's answer after 1970, the experiences of the UAR and Ba'thist rule in the 1960s had left a bitter taste in the mouths of both the regime elite and the urban establishment. A low-trust system seemed to be irreversibly in place at the time. Most social sectors, feeling disempowered and disenfranchised—politically, if not economically—were helplessly resigned to the dominance of a fringe that promised national unity and economic progress.

As Batatu, Hinnebusch, Perthes, and Heydemann have all rejected the sectarian argument for explaining Syrian politics, so does this study. What is being emphasized here is not that sectarianism was an intended goal of the increasingly 'Alawi-dominated leadership. Rather, the rural-minoritarian historical background of this otherwise nationalist-populist leadership was a catalyst in radicalizing Syrian politics in the 1960s, in which the principal culprits were the urban bourgeoisie and the landed establishment. This sociocultural opposition was reinforced after 1966, but particularly after the Asad takeover in 1970, leading to a near civil war in Syria between 1976 and 1982. As discussed above, the challenge of consolidating populist rule in a fractious environment led the increasingly rural-minoritarian leadership to rely on sectarian background as an associative mechanism that reduced the risk of further divisions and increased cohesion in confronting what seemed to continue to be a resilient socioeconomic establishment. The systemic imperatives of capital accumulation and legitimation compelled a firmly saddled regime in 1970 to contain important parts of the establishment (more the bourgeoisie than the landed strata) by establishing a détente of sorts with them. For in Asad's view at the time,

> the regime could only ride out its difficulties by switching into the channel of compromise politics on both the regional and domestic fronts, thus enabling the country to concentrate on rebuilding and strengthening its defenses. Internally this meant, in essence, toning down the urban-rural conflict and conciliating the urban middle class.[71]

The manner in which this détente was established domestically and regionally reflects the import and impact of the historical sociocommunal and socioeconomic antagonism between state power holders and the business community at large.

The need to preserve the decisional autonomy of the Syrian regime after 1970 led its leaders to pursue patterns of recruitment and promotion that reinforced the confinement of most high posts to 'Alawis, thereby exacerbating the dissonance between officials and capitalists. From the perspective of the urban-Sunni establishment and its dependents in the traditionally conservative urban *suq*, the leadership was responsible for wresting—many say stealing—their economic power base and, by association, their political power. Thus, resentment of the Ba'th ran deep among both the bourgeoisie and the conservative urban quarters, who saw their fortunes and social prestige lose ground to what they described as a formerly obedient and downtrodden community from which they used to hire their maids. This intertwining of political, socioeconomic, and sociocultural factors acted to create and perpetuate a legacy of deep-rooted mistrust between the state and the business community.

FAILURE TO DISCIPLINE THE PRIVATE SECTOR: BALANCING POPULISM WITH THE BOURGEOISIE

After the 1963 coup, the role of the private sector was gradually limited, but preserved. The regime could neither offer the private sector collective benefits (as an incentive for cooperation) nor do without private capital and entrepreneurship. According to Hinnebusch," [w]hile socialization of the entire economy was seen as the ultimate goal, in the interim, a role for the private enterprise in internal trade, construction, tourism, and small industry would be preserved under state regulation; the petite bourgeoisie would be socialized only gradually and by persuasion."[72] After 1970, however, further socialization was dropped, and parts of the business community enjoyed more power than the Ba'th had ever envisioned before 1970 or admitted hitherto.

Why did the regime not engage the private sector as a whole? Is it because it was unwilling to do so, or unable to do so? In retrospect, it seems that the regime, ultimately, had the ability to further confine the role of the private sector, but did not. On the other hand, throughout the following years the regime was able to extend more "rights" to the less privileged social classes and monopolize more of the commanding heights of the economy for their benefit. But it did not do so either. What, therefore, accounts for the self-limiting behavior—both early on as well as after the Asad takeover?

Two factors are prominent in accounting for the regime's self-limiting behavior: first, the increasingly rural-minoritarian status of a leadership confronting a hostile and potentially powerful business community, and second, the related rational preference on the part of the leadership to maintain both legitimacy and autonomy. As a populist regime that also suffered from an increasingly rural-minoritarian status, it established its legitimacy by embarking on popular social and economic reforms in the early 1970s—labeled the "first *infitah*" by Perthes.[73] But because the deepening of these reforms risked both the regime's loss of autonomy from new beneficiaries—labor did not consent, and its leaders were co-opted—and its loss of internal and external support from functionally conservative forces, the leadership opted for a balancing game, of which self-limitation was an unintended by-product. According to Hinnebusch, "as Syria's power elite became bourgeoisified, it sought a modus vivendi with the bourgeoisie. However, to avoid becoming dependent on a class it still cannot trust, it seeks to maintain its populist constituency and preserve its autonomy by balancing between rival bourgeois and popular forces."[74] This is what Hinnebusch, Ayubi, and others studying Middle Eastern states such as Syria or Egypt have called Bonapartism or a Bonapartist state, a state that stands above and manages social conflict.[75]

PATRONAGE AS A PRICE FOR SECURITY: HOW THE REGIME ACHIEVED THE BALANCING GAME

Essentially, short of the necessary economic and social resources in 1970, the regime opted for a careful lose-lose scenario where both it and its opponents lost the opportunity to establish hegemony: its mixed ideological canon after 1970 diluted its force of persuasion and prevented it from creating an organic and broad-based "historical bloc." For their part, all opponents of the regime lacked the institutional means to achieve any kind of domination, let alone hegemony. Only the regime possessed these means and manipulated them to its advantage and toward its goals in the service of bolstering its autonomy from social forces.

The regime's notion of "leveling egalitarianism" was instrumental in keeping the masses under control but also stripped the regime of much of its mobilizationary potential by failing to provide collectively beneficial selective incentives to cooperative or productive social sectors. Faced with what can be called a "strong society," the regime was less intent on empowering certain segments (including its own constituency), and more intent on equally disempowering and balancing all sectors for the purpose of maintaining its autonomy, for which the regime's rhetorical euphemism was "social peace." Ultimately, this was achieved by stripping popular sectors, groups, and organizations of any meaningful autonomy while connecting their livelihood to the state,[76] and by wresting all institutional power from the big bourgeoisie and confining its economic role to activities that were heavily regulated or subordinated to high policy. Hence, the post-1970 trajectory was one of institutional demobilization of populist forces and selective extrainstitutional mobilization of parts of the business community in the form of budding economic networks. These networks, though only informally tied to the heights of power, would have a decisive impact on the pattern of economic change in Syria for more than three decades to come.

The nature and dynamics of these economic networks reflect the calculus of the regime in attempting to bring a traditionally hostile and antagonistic business community back into the political economic formula without incurring the attendant risk of being overtaken or subsumed by capitalist social forces and their urban allies from traditional quarters. The rural-minoritarian character of the leadership and the history of sociocommunal antagonism, which is still felt at the time of this writing, rendered the regime highly risk-averse vis-à-vis the reincorporation of the urban-Sunni-dominated business community. The security of the regime, however, was maintained.

Select members and groups in the business community, as well as lay opportunists, came to form intricate webs of interests with regime officials and, more important after 1970, with strongmen in the mushrooming security apparatuses. These networks, however, would remain largely uninstitutionalized and operate behind closed doors until 1990–91, when the government officially acknowledged the role of the private sector in the national economy. The lack of trust that characterized the relations between the state and the business community as a whole pervaded these networks as well, preventing the exchange of information and the transparency needed to conduct collectively profitable business and leading to a pattern of collusive rent-seeking of the worst variety,[77] one that further fragmented the economic bureaucracy and produced tailored policies accompanied by contradictory laws and regulations. Despite a speculative boom in the early 1990s—akin to that of post-Nasir Egypt's *infitah*—the outcome in Syria between 1995 and 2005 was economic stagnation against the backdrop of inefficiency[78] and developmental woes.

CONCLUSION

The Ba'th can be viewed as a vehicle for rural uprising against the urban-Sunni establishment. Hinnebusch points out that the "radical Ba'th enterprise" reflected both Syria's urban-rural cleavage and class antagonisms.[79] Suffering immensely from hardships in rural areas and from their disadvantaged class status, the 'Alawis in particular stood to gain from virtually any change in the status quo, and were thus in the forefront of revolutionary currents. Though often at odds, the urban establishment and the landed notables were viewed ultimately by the rural peasantry and underclasses as partners in their exploitation. The turbulent events in the early 1960s, including the resilience of the urban establishment, convinced the emerging rural revolutionaries of a zero-sum game between themselves and the urban establishment and their allies. Compromises were both unlikely and dangerous, especially in the first half dozen years of Ba'thist rule after 1963. Building on the reforms initiated by the UAR, Ba'thist socialist transformation achieved social leveling and significantly reduced the rural-urban gap, thereby empowering the majority of excluded sectors of Syrian society, most of whom, even in rural areas, were Sunni. The social cost of this leveling was a disempowerment of the urban establishment, which for a long time to come scarred the relationship between the state and the business community at large. Moreover, the 1967 by Israel isolated the regime politically until 1970, both domestically and regionally. Asad's détente with conservative forces was both bold and necessary, and proved enduring four decades on.

Making the economies of LDCs more efficient is a formidable challenge, given the simultaneity of crises these countries face. Most important, the task of making economies more efficient and productive requires kinds of collective action, signaling, transparency, information exchange, and reciprocity that are difficult to achieve in the absence of trust between power holders and capitalists. Until there is a homogeneity of sorts between the social carriers of power and capital, economic efficiency is likely to remain elusive and subordinate to the imperative of maintaining autonomy. The dynamics of populist-authoritarian rule further exacerbate and politicize issues of trust and collective action because authoritarian rulers possess a low tolerance for uncertainty and tend to discount long-range payoffs. On the other hand, the redistributive commitments of populism prevent the regime from engaging the private sector as a whole, opting instead for informal relations that take on network-like structures.

3

THE POLITICS OF
PRIVATE SECTOR DEVELOPMENT

There is no "private sector proper" in Syria since 1963.

**—Muhammad Ghassan al-Qalla', Syrian industrialist and chief
academic consultant for the Damascus Chamber of Commerce**

*In its majority, the private sector is the product of aberrant [shaththa]
conditions . . . chained by basic political factors.*

—Ma'moun Tabba', Syrian lawyer and businessman

*Our regime is unable to tolerate a strong private sector, a giant. Either it
must remain a dwarf, or it may grow in the shadow of the state, but it must
not operate in the open, under the sun. . . . [I]t must operate only through
[committing] collective violations and chaos, so as it can be taken out at
any moment.*

—Riad Saif, Syrian industrialist and parliament member

There is no conflict of interest between the state and the private sector.

**—Ratib Badr al-Din al-Shallah, president of the Syrian Union of
Chambers of Commerce**

The private sector has indeed developed and assumed its role.

—Abdul Rahman al-'Attar, Syrian businessman

*The private sector today is in better shape than it was in the 1990s, but it has a
long way to go.*

—Nabil Sukkar, Syrian economist

THE SYRIAN PRIVATE SECTOR, much like its counterparts in the region, does not
exist in a vacuum, nor do its properties derive from abstract roles that have
come to be read onto it. It is very much an outgrowth of particular struggles
between state and market, politicians and capitalists, and reflects a particular
history of contention that continues to color the interaction between state officials, political elites, and businessmen. State officials within unraveling state-

run economies usually view the private sector with suspicion in fear of collective action among its members that might compromise the state as well as the officials' own interests. More deeply vested in the longer term, the political elite in authoritarian regimes eventually see the private sector as a reservoir of potential and willing partners in mutually beneficial alliances and economic schemes. For businesspeople, states pose either opportunities or constraints, depending on an individual's proximity to state officials or political elites. In Syria, the deep-seated legacy of state-business antagonism and the subsequent unraveling of the state-run economy exacerbated these modal preferences and pushed state–private sector relations to the informal realm for quite some time before we began to see a resurgence of formal, institutionalized relations. The unraveling of the state-run economy is colored by an enduring legacy of political antagonism and in some measure continues to be fed by the very factors that marked that legacy.

Despite the bitter state-business legacy, Syria falls on the same spectrum of state–private sector relations that encompasses similar cases in late-developing countries, notably in the Middle East and North Africa.[1] Research on private sectors and state-business relations in the Middle East is growing[2] and approaching the point where cumulative knowledge will soon allow analysts to develop more sophisticated theoretical frameworks on the topic. The relationship between the state and the private sector in any of these countries is fraught with contingencies and constraints, and is usually governed by historical and systemic factors that must be addressed on a case-by-case basis. And though private sectors in neighboring economies have had an earlier resurgence and have therefore attracted considerable analysis and research, not enough is known about the specific contours of the private sector.[3] Aside from its comparatively more restrictive research environment, Syria's actual "private" business power has seldom resided in formal private sector institutions. And though the formalization of state-business institutions is well under way, it is by no means near complete.

Despite vastly improved relations between the regime and the private sector, it is still evident that the current Syrian regime has not broadened its rule sufficiently to contain the entire private sector. Until such time—until the social and political gap between the regime and the business community *as a whole* is narrowed, or until external pressures force a change on elite preferences—the Syrian regime will persist in avoiding normalized engagement with the private sector and continue to interact with select moguls through informal economic networks. It is therefore not surprising to witness the often sharp opposition between independent businessmen who constitute the numerical majority in the private sector and the few remaining businessmen who possess the plurality of big business assets and who are beholden to their partners in officialdom. We must thus examine the various social segments that constitute the private sector, particularly its upper crust, and shed light on the political conditions under which the private sector developed until 2005, including the institutional context that stunted its development.

THE SOCIAL BASIS OF SYRIA'S PRIVATE SECTOR: POLITICALLY CONSTITUTED SOCIAL STRATA

The new economic elite in Syria comprises both a private and a "public" component: private businesspeople and state officials, the latter who are either partners with private sector actors or who themselves have gone into business since the late 1980s. The new economic elite, therefore—its state and private varieties—is a relatively recent social phenomenon. It emerged with the acceleration of statist economic policies during the Hafiz al-Asad era, particularly after the heavy inflow of capital from Arab Gulf countries in the aftermath of the 1973 Arab-Israeli war. Referred to as *al-tabaqa al-jadida* (the new class), or *hadithi al-ni'ma* (those with new wealth), the new economic elite qua social category grew rapidly as a result of a number of factors involving the expansion of the state, public investments, (semi)legal business ventures across Syria's borders, and exceptional domestic "business" deals, all of which brought together officials and private partners in largely commercial ventures that provided little added value to the economy.[4] The new private bourgeoisie is largely a creation of the regime, while the state bourgeoisie has been an outgrowth of statist policies and risk-averse regime strategies that emphasized capital accumulation within regime orbits—that is, industrial expansion rather than industrial deepening.[5] These strategies were intended to create a new economic elite in the image of the new, more rural, more minoritarian state elite, one that is juxtaposed to a traditionally resilient urban-Sunni bourgeoisie. Though this social divide was not the only concern of the regime—there are other political concerns associated with the developmental dilemmas of populist-authoritarian regimes like Syria's—the social factor emerged as increasingly decisive for an individual's inclusion among the top ranks of the political and economic elite, especially as liberalization policies expanded in the late 1980s and early 1990s.

Amounting to no more than 1 percent of the population,[6] the new economic elite (in both its private and public/state varieties) wields tremendous power, especially at the level of medium-range economic policies. Its power is derived not from the institutions that represent and support private business, for such institutions are rarely representative of the private sector or the business community as a whole. Rather, its power emerges from both its access to the highest power centers in the regime and the positions that members of the state economic elite themselves hold simultaneously in government, party, and the army and security services. The most powerful among the new economic elite are by far the state officials who went into business, followed by a small number of surrogate private businessmen who are beholden to the regime and whose fortunes are a direct result of such relations.[7] The remaining parts of the private economic elite are economically more enterprising than either of the other groups but wield far less influence on economic policies and are far less wealthy.

The most powerful segment of the new economic elite thus derives its fortunes primarily through its political positionality, and is itself politically rather than economically constituted: without access to, and the blessing of, the political and military elite, opportunities for significant private capital accumulation are quite limited. It is political position or connections, not entrepreneurship, which determines membership among the top echelons of the business community. Though powerful politically and economically, the new economic elite as a whole is dependent on rents (politically created and expedited economic opportunities and income), remains largely undifferentiated sectorally,[8] and lacks a common interest in sustainable collective action.

Private Sector Actors

The private economic elite, or the new business elite, is divided politically into three broad categories, defined largely by their proximity to the state bourgeoisie and the economic networks that bind them.

The Big Business Elite   The most influential and wealthy group of private new businesspeople consists of those who managed to establish the coziest relations, including business partnerships, with the various state agencies and regime personnel since the 1970s. This group's loyalty to the regime has been time-proven. These Syrian tycoons constitute the first and most powerful economic line of defense for the regime. Their economic desires are prioritized by the state, not because the state is able to mobilize them or because they believe in the regime; rather, it is because their interests derive from the economically restrictive status quo over which the regime presides, one that provides them with exceptional business opportunities. This stratum of the business elite enjoys the largest portion of privileges, and its income includes a substantial amount of rent derived from protection, monopolies, and exemptions.[9] Sa'ib Nahhas, a businessman who became one of the "troika"[10] in the 1970s, is an example.

The Small Business Elite   The second category includes businessmen who have accumulated significant fortunes (though smaller in scale than the aforementioned group) and who tend to be close enough to the tentacles of power to keep on doing business. This category includes individuals who rose to prominence beginning in the early 1980s through all kinds of illegal and semilegal economic activities. Although apparently loyal to the regime, individuals in this group are usually connected to certain personalities within the regime elite across the board, including their relatives. In other words, their relations with the regime are not direct and general but rather indirect and particular, perhaps shying away from, or incapable of achieving, a more general and official presence there. This stratum also includes those whose income is derived primarily from rent. However, it is this group of individuals that has faced grave difficulties in competing with the offspring of the state bourgeoisie in the late 1990s and into the new century. For the most part, the offspring of the state bourgeoisie are entering the market at the expense of these former protégés of their fathers. Ma'moun al-Homsi, who served a five-year prison sentence for speaking out (belatedly) against the regime, is an example of the small business elite.[11]

The Relatively Independent Business Elite   The third category includes individuals who have accumulated even less wealth but enough to be considered in the upper socioeconomic segment of Syrian society. These businesspeople, often by virtue of social ties (status, sectarian, even ideological) or mere personal preference (for example, to stay away from the risk as well as peril of closeness to the regime), remain outside regime circles. Although some are more independent than others, most are able to exploit the privileges and distinctions available to big capital via legal or quasi-legal practices. This may and usually does involve dealing with public sector companies and officials by virtue of procedural and business requirements. Many of the individuals belonging to the new business elite, especially in this third category, were in fact part of the old bourgeoisie. They either rejoined ranks in the 1970s after a hiatus of more than a decade, came back from abroad after 1991's more open investment climate, or remained in their nationalized companies (such as banks and foreign companies) and were in time catapulted into the new business elite by virtue of their local

Table 3.1. Attributes of the Syrian business community, 1986–2005

Social stratum	Social origin	Position vis-à-vis regime	Nature of position vis-à-vis regime	Politics	Economic orientation	Institutional expression	Dominant economic activity
New economic elite							
State	Predominantly rural/Alawi	Solidarity	Organic	Pragmatic/"left" (proclaimed)	Mixed command/market	State agencies	Oil, contracting, telecom, duty-free zones, auto advertising, pharmaceuticals, chemical industry
Private sector	Urban cross-sectarian	Partnership	Strategic	Pragmatic	Mixed command/market	Chambers/Guidance Committee	Imports, electronics, agro-business, tourism, protected manufacturing
Old bourgeoisie	Predominantly urban-Sunni	Antagonistic	Social/political	Conservative/right	Liberal	Family networks	Textiles manufacturing, internal trade
Independent businesspeople	Urban cross-sectarian	Antagonistic	Political	Pragmatic/center-right	Liberal	Private forums	Import/export, high-tech contracting, light manufacturing

experience and international connections. This stratum also comprises individuals whose income includes rent, but most run comparatively productive business operations, including in new sectors such as information technology. This is the most entrepreneurial group within the private sector as a whole and is poised to take on a weightier role in building Syria's economic future.

Finally, it is noteworthy that capitalists who have maintained or were allowed to maintain part of their businesses throughout the era of nationalizations, and those who have sprung up by association, all remain rather modest and undercapitalized. They consider themselves part of the old bourgeoisie that is persevering in the hope of a return to "good old business" practices and ethics. Politically, however, they are not quaint. They are slowly aligning themselves with members of the new business elite who claim to have roots in traditional business families by virtue of city quarter origin, extended family networks, or the maintenance of "good old business ethics." Otherwise, for all intents and purposes they have melted into the growing ranks of the petite bourgeoisie. The petite bourgeoisie is, at the time of this writing, quite vulnerable economically, suffering from the inflation of prices that is far outstripping their income. But they remain a social force that can easily be activated if the "right" leadership is provided, that is, if the leadership addresses both their economic *and* social concerns, which tend to be liberal and conservative, respectively (see Table 3.1).

Business Actors Among the Political Elite

Business actors who have their origin in the political elite are drawn from four relatively well-defined categories associated mostly with officialdom through professional or business ties.

Top Leadership   By all indicators, the most powerful segment of the state economic elite is drawn from the ranks of the top regime leadership, though not all these individuals have been constantly in charge of an official post.[12] Comprising a few dozen individuals who control the commanding heights of the Syrian economy within and outside the public sector, this stratum is united by its direct relations with the ruling family. Defections or exclusions within this category have been few and far between, epitomized by the expulsion of Rif'at al-Asad, the former president's brother, from official and nonofficial positions of power in 1998.[13] Important, however, were the growing tensions within this category in the late 1990s when the succession crisis reached its peak and led to an intrafamily shooting at the Presidential Palace.[14] Nonetheless, this stratum has experienced the least turnover and has thus been able to accumulate the largest fortunes over a period of more than three decades. Though these individuals are in control of public sectors such as oil, they are increasingly deriving their wealth from relatively recent entries into various lucrative private sector markets, including those of communication, information technology, car dealerships, and the free trade zones that were liberalized and expanded in 2003. Their relations with individuals and institutions in the private sector remain informal at virtually all levels, though some of the partnerships with private sector individuals are becoming increasingly public.[15]

Army and Security Services   Directly below the top leadership category is that of the army and security services. This category includes not only top generals and heads of the nine major security apparatuses but also their deputies, loyal underlings, and former heads of security. Numbering several hundred, with a few dozen exceptional strongmen at the helm, these individuals have been able to convert their coercive power, and in some cases their institutional positionality, into significant wealth.[16] However, due to the military nature of their work, their involvement in private business is usually through partners.[17] In that capacity they act as the "protectors" of businessmen, who usually compensate them handsomely. Not surprisingly, most of the offspring of powerful figures in the army and security services have opted for private careers as they came of age in the mid- to late 1990s. Together, fathers, sons, and daughters form a significant power and financial bloc among the state bourgeoisie as a whole, and it is difficult in this "familial" context to separate the public and the private. With the passage of time, however, the general movement within the families of state officials is clearly toward the "private" sector.

Administrative and Bureaucratic Sectors   This third tier among the state's economic elite includes several hundred top civil servants, cabinet members and their deputies, provincial governors and high-profile mayors, and heads of labor and peasant unions who after 1985 gradually became part of what Hinnebusch calls "the embourgeoisied elite."[18] Also included in this category of the state's economic elite are dozens of high-ranking party functionaries—many having no official governmental posts—and their cronies, most of whom are associated with the Regional Command of the Ba'th party, the official decision-making body in Syria. What is significant about the civil servants in this stratum is that they are slowly but steadily moving to the private sector and leaving behind their political careers. This move, usually typical among those without close regime ties, is a phenomenon that started in the 1990s when opportunities for success in the private sector became available, especially through their own ties to business actors.

Economic Public Sector   The move of civil servants into the private sector is not unique. Long before this trend, former *and* incumbent managers in the economic public sectors had been entering into private business with far more skills, relations, and eventually, economic success. These managers, along with some of their deputies and other economic bureaucrats, have historically operated the eighty-odd state-owned enterprises since the mid-1970s. Many of their positions are akin to limitless tenure, with minor revisions since President Bashar al-Asad took the helm. Even those who are removed from their posts as managers usually remain within the same economic sphere, institutionally or informally, on the basis of ties they have woven during their tenure. Numbering in the hundreds (considering the boards and committees that run the public economic sector), former and current high-level economic public sector managers and bureaucrats have been most successful, not only in making the move to the private sector but also in competing effectively, even with better-positioned businessmen with ties to the core elite. Specifically, economic public sector managers and officials have benefited from years of experience in a rather closed economic system, working under conditions of severe product shortages and decisional constraints. They have established the skills, relations, and contacts—domestically and abroad—that have prepared them for both honest and "subsidized" competition.[19] Some of them, however, have decided to abandon their privileged relations, and their official posts, in favor of independent economic futures unencumbered by political ties and loyalties. This trend continues, as the opportunities for capital accumulation in state-owned enterprises shrank in the late 1990s as a result of the economic recession that started in 1995.

THE PRIVATE SECTOR VERSUS THE NEW BUSINESS ELITE

The Syrian private sector, thus, is a heterogeneous amalgam of various social components that are brought together under the umbrella of the word "private," when nominally defined as those components juridically separate from components owned by the state.[20] In reality, the larger segments of private sector assets and capital belong to individuals contained within the umbrella of the regime; they are often directly accumulated in the shadow of the state, through the exercise of state authority and via the state's own mechanisms and agencies.

This gives a more nuanced meaning to the phrase "private sector," especially as the literature on the politics of economic reform struggles to interpret and predict reform outcomes that are associated with liberalization policies and expansion of the "private sector" in developing countries.

Such liberalization policies have led to an increase in the size of the private sector in nearly all cases, which invariably occurs at the expense of the public sector's share of the economy. These shifts in ownership have been associated with growing demands for more accountable government on the part of private business. But in most late-developing countries, as the 1990s revealed, the link between privatization and government accountability was not systematically present, and in some cases the most powerful elements within the private sectors have favored the status quo. Syria represents one example of this phenomenon. The reason for Syrian economic outcomes, however, lies beyond the customary explanation put forward long ago by Jean Leca[21] and quoted by many political economists studying economic reform—namely, that such businessmen prefer to seek rents through privileged networks in the shadow of the state rather than to have to compete in an open market.

The more weighty explanation for economic outcomes in Syria lies in three additional factors: first, in the kind of strategically loyal economic networks that developed between the regime and the new private economic elite (itself largely a creation of the state); second, in the fact that the largest parts of the private economy in Syria are operated or owned by the state's economic elite; and finally, in the fact that the continuing mistrust between the regime and the larger business community has further altered, albeit grudgingly, the preferences of the new economic elite in favor of the status quo. The first two factors characterize, in kind if not in degree, state-business dynamics in many developing countries, certainly in those across the non-oil-rich Arab world. The third factor, in Syria, is the mistrust between power holders (rural-minoritarian) and capital holders (urban-Sunni) historically. This added dimension of antagonism sharpens further the conflict between state and market, or between the regime and the independent private sector, and has led the regime to view the relationship between itself and independent capital in zero-sum terms.

As is the case currently in comparable countries, like Egypt, the "new" state-created and state-protected business elites in Syria favor the status quo because their own preferences are privileged over the preferences of the entire business community. Thus, the new economic elite (those Hinnebusch refers to as "crony capitalists"[22]) and the private sector as a whole (everyone else) are at odds. While the new economic elite has been content with proximity to the state and membership in the economic networks, where rents are distributed and laws transgressed, the rest of the business community has to play by the rules, contend with endless bureaucratic procedures, and negotiate its way through a contradictory legal environment.

This state of affairs started in the late 1980s with the advent of informal liberalization and continues, until the time of this writing, with little variation since 2005 in being more open to the broader business community. More significant is the fact that privileges and rents were doled out by regime potentates to select business partners without any expectations of reciprocity by way of economic performance.[23] The state's economic elite—or the political elite who also went into private business—and their offspring have been in the forefront of those receiving special privileges, often being the same individuals who were distributing those privileges, making rent-seeking extremely efficient! The result was a massive level of formally private investment in the early 1990s, most of which was either in nonproductive sectors or in one way or another protected from competition by tailored policies.[24] Since 1991, and more recently since 2001, the lion's share[25] of new opportunities and new markets went to a small group of individuals associated in some way with the regime, either through familial ties or through public, governmental, or military/security sector posts. Syria thus has a private sector that is not "private," in the sense that much of its assets are owned by individuals who still either occupy official state posts or are close relatives of the top regime officials.[26] Hence, an opposition develops between the interests of the new economic elite (including the state bourgeoisie) and those of the rest of the business community composing the private sector.

Nowhere is the opposition between the new economic elite and the private sector proper more evident than in the largely inconsequential pattern of distribution of assets between the private and the public sectors in the 1990s. Whereas the public sector had maintained the upper hand in fixed capital formation since 1963, relegating the private sector to small and medium business ventures, the situation was reversed in the early 1990s.[27] The immediate cause was Investment Law No. 10 of 1991, which encouraged private domestic and foreign investment by providing tax and other incentives.[28] The contrast between the shares of public and private assets over time becomes stark when one considers the dramatic reversals in fixed capital formation figures between 1985 and 1992 (see Table 3.2). Whereas the public sector's share in 1985 (66%) was nearly twice that of the private sector, which contributed 34 percent to gross fixed capital formation, the

Table 3.2. Syrian gross fixed capital formation

	Percentage by sector			Percentage by sector	
	Private	Public		Private	Public
1963	45.62	54.38	1996	52.00	48.00
1970	29.58	70.42	1997	42.00	58.00
1975	29.19	70.81	1998	41.00	59.00
1980	37.23	62.77	1999	40.43	59.57
1985	33.73	66.27	2000	36.42	63.58
1990	55.01	44.99	2001	40.87	59.13
1991	58.00	42.00	2002	39.22	60.29
1992	67.00	33.00	2003	34.35	65.65
1993	65.00	35.00	2004	52.94	47.06
1994	58.00	42.00	2005	52.34	47.23
1995	56.22	44.00			

SOURCE: Central Bureau of Statistics, "National Accounts," in Statistical Abstract, 2005, 546; International Monetary Fund, "Syrian Arab Republic: Statistical Appendix," 9; International Monetary Fund, "Article IV Consultation Staff Report: Syrian Arab Republic," February 2009, 21.

opposite situation prevailed in 1992, by which time the private sector had nearly doubled its share while the public sector had halved its own.[29] Investment and trade figures reveal a similar pattern of nominal private sector growth.[30] However, fluctuations in the size of the private sector seem to have had little effect because the majority of new private sector assets are controlled by actors who are associated with the regime in one way or another. Hence, the power of the private sector proper in its influence on policy is not enhanced because the biggest private sector *winners* do not share the interests of the private sector as a *whole.* There is one caveat: ownership reversed again between 1997 and 2003 in favor of the public sector (although the private sector lead was restored after that). This public sector spike was due primarily to the top regime leadership's decision to increase public investments dramatically in 1996–97 as a response to the economic crisis. It persisted for a period after Bashar's assumption of power because it was part of the new regime's consolidation and retrenchment strategy, one that gave way to the post-1991 pattern once he was firmly in the saddle.[31]

Yet, in contrast to the spate of optimistic reports and articles published in the mid-1990s, which projected a decisive victory for private sector evangelists (both analysts and businessmen alike), these numbers were quite misleading in and of themselves *and* in terms of the changes they portended. Despite a burst of energy in the early to mid-1990s, the private sector remained quite modest in its contribution to added value, which explains, in part, quick regressions and reversals at least until 2005. Furthermore, notwithstanding the boost the regime leadership gave the public sector in 2006, most observers discounted the argument that the rise of the private sector was due to the relative decline of the weakened public sector, which in 1991 was beginning to strain under the weight of its social obligations and the lack of revenue generation.[32] A decrease in the role of the state was thus witnessed, but not necessarily a change in the identity of those who made decisions regarding the sectors that the state presumably ceded to the "private sector." This state of affairs reflects a regime survival strategy that eschewed the broadening of the role of the private sector proper, a strategy which continued until 2005.

STRATEGIC REGIME RELATIONS WITH THE PRIVATE SECTOR
The Secondary Role of Private Business in the 1970s and 1980s

The relationship between the state and the business community in Syria has been historically quite strained, as discussed in the foregoing chapter. Despite ebbs and flows, usually associated with economic booms and busts, the general sense in structural terms, and at the level of individual officials and businessmen, is that the two social forces are at odds. Some analysts, and certainly most hardliners within the previous regime of Hafiz al-Asad, viewed the relationship in zero-sum terms: that the rise of the private sector could occur only at the expense of the regime. Conversely, it is evident that the consolidation of the regime itself, beginning in 1963, occurred at the expense of the traditional private sector, symbolized by what is called the "traditional" or "old" bourgeoisie.

While its strategy shifted slightly in 1970, the Syrian Ba'th regime has related to the private sector through the prism of security since assuming power in 1963. All along, the regime would give either moderate concessions to the private sector as a whole, or dole out "magnanimous" privileges to a select few therein, for the purpose of preserving its autonomy at the macroeconomic level. Such tactics occurred (and continue to occur) undoubtedly at the expense of the health of the economy. With the economic price that the regime must pay to preserve its decisional autonomy and ultimately its security comes another administrative cost: its decreased capacity to run the economy, outside of the blunt exercise of prohibitional and punitive power. Though administrative costs can be compensated for in the short and medium run by increasing oppressive measures and dependence on external sources of income, the use of such measures eventually comes back to haunt regimes when rent dries up, a prospect that the Syrian regime will have to contend with in the not-so-distant future.[33] Until such time, however, it is unlikely that the regime would voluntarily change its strategy for dealing with the private sector, a strategy that is as old as the regime itself.

Directly after the "Corrective Movement" of 1970, the new Ba'thist regime under Hafiz al-Asad was less ideologically inclined, more pragmatic politically, far more careerist, and most important, outward-looking toward the region as a whole. The regime recognized its social and political vulnerabilities: it was a radical rural-minoritarian regime largely cut off from the rest of Syrian society by virtue of its own radicalism, which had polarized the country for half a dozen years; it was in charge of an embattled state that had suffered a grave defeat only three years earlier at the hands of Israel; it ran an ailing economy that was not likely to receive support from conservative Arab states. The Syrian regime of 1970 rose at the expense of the party[34] *and* to a great extent the army, and was supported primarily by the security apparatuses and "special forces" that warring regime strongmen had been busy setting up in the late 1960s.

Given the longstanding animosity with the private sector and the preoccupation of the regime with its own security and its decisional autonomy, it was disinclined to offer the private sector any legitimate representation or allow it to erect its own expressive institutions independent of state control and scrutiny. Instead, until 1973, when foreign aid swamped Syria in the aftermath of the October war against Israel, the state preferred to keep the once-thriving private sector under control. Against this background, the regime attempted to create a new economic elite in its own image, but it was encumbered by the turbulent events of the 1970s and early 1980s.[35]

State-business relations that existed between 1970 and the late 1980s remained largely informal, with the exception of a few notorious cases that have been overemphasized by analysts because they were among the few that were visible and accessible.[36] The "troika," as they are often labeled, included 'Uthman al-'Aidi, the tourism mogul; Sa'ib Nahhas, the transportation mogul; and 'Abdul-Rahman al-'Attar, a businessman of a comparatively lower order. Though these cases were more or less visible, the majority of businessmen working with or in the shadow of the state and its personnel remained faceless for more than a decade. Only in the late 1980s did one witness the emergence of relatively more visible relations between the regime and individuals in the private sector, usually through patronage relations associated with the Chambers (of Commerce and Industry) or during the rejuvenated parliamentary elections, beginning in 1991. Even then, it was difficult to link state officials and businessmen, especially for outsiders. The protégés of security service strongmen in the Chambers, for instance, are quick to condemn the hold the state has on the economy,[37] naturally leading the "uninitiated" to conclude erroneously that they are rivals.

The Improved Status of, and Ambivalence Toward, the Private Sector in the Late 1990s

In the late 1990s, the strategic situation was slightly different as private sector actors acquired more legitimacy, if only because of the growing state-business alliance. While in the 1970s, for instance, the only conspicuous "representative" of the private sector, a man by the name of Tahsin al-Safadi, would have to gather the courage to ask for a reduction in inspection campaigns by the Ministry of Supply, in the late 1990s business "representatives"[38] were established parliament members and board members at the various Chambers, supported by political power and able to make policy recommendations at high-level institutions connecting the state to the business community.[39] By 2005 we began to see business and "market" interests represented directly in government, as in the appointment of the reformer Abdallah al-Dardari to deputy prime minister for economic affairs. The official pronouncement of the Social Market Economy at the Ba'th party's tenth Regional Command Conference during that same year effectively turned the page on the previous era. But these are relatively recent developments.

The regime's historical ambivalence toward the private sector was evident in the snail's pace at which the government moved in formulating and implementing liberalizing economic policies of any sort or magnitude in the 1980s and into the better part of the 1990s. The political elite were and continued to be caught in a dilemma governed by three constraints: first, they needed the private sector for generating foreign exchange and jobs; second, they were unwilling and in their view unable to share power safely with broader sections of society; and third, the private sector's economic power—for example, its share of GDP, investments, employment generation, exports, international connections, and know-how—was growing (however imprecisely measured) as a direct result of the regime's rational if slow retreat from the economic sphere. Thus, the optimal outcome for the regime, given its security preferences, was to encourage private sector growth to the extent that it could ameliorate the economy, but not so much that it threatened the balance of power[40] between state and business.[41] In order to achieve this, the regime selectively networked with the most economically significant individuals in the private sector, individuals who owed their initial rise to its patronage and blessing, if not need.

The Bottom Line: Economic Power Bereft of Political Power

Since 1973, the regime has adopted first informal and then formal methods by which such networks developed. First, informally, the state created and re-created an incentive structure that renders rational or necessary the voluntary cooperation of a select group of businesspeople (that is, without some form of cooperation with or blessing from the state, medium to large private business cannot survive). Then, in the late 1980s and throughout the 1990s, the state began mobilizing particular members of the private sector into the formal political process through participation in the defunct People's Council,[42] through election to the boards of Chambers of Commerce and Industry, and through representation in the Guidance Committee that links the private sector to the state. The guidelines set for these institutionalized networks are, essentially, that private money is left in private hands so long as it does not encroach upon the regime's domain—politics. Otherwise it becomes "public" money and is seized by the regime through the selective invocation of laws and regulations that big businesses are bound to have transgressed in the context of the contradictory legal environment described above. By the end of the 1990s, the portion of the private sector that was somewhat independent from the regime became more aggressive. However, despite the regime's suspicion of the private sector in general, it could no longer reverse the growth of the private sector and was becoming far more dependent on it for investment, job generation, and foreign exchange procurement than it had ever been since 1963. Nonetheless, according to insiders who were privy to intraregime discourse, especially regarding the looming issues of succession at the time, there was a renewed, creeping ambivalence among some regime strongmen toward those parts of the private sector that were independent of the regime's sphere of influence. For the most part, this ambivalence was dealt with by an aggressive promotion of business actors directly connected with the regime, even the family, notably the likes of Rami Makhlouf, Bashar's cousin, whose business empire spanned nearly all sectors of the Syrian economy by 2005. By then, Syria's political economy began officially to head in a different direction, even if, again, at a slow pace.

The ultimate challenge for the regime is determining how it can benefit from private economic initiative without paying a political cost. When the state succeeds in mobilizing the private sector, both state and private sectors benefit economically, and the state benefits politically—at least in the short run. In the long run, the calculations are likely to change. For big business, the opportunity cost of cooperation over time is likely to increase at the same time that the regime's need for big business cooperation increases, thereby giving leverage to big business—assuming a minimum level of tacit organization, or even mutual understanding. For the time being, we remain in the short run, where observable gains accrue to the state. Economic policy developments since the creation of the Social Market Economy may begin to reduce the ambivalence toward the private sector simply because this sector is increasingly dominated by "friendly" economic actors, a reality that continues to respond to the "cold feet" the regime experienced at the turn of this century.

PRIVATE SECTOR "INSTITUTIONS"

An important characteristic of the Syrian private sector is that until 2005 it did not have genuine representation as such. Existing institutions such as the Chambers of Commerce and Industry represented only portions of the business community, despite appearances to the contrary. The Chambers' role ceased to be effective in 1963, when the Ba'th took power, and their rejuvenation after the Corrective Movement of 1970 left much to be desired by the business community. It was not until 1982 that the Chamber of Commerce in Damascus (this does not apply to the Chambers of Commerce elsewhere or to any Chamber of Industry in Syria) acquired an elevated political, though not economic, status. This upgrade was a direct result of the alliance of the Damascene bourgeoisie—then associated with the Chamber of Commerce and led by Badr al-Din al-Shallah—with the regime in its confrontation with the Islamists.[43] However, Damascene traders are ambivalent about the close ties between the top regime leadership and the Damascus Chamber of Commerce. Some are proud to announce that the rapprochement was also a product of al-Shallah's personal relationship with former president Hafiz al-Asad, while others consider the relationship to be a form of co-optation that further crippled the business community as a whole. According to a well-spoken Damascene member of the traditional bourgeoisie who trades in textiles,

> [w]hen the Hama incidents occurred [late 1970s], Damascene traders stood their infamous stand alongside the regime, and the President acknowledged this stance in his famous speech at the stadium of Damascus University. After this "stance,"

the regime's view of the Chamber changed, and they started to regard them [the traders] with respect. When a dear visitor would arrive in Syria, they would take him to the Chamber.[44]

Nonetheless, the Chambers seem to be more popular within regime circles in general than among the traders they claim to represent. The above-quoted merchant, along with many others who have a distinctly sound reputation as well as a substantial portion of the market in the subsectors in which they operate, remain suspicious of the Chambers' role and dynamics. Though they attend special Chamber lectures and meetings from time to time, they are aware that their voices or interests, while "heard," are usually only heard. Some say that this is why "we say nothing. I'd rather work on my next shipment than to plead for the fiftieth time for the most simple and rational of requests."[45] The situation is similar in kind, if only much worse in degree, in the Chambers of Industry across the country. Even board members at the Chamber of Industry in Damascus voice their ineffectual role: "We are not decision-makers even regarding Chamber issues; we are neither an executive nor a consultative party. . . . [W]e examine economic matters and forward them to the 'decision-maker.' We do not make any decisions."[46] According to Riad Saif,

[t]he Chambers are akin to "populist organizations" that the government creates and they do not possess any power to actualize their demands. Membership in the Chambers grew beginning in the late 1980s because it was a necessary prerequisite for acquiring a commercial or industrial record and a variety of licenses to do business.[47]

Economists concur. Rizqallah Hilan, a respected Syrian economist, related increases in Chamber membership partly to the satisfaction of everyday needs that are independent of business:

Products in general were very expensive in the early 1990s because of high custom duties irrespective of who is benefiting from higher custom duties or whether they went into the state's treasury. The result was that people would try to get around such duties. For instance, people would sign up with the Chambers of Commerce so they could get a pickup truck with reduced custom duties, supposedly for business use.[48]

This is a prevalent view in the business community in Syria, from Aleppo to Hama and Damascus, and it applies to both the Chambers of Industry and the Chambers of Commerce, though industrialists' complaints and disillusionment are far deeper. After a lengthy discussion on the conditions of the Damascus Chamber of Industry, Muhammad Saraqbi, a former vice president of the Chamber, stated that the objective at the Chamber is to attain the status of the Chamber of Commerce in Damascus,[49] a reputedly ineffectual and scarcely representative organization.

What many in the private sector consider a far more effective, though far less accessible, institution is the Guidance Committee, the only institution that officially links the business community to the state. But the picture is just as cloudy there. According to independent Syrian economists and former public sector officials working in economic affairs, the Guidance Committee has effectively taken over the role of legislative *and* executive authority with respect to a wide range of policies spanning tax exemptions and selective licenses for import and export commodities.[50] Some businessmen accord it supreme importance: "[T]he Guidance Committee is the most important economic institution in the country because, as opposed to the governmental Economic Committee, its decisions acquire a legal form. Its decisions are intended to be general and strategic."[51]

The Guidance Committee became effectual at a particular juncture shortly after the 1986 crisis, when the state needed to mobilize investments to compensate for dramatic reductions in public sector access to foreign exchange, and hence investments. For the regime, the caveat was to do so without empowering the private sector as a whole. In practice, this translated into efforts at mobilizing investment either without relinquishing more economic levers than necessary, even to ostensible regime allies in the private sector, or to worse effect, without creating new winners from outside the economic networks in the private sector on which the regime had depended since the late 1970s. The result was the effective supplanting of the governmental Economic Committee (which persisted as an organizational shell dealing more with ideological policy issues far removed from daily economic operations; for example, that Syria is a socialist economy led by its "nationalist" public sector) by the Guidance Committee, which represented the formalization of hitherto informal relations between the regime and its select partners and protégés in the private sector. Though it was created in 1981 for the purpose of "encouraging exports and designing more rationalized import policies,"[52] the Guidance Committee—officially titled the Committee for the Guidance of Imports, Exports, and Consumption—became after 1991 the hub for the distribution of rents, especially in the form of selective liberalization of import commodities associated for the most part with existing or new businesses owned by various regime officials and their partners in the private sector.

The incarnation of the Guidance Committee is officially headed by the prime minister and his deputy for economic affairs, and is presented as the only governmental institution in which private sector representatives are full participants and where they have the opportunity to address their grievances in a pluralist and national context that includes representatives from other social sectors, including the economic office of the Ba'th party, the General Federation of Trade Unions, the Peasant Union, and the presidents of the Damascus Chambers of Commerce and Industry.[53] Among the larger business community and its proponents, the Guidance Committee is understood as the tacit institutional arm of economic networks,[54] where "corridor policies" take shape.[55] According to Syrian economist Khalid Abdul Nour, among others,

> though the Guidance Committee was created to serve a macro-function, its behavior [sulukuha] serves a micro-function by tailoring policies. . . . In the end, the Guidance Committee is concerned with simple matters, and even these simple matters reflect the interests of power centers that are in harmony with the interests of the beneficiaries.[56]

Thus, until 2005, independent businesspeople in the private sector did not consider the available institutions representative, nor were they allowed, or even willing, for fear of regime reprisal, to erect their own. Many were indeed waiting for a time when these same private sector institutions could assume their intended role, or when they could erect their own institutions.

Two general outcomes have resulted from a lack of credible private sector representation and the search for alternatives. First, the larger business community remains fragmented sectorally, politically, and geographically. The private sector is sectorally fragmented and underspecialized. Businessmen with capital work in various sectors simultaneously to avoid complete collapse in the event that one of their businesses fails due to government crackdown or an inability to compete in a market because of excess supply. Such excess supply results from a lack of effective institutions that would channel information between the government and the private sector, and within various private sectors. Politically, there is a major division between regime supporters and detractors. Within each of these categories are further divisions that reflect the nature of support (for example, strategic, organic) and opposition (political,

social-ideological, economic). In the Syrian political context, economic rationality does not always make for productive partnership or fruitful collaboration, even among regime detractors who belong to the same subsector. By the
same token, regime supporters belonging to the same economic networks that
allow them to transgress laws and regulations are themselves competing for
rents and protection, making their sectoral collaboration far less likely. Finally,
geographically, the private sector in Damascus in general is more beholden to
the state than its counterparts in Aleppo, Homs, Hama, and the rest of the
country (excluding the coast generally and Latakia in particular). At the same
time, the private sector enjoys a greater presence (if uneven) in both Damascus
and Aleppo compared with the rest of the country.[57]

A second outcome related in large measure to the lack of representative institutions for the private sector is that both large and small ventures remain
family-oriented. More than religion, sect, or region, the extended family, and
increasingly the nuclear family, represents the most trustworthy social framework for a business community operating under serious constraints which
compel most business operations into the semilegal or wholly illegal arena
(see Figure 3.1).[58] This is certainly not unique to Syria, but the lack of trust between the Syrian regime and the larger business community is an additional
factor reinforcing family patterns of business development. "Economically
speaking," as al-Hayat titled one of its articles on Syria, "[t]he dependence of

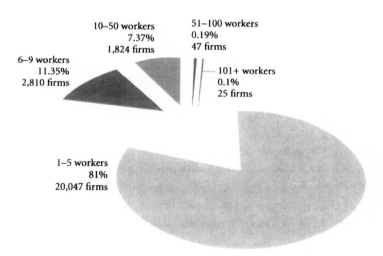

Figure 3.1. Private sector firms. Percentage of distribution by number of workers. Data from
Syrian Central Bureau of Statistics, 2001.

the [Syrian] private sector limits its ability to expand its investments and its capacity to absorb labor."[59] Thus, the expansion that the private sector witnessed in the early to mid-1990s, in terms of domestic investment and gross fixed capital formation as well as in the number of private sector firms, was not accompanied by a proportional reduction in unemployment, because 90 percent of the firms were family-run.[60] Besides the fact that most of the expansion occurred in non-labor-intensive sectors, the new businesses that emerged tended to rely first and foremost on family members, many of whom already had a job in the public sector, which left most of their afternoons free for a second job in the private sector.

POWER AND THE PRIVATE SECTOR

Economically, the private sector as a whole indeed has very little autonomy. It is unable to invest properly, unable to employ its credentials, and unable to articulate its collective demands in a prioritized manner. It is thus unable to become a viable "economic sector" unto itself. As Riad Saif describes from experience, "[t]he private sector is an abnormal [*ghair tabi'i*] sector that grew and developed under abnormal conditions and under abnormal circumstances."[61] Politically, a remarkably weak organizational capacity results from the above characteristics, leaving private sector independents isolated from one another, or atomized.

Most significantly, the private sector is not only small and divided, but it is also not quite "private," in the sense that much of the assets therein are owned or controlled by state officials, the state bourgeoisie, and their partners in the private sector. These conditions of institutional representation and resource distribution persist for the most part, notwithstanding the strides the "new" leadership has taken since 2005 in allowing for more genuine private sector representation under the rubric of the Social Market Economy. Whether this will result in a robust private sector remains to be seen, but most indicators suggest moderate expectations under conditions where regime security continues to reign supreme. From the perspective of the regime elite, the only private sector it could allow for is a subservient private sector, stripped of the instruments of genuine expression, representation, and collective action.

It is therefore not prudent to consider state-business relations in Syria—as well as in many other LDCs (late-developing countries)—as synonymous with state–private sector relations. However, the relationship between the state and the private sector constitutes the context within which state-business relations emerged. Faced with the economic need for private sector initiative, the regime opted for selective informal relations with individual business actors, while the private sector was left to limp along. The selective relations that state officials developed with private business actors after 1970 took the form of informal economic networks, the arena where considerable economic decision-making power resided for at least three decades.

4 THE FORMATION AND DEVELOPMENT OF ECONOMIC NETWORKS

IN VIRTUALLY ALL DEVELOPING COUNTRIES,[1] and perhaps beyond,[2] relations between the state and business have taken the form of what can be called economic or policy networks that may or may not operate through formal institutions. Though networks are ubiquitous in nearly all settings where state and business cooperate, their impact on economic growth and development can be more or less detrimental or positive depending on the conditions of their emergence, their internal dynamics, and their relation to the broader institutional and social context.[3]

Notwithstanding potential reductionist tendencies in the political economy literature dealing with economic networks in developing countries, the resilience and policy impact of such networks is well-founded and well-documented.[4] For Syria in the late 1980s, I argue that the effects of the maturing economic networks—combining the political and economic elites—became extant in the economic, regulatory, and fiscal policy reforms of the late 1980s, the 1990s, and through the early 2000s. The foreign exchange crisis of 1986 marks the acceleration of consolidation and influence of economic networks, albeit at an informal level until 1991 when these networks co-opted the official institutional expressions of the "private sector." They did so under the rubric of the government's reform policy, *al-ta'adudiyya al-iqtisadiyya* (economic pluralism). Although the impact of such networks has been largely limited to middle- and lower-range policies, their ability to bypass or manipulate laws and regulations has significantly widened their reach. This has allowed them, intentionally or inadvertently, to shape general developmental change in idiosyncratic ways that were ultimately detrimental to economic efficiency and productivity.[5] These economic downturns were not desired or intended by the state, the broader business community, or the participants in these networks, who represent the primary beneficiaries of the reform process. Economic decline was largely a result of rampant rent-seeking and rent allocation that was misdirected by a widely penetrated and

incoherent bureaucracy.[6] The proximity of these networks to decision
bodies, and the participation of decision-makers and top officials in th
works, made rent-seeking and rent allocation an extremely efficient proce ___ __ring the post-1986 reforms.

NETWORKS AND INSTITUTIONS: WHY DO ECONOMIC NETWORKS EMERGE?

Pervasive and powerful economic networks combining webs of bureaucrats
and capitalists have been prominent features of political economies in transition from a centralized arrangement to a more decentralized and not necessarily market-oriented one.[7] In this sense, networks become the dominant form
of state-business interaction during the earlier phases of reform as both the
political and economic elites deal with new forms of economic governance and
their attendant legal, institutional, and organizational correlates. During these
earlier phases, networks do not "replace" existing institutions. Rather, informal state-business networks emerge and operate alongside institutions as an
alternative form of agency that reflects a regime strategy of encouraging capital accumulation while maintaining its distributive image, commitments, and
governance structures. Such informal networks are largely responsible for the
dramatic growth of shadow economies so pervasive in reforming states, from
Russia to Egypt.[8]

As members of these networks accumulate capital and gain confidence as
business actors, and at times as public figures, and as regime officials themselves
enter into business directly or indirectly through private partnerships, we begin
to witness a more organic phase of institution-building emanating from existing networks. Increasingly, more emphasis comes to be placed by both the political and economic elites who are part of these networks on market and business
institutions that will cut transaction costs while maintaining special informal
relations and privileges for the select few. Informal relations—which often take
the form of institutions in and of themselves—persist and are simply complemented by more formal and relatively representative institutions that are better capable of handling the growing volume of economic transactions. This is a
drawn-out process; formalizing relations in an organic and representative manner did not begin in Syria until after 2005, a period that is not as amenable to
scholarly investigation as the period examined in this book (1970–2005).

The question remains: Why did the state elite choose to forgo the option
of formally extending or reforming its own economic institutions to include
all possible investors and generate opportunities for the entire business com

munity? Or, why did it opt for informal network-like relations with members of the business community starting in 1970? In the case of Syria, networks did not precede the state or the market (however limited the latter), nor were they merely the product of economically inefficient institutions, as the case might be elsewhere. Networks emerge within existing states and markets as a means for state elites and business partners to secure extraordinary benefits that neither could obtain under formal state-business arrangements. However, the motives for each party differ: state elites look for security, first and foremost, and business partners seek profits that cannot be obtained under the constraints imposed on the private sector as a whole. Without examining the institutional and social contexts in which state elites and business actors operate, we would find the development of pervasive informal and selective relations between state and business incomprehensible.

The institutional context in which these networks emerged in Syria is what can be called populist-authoritarian unraveling or dilution, whereby the distributive commitments of populist-authoritarian states begin to give way to populist demobilization and alliance-shuffling in favor of hitherto excluded business actors. Although ideological constraints related to distributive commitments and the exclusion of business from the state's corporatist structure proved surmountable in the case of populist-authoritarian regimes like Egypt,[9] the challenge remains one of security for cases such as Syria.[10] The lack of trust between the regime and the business community, based on deep-seated historical antagonism, has prevented the state elite in Syria from pursuing rapprochement with business à la Egypt: the Syrian regime could neither dissolve its ruling Ba'th party (as the Egyptian regime did with the Arab Socialist Union) nor replace it with a new one (such as Egypt's National Democratic Party) that is institutionally and ideologically more amenable to the official incorporation of business interests. The Syrian political elite had reasons to fear a resurgence of the traditional business community, despite its institutionally weakened position since the 1963 Ba'th takeover. According to Heydemann,

> [t]he union [United Arab Republic] educated this generation of radical reformers about the resilience of the private sector, the intensity of business opposition to social reform, and the strategies capitalists could employ to undermine the radical restructuring of Syria's political economy. . . . [T]he union experience became its [the Ba'th's] touchstone and its antimodel, the crucible within which many elements of the Ba'th's political repertoire took shape.[11]

By 1970 the socio-institutional context made some informal networking in the service of capital accumulation and security rational, but it also prevented the Syrian regime from safely mobilizing the business community as a whole. As a result, the official institutions of the business community were further suppressed and contained at the expense of collective collaboration and efficiency. Ironically, or perhaps not, it is these emerging informal state-business networks that developed an interest in rejuvenating decrepit business associations after the late 1980s, particularly in 1991 when the first reform measures were formally formulated and implemented. That process, however, constituted window dressing much more than the development of representative institutions.

Because networks operate as alternative mechanisms of association, their conditions of emergence are not the sole reason for their development and consolidation.[12] In the Syrian case, where networks are quite pervasive, they were also spurred by a political and legitimation crisis with institutional reverberations. The conflict between the state and the Islamists in the 1970s and early 1980s was in many ways spurred by the perceived lack of legitimacy of the regime, both politically and economically, from the perspective of excluded traditional sectors and most small businesses in the urban *suq* (traditional market of manufacturers and artisans). The showdown between the state and the opposition between 1979 and 1982 further catalyzed selective rapprochement between state and business in the form of informal networks.[13] The civil unrest, very much tied to the power of the then-weakened traditional business community, accelerated the formation and consolidation of economic networks, which by that time began to take on a life of their own: state elites would try to create a business elite in their own image, and they would themselves become even more heavily involved in business.

The Genesis of Economic Networks in Syria

As part of the regime's retrenching strategy after Asad's 1970 coup, top elites led by Hafiz al-Asad himself took initiative to bring part of the business community back into the political economic equation. Unable to officially incorporate the business community as a whole for security concerns, state elites embarked on the creation and development of informal ties with particular established and ascending business actors. More broadly, we witness the formation of key economic networks in the mid- to late 1970s, comprising top state officials (including military, security, and bureaucratic personnel), select business actors, and paraofficial actors connected to the regime mainly through familial and communal, but also through professional, ties (for example, former teachers, doctors, engineers). Significant here is that early on these networks included state actors (including well-known figures like former vice president Abdul Halim Khaddam and former head of military intelligence Ali Duba) who had little or no professional business experience and were thus more dependent on their proximity to the state for "staying in business." Also included in these networks were lay individuals who had largely been catapulted by state officials from various professional or blue-collar backgrounds into the business world during the investment boom of the mid-1970s,[14] and later through mixed-sector ventures, smuggling, black marketeering, and cronyism. These actors were seen by the regime as loyal, because they had few or no options compared to formerly more established and trained business actors drawn from the ranks of the old, but culturally vigorous, bourgeoisie.[15] By the same token, the adversarial state-business legacy left an evident imprint on emerging state-business networks, not least because of the communal as well as the socioeconomic differences between the political elite and capitalists in the prepopulist periods (1946–58 and 1961–63). Institutionalized as they became after 1970,[16] such differences reinforced the narrowness of the ruling coalition at the top rungs, and rendered the regime vulnerable by reducing its capacity for incorporating or absorbing social forces without being overtaken by them. Hence, the pattern of incorporation the state pursued included similarly vulnerable individuals and groups that generally lack strong social bases of support.

Sustained by a particular configuration of factors and interest,[17] this situation of mutual dependence within state-business networks shaped their development and consolidation throughout the 1970s, 1980s, and 1990s. Mutual vulnerability fostered the conditions for collusive relations between state and business and by the mid-1990s contributed to costly outcomes, socially, administratively, and economically. The operating dynamic has been the organization and reorganization of rent-seeking opportunities in the context of protracted economic liberalization. Economic networks acted as a form of agency in carrying out this process, even if in fragmented form where actors were not working in unison.[18] Exacerbating collusive state-business relations is the fact that a growing number among the political, military, and bureaucratic elite, later including their offspring, went into business either directly or through protégés in the 1970s, and more vigorously in the 1980s and 1990s. The fusion of the roles of public decision-maker and capitalist in the agency of officials and paraofficials has had a tremendous impact on the economic decision-making process in its formulation and implementation phases.

Notably, state-business networks did not acquire any sort of formal expression until the early 1990s when the government implicitly proclaimed a shift in its economic policy and development strategy, one that gave recognition to, and conferred legitimacy on, the developmental role of the hitherto constrained private sector. Not only did these rent-seeking networks survive this shift, but they actually participated in shaping it and in shaping the ensuing process of liberalization, if not by dominating it wholesale then by circumscribing further the limits of economic liberalization by diverting resources from collective to private targets. As a result of the particularist policies brought about by the influence of these networks in the early 1990s, unintended economic and institutional consequences started to take effect, and the Syrian economy entered a deep slump beginning in 1994.

By the end of the 1990s, a serious liquidity crisis led to the dramatic shrinking of rent opportunities, all spurred by a decade of misallocation of resources and policies that had been tailored to fit particular individuals. Current account surplus dropped sharply starting in the early 1990s, plummeting from a surplus of $700 million in 1991 to a deficit of close to $800 million in 1994 (see Figure 4.1). Liquidity surplus remained under 1.5 percent of GDP for most of the 1990s, only breaking 2 percent again in the mid-2000s.[19] Although regionally a decent performer in terms of real GDP growth in the early 1990s, Syria dropped behind its closest comparatives—Egypt and Tunisia—after 1994 (see Figure 4.2). Record lows in economic productivity and public/private investments were evidenced by potentially destabilizing widespread unemployment, which reached 20 percent in 2000 by nearly all non-government estimates.[20]

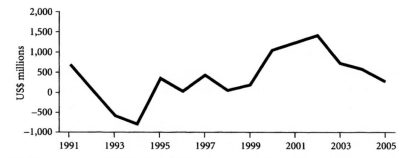

Figure 4.1. Syria: current account balance, 1991–2005. Data from Economist Intelligence Unit, "Syria Country Report," 1991–2009.

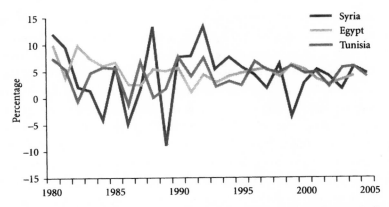

Figure 4.2. Real GDP growth, 1980–2005. Data from World Bank, World Development Indicators Database.

Throughout the period of economic decline, the impact of rent-seeking economic networks was colliding with the broader political logic of regime maintenance: the detrimental developmental cost of rent-seeking started to outweigh the benefits of instrumental reform as a regime maintenance strategy. Such notable downturns sounded serious alarms to the regime, especially in the absence of new oil finds as an alternative source of state revenue, in contrast to the case in 1991.[21]

Despite competition for shrinking rent opportunities within economic networks in the late 1990s, individuals[22]—especially the private component—found common cause amidst calls for the overhaul of the entire economic system that were emanating from the larger business community and the (re)emerging civil society. Opportunities for alternative social alliance-making, which included calls for the reorganization if not dissolution of these networks, coincided with—and were tainted by—the presidential succession struggle, which short-circuited efforts at mobilizing an alternative center of economic power led by urban-Sunni businessmen and some of their counterparts within the regime. Many of these businessmen had ties to the former vice president, Abdul-Halim Khaddam, and former chief of staff Hikmat al-Shihabi. Preparing Bashar al-Asad for the presidency involved paving the way for him, which meant sidelining, perhaps prematurely, a number of vociferous opponents to his succession, especially among the so-called Sunni "old guard." Until Hafiz al-Asad's death in June 2000, the economy was at a standstill, but it was poised to undergo some change in the medium run. Entrenched economic networks, most of which stood on the sidelines during the succession crisis, were able to survive yet another challenging transition. Notable, however, is the regime's recognition of these political developments and its attempt to further constrain rent-seeking networks and the exclusive doling out of benefits, contracts, and distinctions to individuals close to the top rungs of power.[23] During Bashar's first five years in power, state-business relations underwent little change or turbulence beyond the shrinking process discussed above. More pressing issues were on the table for the regime, especially how to (re)consolidate power for the long term amidst a growing civil society campaign to do away with Asad's legacy altogether in the name of Bashar's own modernization and reform platform.[24] Meanwhile, privileged network members were beginning to think outside the box by pressing for market mechanisms and reforms—including private banking, dealing in hard currency, and the establishment of holding companies and a stock exchange—that would replace state-centered mechanisms of economic control. Though such policies were being formulated quietly and diligently in the background, none of them saw light before 2005, the year when Bashar finally consolidated his rule and called for the launching of the Social Market Economy, which was amid international and regional calls for Syria's isolation as a political player in the region.[25]

Economic Origins of Rentier Opportunities and the New Economic Elite

In examining the recent history of the new economic elite in Syria, we find its origins in a series of windfalls and opportunities that vastly expanded the domain and scope of rent income. These opportunities coincide roughly with three periods of state-business relations, each with its own landmark for the nature of the relationship, rent-seeking opportunities, the role of the state, and the resultant reform pattern (see Table 4.1). It is important to note the relationship between the timing of these windfalls and the burgeoning of the networks: economic networks were formed largely for security reasons initially, but later on grew tremendously in order to capture the benefits of chaotic investment and reforms, including debt-reservice agreements and various decrees and laws that opened up sectors of the economy to private business. When such opportunities subsided in the early to mid-1990s, so did the vigor of the networks. But there's another reason for the dip. These informal state-business networks served another purpose, especially before 1991: they camouflaged the state's permissiveness in expanding private activity during the heady socialist days of the 1970s and 1980s, and they acted as a cover for the direct or indirect involvement of various officials in business.

Table 4.1. Patterns of state-business relations: networks, rent, and economic change

| | Development periods | | | |
| | 1970–1990 Informal | | | 1991–2005 More formal |
Nature of business incorporation	1970–1977	1978–1985	1986–2000	2001–2005
Character of state-business relations	Rapprochement	Selective cooperation	Fragmented collusion	Semiformal collaboration (to protect capital gains)
Type of economic reform	Controlled liberalization	Selective liberalization	Circumscribed liberalization	Eclectic transitive stage (leading to Social Market Economy in 2005 marked by financial liberalization)
State's role	Producer	Midwife (creating private wealth)	Active guarantor of rent	As in earlier period, plus: Manager/regulator of rents
Rent opportunities	Public investments/ purchases/ contracts with foreign agents	Mixed sector ventures, smuggling/ black market, USSR debt repayment (D/R)	Tailored reregula- tion (imports/ exports), Invest- ment Law No. 10, USSR D/R, duty-free zones, construction, telecommunica- tions, tourism	Telecommunications, tourism, private banks, transportation, regional schemes
Formation/ consolidation of economic networks	Consolidation: within the state	Formation: between state and private sector	Consolidation: within economic networks	Shrinking and realignment of networks (based on potential economic independence and/or protection from the state)
Formal business incorporation/ expression (additional sites)	—	—	Chambers of Commerce and Industry, Guidance Committee, Parliament (1991)	As in earlier period, plus: Preparations for: holding companies, Syrian Business Council, and Damascus Stock Exchange; joint business associations (all materialized after 2005)

NOTE: This table encompasses relationships that will be discussed in both the current and the following chapters.

The first stage extends from 1970 until 1977. It is perhaps the most important period in the subsequent relations between the state and the private sector, as it constituted a model for cooperation that has been repeatedly emulated since. First and foremost, this period is marked by state-business rapprochement fol- lowing the "Corrective Movement" that was led by Hafiz al-Asad: "In 1970 a re- gime split, partly precipitated by urban opposition, resulted in a tacit alliance between Asad, then a 'reformer,' and the 'moderate' Damascene bourgeoisie, in which Asad came to power and initiated limited economic and political liberal- ization."[26] Although the word "alliance" is an overstatement, it became clear that the new regime was intent on mending fences with some of the icons of the business community.[27] The rapprochement took place indirectly, however, through what can be called a mild loosening of government controls on private economic activity, mainly in imports, internal trade, and contracting regulations involving foreign companies.[28] As liberalization measures were under way, however, a more important process was taking place within the state: the partitioning of various state sectors into feudalistic estates or domains among the various centers of power in the army, party, bureaucracy, and most notably, the security apparatuses.[29] This process of internal distribution of domains (*tahaasus*) occurred with the blessing of the leadership, which was concerned with the further consolidation of populist rule. Notably, this process facilitated cooperation with various private sector representatives by streamlining lines of communication and exchange. It was a customary practice for middle- and high-level officers in the security apparatuses to be "commissioned" as protectors of particular private sector individuals.[30] At the time, the authority for such practices (for example, commissioning, protecting "businessmen") was confined to the first three tiers of power in the Syrian regime: the top leadership, top security apparatus chiefs, and top army officers.[31] With time, however, as the windfalls and rent opportunities increased, both the practices and the category of those empowered to carry them out expanded considerably.

Beginning in 1973, the first windfall occurred as a result of the enormous capital inflows from the oil boom and from Arab aid after the October Arab-Israeli war. This period led to unprecedented and rather anarchic (decentralized) public expenditure on an unprecedented scale in a country accustomed to, and hitherto comfortable with, rather modest budgets: "[I]t can be estimated that, throughout the 1970s at least, some 65 percent of all investments, and some 80 percent of all public investments were actually financed from external resources,"[32] primarily from the Arab Gulf countries.

As a result of these enormous capital inflows into Syria after 1973, government spending soared and public sector projects were hastily established in practically all economic sectors, especially in the so-called strategic sectors and commodities (electricity, cement), which required high start-up costs.[33] Investment chaos ensued. Adding to the haste was the fact that Gulf aid would have a short shelf life. Therefore, Syrian decision-makers were more interested in executing various under-studied projects so as not to lose the aid that had been earmarked for Syria, often for particular projects. Experts from Bulgaria and Romania, in addition to local experts, would prepare feasibility studies in a hasty manner, not considering all the practical aspects of projects.[34] Such practices led to the creation of inefficient factories, often side by side or in the same city, producing similar products, with no links upwards or downwards. Cement, paper, sugar, and other factories were erected in improper locations, on the wrong soil, and with no environmental considerations.[35] For instance, four shoe factories were created in the same general area during this period; not only did they quickly fail, but they also caused the shutting down of authentic Syrian-made factories that had been producing high-quality products. Other examples abound; in short, external aid was not invested efficiently. Instead, the government sought a policy of *tawteen al'amala*, or providing jobs in various locales. This occurred in an economically irrational manner that did not serve labor, because many of these projects were short-lived. In fact, the policy of *tawteen* was a form of compensation for the corruption and excesses taking place within the state. By the mid-1970s, the state's social vulnerability had started to emerge. Not surprisingly, in the meantime, state–private sector relations were flourishing.

The public sector's share of external trade was 90 percent. Many of its new deals with foreign companies for the establishment of various new businesses, or the importation of new machinery and products, took place through various intermediaries, most of whom were private citizens and hitherto unknown to the public.[36] These intermediaries possessed the knowledge, training, and experience that the regime lacked, particularly in the areas of economic policy-making and international relations. They had international connections, expertise, experience, and domestic connections, which were needed to conduct mediation. This first crop of rentiers was for the most part composed of skilled or professional entrepreneurs who had a low opportunity cost in the existing national market. Though many of them were descendents of old bourgeoisie families (who themselves owned and ran similar establishments before the 1965 wave of nationalization) and were actually involved with the same companies they were asked to work with again, some were from modest urban backgrounds and benefited from opportunities offered by the significant expansion of state bureaucracy and free college education. Their participation in government-sponsored projects was not entirely by regime choice; rather, it was the regime's need.

Most of these individuals had lost their assets and their jobs but naturally retained the experience as well as contact with these companies. In fact, many members of this group were themselves being sought after by both the nationalizing state and the foreign companies that had lost their business or had the terms of agreement change according to the needs of the new local "owner" or agent. Thus, many were "kept" and employed by the state in the same postnationalization state-owned enterprises, and others were simply considered by the foreign companies to be their ticket for a future reentry. Changing politico-ideological circumstances after the Corrective Movement in 1970, but more significantly new capital inflows after 1973, led to the dramatic reemergence and rapid rise of such individuals who otherwise had their wings clipped. They would mediate with foreign companies on behalf of the state, or they would help manage, if not themselves manage, the new projects that were established.

The private businessmen who were given (or retained) direct managerial or senior positions became part of the public sector. Others—those who continued to (re)mediate as agents or who established their own companies with usually vertical economic production or service relations with state-owned enterprises—grew as part of the private sector but very much in the shadow of the state. Ultimately, many of these individuals entered into effective business partnerships with political (official and unofficial) or military elites on the following basis: the businessperson in a private capacity would provide the managerial or technical skills, the entrepreneurship, and some capital, if any, depending on the nature of the projects; on the other side, the "official" or "quasi-decision-maker" would guarantee the licensing, the winning of government bids and tenders, the bureaucratic shortcuts, and the "legal" cover for assorted semilegal or illegal transactions (for example, dealing with foreign exchange).[37] As will be discussed below, this model developed in the 1980s to include a third party, the technocrat, who is an invariable part of the economic decision-making bureaucracy.

The second period that provided opportunities for the rapid, if not risk-free, accumulation of wealth was from 1978 until 1986, when the Syrian market increasingly experienced severe shortages in consumer products, producers' means of production, and raw materials. Combined with the Syrian intervention in Lebanon from 1976 and the ensuing smuggling and black marketeering there and over the Turkish border in the early 1980s,[38] the shadow economy in Syria grew dramatically.[39] The most notorious smuggling and black market network was constructed by the then-president's brother, Rif'at al-Asad,[40] whose network included army generals, security services barons, and their private partners. This network became a model for other networks.

Another landmark of this period is the beginning, in the 1970s, of cooperation through mixed sector ventures in tourism and transportation between the state and what is referred to as the business troika: 'Uthman al-'A'idi, Sa'ib Nahhas, and Abdul Rahman al-'Attar. Although the coincidence of mixed sector ventures—which involves the cooperation of the state and select members of the business community—with a shortage economy and smuggling seems counterintuitive, since the private sector could have easily supplied the national market, it actually is not. In practice, these activities were intimately related.

As capital inflows increased dramatically and as the new regime consolidated its rule in the mid-1970s,[41] its leadership was becoming increasingly detached, socioeconomically, from the social base of the Ba'th party (workers, peasants, and the intelligentsia). According to Hinnebusch, "state-led economic growth in the 1970s fostered bourgeoisification of the political elite, a state-dependent bourgeoisie, and alliances between them and elements of the surviving private bourgeoisie."[42] The regime launched the mixed sector ventures as part of a strategy to appease the private sector and to bring elements within it to its side. However, when corruption became rampant and when chaotic industrial and other investments began to gore the interests of a significant number of the traditional artisans and shopkeepers within the *suq*, calls were made to put an end to such practices. It is significant that some calls were made from the Ba'th party, an indication of the resilience of committed Ba'thist elements.[43] In any event, the government responded with its recurring "anticorruption" campaign; seized the assets of various businessmen;[44] and put the business troika in jail. When the clamor for more crackdowns and arrests grew louder and then coincided with an escalation of the civil disturbances and assassinations by the Muslim Brotherhood, the "corruption file" faded to the background, or was "stopped," with no explanation: "The corruption file was opened because it was unavoidable. But it stopped because it reached high enough to taint the core of the regime. Usually, when matters escalate to that level, from that time until now, they stop and end [lapse]."[45] Henceforth, elements within the new business elite that were benefiting from both the shortage economy and the Lebanon intervention realized that they could not conduct their business in the open; they, and their partners in the private sector, went underground and carried out their business operations and expanded their relations in an informal manner. The economic and political impetus for network formation was at full force. Socially, the mistrust between the regime and the traditional segments of the business community grew and deepened in response to both the government's economic policies and alliances, and the increasing hostilities between it and the Islamists. The political elite grew increasingly rural and minoritarian.[46]

This period created the material grounds for the activation of various public-private ties in establishing sophisticated smuggling and black market networks, primarily through Lebanon.[47] It is during this period that laws were broken to an unprecedented degree, and ties strengthened or created between military[48] and government officials on the one hand, and various groups and individuals in the private sector on the other. The Lebanon intervention provided the military, at practically all levels, with ample opportunities for the generation of modest to significant wealth depending on the level of actual (not official) power one commanded. Invariably, the "front man" (*rajul al-wajiha*) was not officially affiliated with the state. In fact, the crop of state economic elite that this period generated came predominantly from modest and working-class backgrounds, and possessed little education and little else by way of entrepreneurship. But cross-border smuggling did not require those kinds of skills.

There was logic, of course, to allowing citizens in their private capacity to engage in such illegal activities. The government at that time, and since the al-Kasm government's inauguration in 1979, was reemphasizing economic and political centralization and the reactivation of the public sector's role in leading development and growth;[49] therefore, it could not be seen to be engaged in wide-scale smuggling and black marketeering, for these activities, in the end, detracted from the renewed economic attempt for hegemony by the public sector. Officials had to turn a blind eye to such practices, if not directly participate in an official or unofficial capacity.[50]

Third, the period after 1987 was marked by a mixture of opportunities and policy shifts associated largely with the 1986 economic crisis, which prompted a protracted economic liberalization. Two factors in particular, however, exemplify the swelling of the ranks of the new business elite: the debt-repayment-through-exports agreement with the USSR, and various regulatory decrees and legislation, including Investment Law No. 10 of 1991. As the latter source (Law No. 10 and other decisions) is prominently featured in the next chapter, I shall here discuss the more framed opportunities associated with the former source, the debt repayment agreement.

The "private" sector was propelled in this period by the opportunity provided by debt repayment to the Soviet Union through export deals. Although these agreements have their roots in the 1970s, they were stepped up in the late 1980s and even beyond the dissolution of the Soviet Union.[51] Two important consequences marked this prospect. First, it was during this period that literally hundreds of firms were established or revamped simply to satisfy the stepped-up debt repayment agreement between the Syrian government and the Soviet Union. Formed largely through informal networks that were already operating a business, such new, medium- to large-sized ventures catapulted a whole array of "manufacturers" from their small, modestly capitalized firms to large and heavily capitalized industries. Moreover, as opportunity knocked, various merchants and manufacturers rushed to join in by setting up new firms expressly for the purpose of such exports. Among those who were able to capture the greatest benefits of the debt repayment agreement were the state economic elite and some of their maturing offspring. Indeed, it was during this period that the notorious "*awlaad al-mas'ulin*" (children of officials) began to swamp the private sector. Initially, this occurred by proxy, through supporting an existing private sector firm or businessman, but that led to the establishment of factories by the officials (or sons) themselves. Having felt the pressure and unequal competition for such deals, those who worked in textiles were most critical of this type of belated entry into the private sector:

> After the Corrective Movement, several large and medium-sized companies were established but primarily to export to the Soviet Union. Those who benefited were closest to the regime at the time or were willing to work with the regime. Later on, the sons of regime officials started to pay attention to private economic activity, especially between the years 1986 and 1989 when opportunities for a large export market began to emerge. This was largely due to the fact that the Soviet Union wanted to speed up Syrian debt payments. Henceforth, several private companies were established again by regime officials' offspring or friends with the principal objective of exporting to the Soviet Union. Because of their proximity to the regime, they were capable of nearly monopolizing contracts especially in the textile industry. . . . But because of the singular mode and purpose of production and exclusive government deals, these companies grew in an economic environment free of competition and pressures for cost-effective production. They would be contracted to produce a certain number of uniform clothing items by a given date: they did not produce for a variable market and thus remained unready for such an environment.[52]

Second, this period had a dramatic effect on the development of the private sector in general, as well as on various private and public industries in particular (for example, textiles). These export markets, and the kinds of deals that were struck to the mutual benefit of officials, producers, and distributors on both the Soviet and Syrian ends, provided a dubious golden opportunity for Syrian producers: an extremely high "demand" for substandard and uniform products. As a result, standards of cost efficiency and quality within home-grown industries dropped in virtually all such firms; the deterioration of these standards occurred specifically in existing and newly established firms that were at the outset marked by substandard product quality and inefficient production. The effects began to appear in 1989 when such exporters were forced to send 20 percent of their total exports to West European countries. Many of these firms failed to meet this conditionality, and the inefficiency of most others was exposed in the early 1990s when these agreements were terminated.[53]

> Only a few people were able to benefit from the Soviet connection and I was one of them, but that is because I had established a name in the textiles industry beforehand and was ready for competitive production. In short, when those deals fell apart, so did eventually most of the companies that were established on their account. Again, few remained.[54]

At that time in the early 1990s, most debt repayment firms were closed down, either because they could not export elsewhere based on their competitive deficiency, or because their owners had made enough profits and were ready to move to alternative, more lucrative business or deals provided by the celebrated Investment Law No. 10. This law and other similar opportunities have also contributed to the formation of both the new economic elite and the networks themselves, but largely by way of consolidating this stratum and network relations. By 1991 the strategy of economic pluralism had been announced by the president himself, and the role of the private sector had been acknowledged as complementary to those of the public and mixed sectors. Thus, Law No. 10 gave members of already established economic networks the opportunity to legitimize their wealth. Often, private businessmen with partners from within the regime would run failing ventures as fronts for their previous or continuing economic activities.[55] As the relationship between the state and the business community was catapulted from the underground, the rate at which informal economic networks grew slowed, but it did not subside until the turn of the century, after Hafiz al-Asad's death.

It is significant that until 2005 the Lebanese connection continued to provide in various capacities and degrees an arena for wide-scale smuggling, money laundering, foreign exchange schemes, drug trafficking, arms deals, oil deals, and other illegal activities.[56] These activities are closely associated with entrenched networks of military and intelligence officers, bureaucratic personnel, core elite offspring, and private traders and manufacturers on a national and international scale.

In sum, the windfalls from each of these three periods increased the opportunity for rent-seeking and promoted a style of doing business marked by semilegality, quick-profit mentalities, and short-term horizons. Each new opportunity drew more businessmen or new entrants into the respective business, swelling the size of informal economic networks.[57] A new economic elite, not accustomed to competition and not vested in value-added generation, began to consolidate as a distinct, though not cohesive, upper portion of the "private" sector in the early 1990s, spawning its own institutional context and shaping developmental outcomes. Along with various government officials, the elite political and military/intelligence cores, and their offspring, this essentially rent-seeking economic elite had a well-defined interest in defending existing political-economic arrangements, especially until the Ba'th Regional Command Conference in 2005. The strategic recalculations, political realignments, and reorganization of rent-seeking that took place at that conference were governed by the announcement of the new Social Market Economy,[58] which for the first time in the history of Ba'thist Syria officially privileged and legitimated the development of market institutions and mechanisms.

Structural Characteristics of Economic Networks

The combination of regime strategies and economic windfalls led to the rapid expansion of informal interactions between the political elite and both established and new business actors. This web of informal economic ties gradually matured and became increasingly consolidated in the 1990s. Most lucrative economic opportunities and policies henceforth had the stamp of one or another member of these networks, whether in the implementation or formulation stages, and certainly in terms of the beneficiaries.

During the 1990s, state-business networks acquired identifiable operative attributes, notwithstanding the turnover and evolution they experienced. Despite the difficulty in conducting this rigorous kind of field research in network analysis—especially in regard to state officials, whose role is often undisclosed or muted—I have accumulated sufficient data, based on interviews, records, and direct observation, to make preliminary yet solid observations regarding the broad contours of the networks involved. The data lend themselves to a qualitative approach to network analysis. A sample of the public figures came from the following families, and they represent members of the party, bureaucracy, military, and security apparatuses, as well as some of their close relatives: Kanʿaan, Khalil, al-Tajir, Naseef, Suleiman, Huari, Hassan, Khawli, Fayyad, Tlas, Aslan, Abdul Nabi, Fayyad, Habib, al-Safi, Shihabi, Makhlouf, Asʿad, Khaddam, Zuʿbi, Akhtarini, Shaleesh, Zayoud, Ismaʿil, Haidar, Nasir, Qadoura. And a sample from the private actor figures came from the following families, many of whom fell in and out of favor with the regime throughout the years: Al-ʿAttar, Nahhas, al-ʿAidi, Khawandah, Hassan, Hamsho, al-ʿAqqad, Fallaha, Hassan, Homsi, al-Douri, Shura, Ghraoui, al-ʿAqqad, Sanqar, Dakhakhni, al-Mallah, Sabbagh, Sharabati, Mansour, al-Shami.

The characteristics of the emerging networks are dynamic, but basic features are discernible. Privileged economic networks in Syria are strategic in nature (as opposed to organic) and were largely a response to security concerns; that is, they were interest-based—"interest" here is defined broadly to encompass economic, social, and political interests—and instrumentally formed. Empirically, network members have come and gone on the basis of security and other concerns, revealing the loose bonds that often exist between them. Relations within networks are based on calculative trust,[59] which in the Syrian case is further colored by a historical legacy of state-business antagonism (whereby actors confine decision-making to immediate rather than longer-term concerns). The networks include civil elements (public officials and private citizens) and military elements and are cross-sectarian (including Sunnis, Shiʿis, ʿAlawis, and some Christians). Internally, they are informally organized in smaller webs marked by a three-way pyramidical structure that designates "roles" rather than personalities pertaining to particular economic sectors, subsectors, or even policy (see Figure 4.3):

A. *Power.* The military/security service component sits at the top (possessing decisional and coercive power). Usually, it takes only one such figure to act as the "guarantor" of rent or various forms of transgression when needed.

B. *Bureaucracy.* The bureaucratic component acts as a liaison for the most part (possessing administrative power and keys) but often as a silent partner. It was usually connected to the prime minister's office, and in some cases *was* the prime minister or his close aids until 2003–2004.[60] Again, it is usually only one figure who fulfills this role within the bureaucracy.

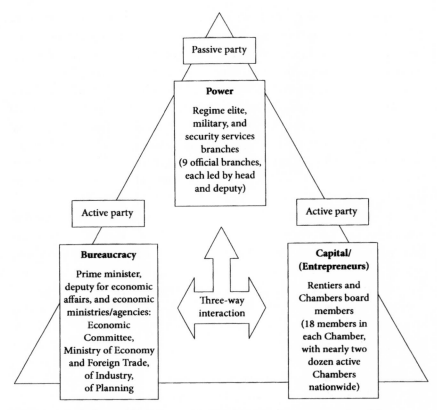

Figure 4.3. Typical pyramidical structure of networks: power, bureaucracy, and capital

C. *Capital.* The "private" component (possessing capital or entrepreneurial skills) is invariably the party involved directly in the day-to-day aspects of the business venture. One or more persons fulfill this role depending on the particular business venture involved.

All actors fulfilling these different roles are in contact with one another. The entrepreneurial role serves as the most active node as a function of its centrality to most transactions.

Externally, the combinations of such networks are organized along the lines of prominent power centers in the top leadership, the military, the bureaucracy, and the party. The manner in which network members relate to one another varies, but direct and personal contact is the preferred form of interaction. The lines of authority also vary depending on the relative economic and political weight of the actors, but the security component is invariably the more authoritative one. The informality and modularity of these networks make it difficult to establish a modal pattern of relations beyond what is specified here. Further field research under changing political circumstances would be required for this task.

These networks' structure is characterized by modularity, that is, made up of various relational parts that can be exchanged or taken out altogether without affecting the structure of the network as a whole. The most stable component of these networks, however, is the top leadership and all coercive apparatuses. Second comes the bureaucratic and ministerial component. With few but notable exceptions, the most substitutable component of these networks is its private component, particularly businessmen who were the product of the shady deals and partnerships of the 1980s. These businessmen tend to have the least legitimacy vis-à-vis the public and thus are most vulnerable to replacement or forced defection (see Figure 4.4). The networks' connection to institutions

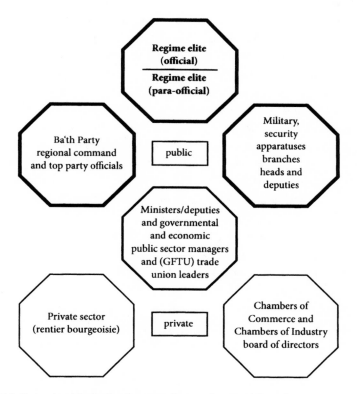

Figure 4.4. Sectoral and institutional sources of economic networks' members

is sporadic, inconsistent, and often unnecessary since informal connection to power centers bypasses institutional authority. Nonetheless, official institutions (for example, Chambers of Commerce and Industry) tend to constitute sites of interaction among network members as well as with other businesspeople. The impact of such interaction was latent and became manifest in post-2005 institutions that demonstrate a more genuine representation of business interests.

These characteristics are not static. In fact, the structure, expansiveness, and prominence of economic networks are temporally qualified. While these networks are ostensibly headed by military and bureaucratic officials, they are by no means always run by them. As both private and public individuals in these networks accumulate capital, their bargaining power increases and they become more attuned to the market, where the criteria for leadership can be relatively less dependent on political will. Furthermore, as the truly private components of these networks (as opposed to their business partners in officialdom) accumulate wealth, they begin to establish interests and relations outside the networks, gradually leading to a situation where membership in or proximity to networks is no longer the sole route to economic prosperity.

As new, more representative institutions and associations emerge, we begin to see a more eclectic business environment in terms of economic influence and governance, even if that environment is ultimately constrained by political elites. This development has been accompanied by a more favorable view of businesspeople during Bashar's rule.[61] Compared to the skeptical gaze that met rising businessmen in the 1990s, several years after Bashar's accession to power, and certainly in 2005, the regime itself began to celebrate the accomplishments of businessmen such as Firas Tlas, the son of the former minister of defense Mustafa Tlas; and Rami Makhlouf, the president's cousin. Though both come from politicized families, they do not enjoy an official political position.

What matters is that the contours of the political logic to which the political elite subscribe have themselves changed, allowing various forms of economic agency to coexist with informal networks, thereby downgrading networks' exclusionary prominence, if not their effect. Though such developments have their roots in the period prior to the Ba'th's tenth Regional Command Conference in 2005, they only became extant afterwards, beyond the confines of this study. To be sure, the particular features of this post-2005 period are still in the making, notwithstanding the uprisings of 2011, which are ongoing at the time of writing. Until 2005, however, policy or economic outcomes reflected a subtle form of intranetwork bargaining and negotiation, where the capital and skills of private business balanced the decisional power of network members in officialdom. The basic structure and characteristics, if not size and strategic position, of economic networks persisted beyond the period directly following the unraveling of Syria's command economy, when their purpose was optimal. Hence, the utility of economic networks leveled, but did not wane, with time, revealing an important pattern of utility of informal relations that merits serious comparative research. It is during that period (from the early 1970s to 2005) that the impact of these economic networks was at its highest. However, the institutional context within which the networks developed continues to be marked by a lack of trust between the political elite and the larger business community, thereby structuring the internal dynamics of these networks.

NETWORKS IN CONTEXT:
TRUST, REGIME SECURITY, AND INSTITUTIONS

The fact that economic networks in Syria have developed an independent internal dynamic, and thus an independent effect on economic outcomes, does not mean that they are impervious to exogenous influence. As with other institutional structures, formal or informal, they are embedded in a larger relational context that at times impinges on their development *and* dynamics. In particular, the context of mistrust between the regime and the larger business community provides a constant reminder to most businesspeople within the networks that there are limits to cooperation: the state will not allow them to acquire political positions (especially for urban-Sunni businessmen), act jointly outside the networks, or convert their economic wealth to political power. Within the economic networks, the ties that bind members in relation to particular economic transactions and partnership are quite stable. With time, however, as the private component of these networks has acquired more wealth, their structural power has increased, but their political solidarity with the regime has been at best questionable.

The top tier of elites within the regime, for their part, began to tread lightly after 2000. In addition to the potential destabilization brought about by the death of Asad senior and the succession skirmishes that took place between the pro-Bashar camp and part of the old guard (for example, between former chief of staff Hikmat Shihabi and the vice president, Halim Khaddam), the regime elite were concerned that the dispersion of wealth might have gone too far. Nonregime elements within the private sector in general and privileged economic networks in particular were poised increasingly to control larger

segments of wealth. At that time we began to see the emergence and gradual "takeover" of increasingly larger sectors and portions of the economy by
regime loyalists, chief among them Rami Makhlouf, the president's cousin.[62]
Such encroachment did come at the expense of some actors within the networks, including the Sanqar group/family, led by Omar Sanqar. Another such
figure is Abdul Rahman al-'Attar, a businessman considered to be one of the
symbols of regime-business partnerships since the 1970s. Al-'Attar came under
significant pressure from the offspring of the state officials who went into
business in the late 1990s, causing him to affirm the obvious: "he who would
like to stay in business, must concede to their [the regime's] politics."[63] This
crowding-out effect continued until 2005 when the networks, though persisting, became increasingly narrow. In turn, private economic initiatives in regard to business ventures and institution-building started to shift out of the
networks, where the spoils were becoming fewer on a per-capita basis. Instead,
the new business elite began to venture into the private sector proper, where
economic reforms were expanding and where market mechanisms were becoming legitimate components of economic life in 2003–2004, leading up to
the establishment of the Social Market Economy in 2005. The historical interplay between mistrust, regime security, and institutions reveals how and when
networks were constrained, if not necessarily debilitated, by exogenous factors.

Economic Institutions as Expression of Networks

Institutions can be conceptualized as forms of organization and rules that are
intended to serve a given purpose.[64] Whether they serve that purpose or not depends on a larger set of factors that are far more complex than the will and the
intention of the powers-that-be. Nonetheless, the raison d'être for institutions
can be gleaned from the interests of dominant actors as well as from the rules
that govern the institutions, officially and in practice.

The manner in which economic institutions—principally the Chambers of
Commerce and less so the Chambers of Industry—were established or rejuvenated in Syria in the late 1980s, along with the rules of participation, inclusion,
and operations that pervade them, reflect the interests of actors that stood to
benefit from the impending formalization of reforms.[65] More significantly, these
institutions represent the organizational expression of maturing economic networks seeking both to secure and to legitimize past, present, and future gains.[66]
Though not all members of these institutions belong to privileged networks,
some do, and some must in order to continue to do business on a larger scale.[67]

The principal linking institution after 1991—the Guidance Committee—is the only governmental body with official private sector representation, where state, capital, and labor[68] come together primarily to approve, disapprove, or ignore suggestions and requests made by private sector or trade union members. But its role is viewed as, at best, vague and reactionary:

> The Guidance Committee aborts the role of the legislature because it also exercises that role in a roundabout way, as when it decided to raise the exchange rate of the customs dollar. . . . [T]his was an indirect infringement of the constitution. . . . At best, the Guidance Committee acquired the role of an ambulance, but one that arrives after the bleeding is well under way.[69]

Although some bargaining takes place during the Guidance Committee meetings, most of the bargaining takes place informally behind closed doors, as it did between 1986 and 1991.[70] Alternatively, bargaining is not always necessary, as decision-makers sitting on the committee are themselves involved in common business ventures. The former prime minister, Mahmoud al-Zu'bi,[71] and the former deputy prime minister for economic affairs, Salim Yassin,[72] were heavily involved in public-private economic networks whose businesses extended from commerce to light (though protected) manufacturing.[73] A favorable tax policy or selective implementation thereof was very much in their own interest as members of these networks.[74] This situation has differed markedly after 2005, when the former deputy prime minister for economic affairs, Abdallah al-Dardari, and the prime ministry as a whole are remote from such schemes. The fact that state-business relations became more formalized with time, and exchange channels were institutionalized within new and evolving market institutions and mechanisms, rendered the utility of the prime ministry almost defunct, if not counterproductive. Historically, however, informal official involvement at the highest level acted as the conduit or liaison for privileged relations between networks and existing business institutions.

In addition to the Guidance Committee, the role of private sector representative institutions such as the Chambers of Commerce and Industry was also rejuvenated in the mid- to late 1980s, just when economic networks began to consolidate. These institutions constituted the primary funneling bodies in which identification, initiation, and recruitment of potential allies occurred. *Official* negotiation and bargaining within these institutions and between them and the government does occur, but on a very limited scale and often concerning the most banal of issues (for example, what time to close the market in the afternoon during the summer!). Generally, the Chambers are not (yet) taken seriously as representative institutions by prominent members of the business community:

> The Chamber of Commerce has approximately 50,000 members, but less than 9,000 actually vote. Why do they join if they don't vote, given that these Chambers are supposed to serve their interests? . . . Also, artisans are registered with both the Chamber of Industry and the Artisans Cooperatives Union. There is no separation between industrialists, professionals, and artisans. There are sectors that are not represented and sectors that are represented more than once. My business [auto dealer] is not represented. There are a thousand reasons why people join or avoid the Chambers.[75]

However, the Chambers continue to be latent arenas of mobilization where, for good or for ill, businesspeople come together. There, in the Chambers, private sector power centers may be lured, co-opted, or manipulated by some regime strongman—or perhaps they play their cards right with the backing of their capital and themselves penetrate the regime elite and state institutions alike. Alternatively, the Chambers represent the strategic arena for those who wish to independently carve out space for themselves in preparation for the coming stages of Syria's liberalization or turmoil.[76] The former tendency represents that of the rentier economic elite, that is, network members; and the latter, that of the recalcitrant old bourgeoisie and the new but largely independent businesspeople.[77] Powerful members of the Chambers are sometimes openly associated with security servicemen or high-ranking regime officials, making the reach of the networks quite deep and debilitating for collective action on the part of any of the Chambers across Syria. More recently we have witnessed the growth of interest in more independent private sector institutions among well-connected and independent businessmen and women alike. In 2007, the Syrian Business Council was established by private sector actors in part as a manifestation of this sentiment, which had lingered for more than fifteen years,[78] reflecting the antagonism between privileged businessmen and the rest of the business community. However, the strategic situation differed markedly in the late 1980s and produced a much less representative set of institutions that did not serve broader private sector interests.

Three factors marked the initial intent behind the establishment or rejuvenation of the first variety of economic institutions in Syria after the late 1980s: (1) access to influence, (2) function, and (3) the top-down nature of rules (for electing board members and granting licenses, for example). For the most part, those parties that the regime favored were able to have *access* to positions of influence within new economic institutions. Access alone was necessary but insufficient for pressing demands: only what is called "subsidized access," that is, access supported by strong elements within the regime, could guarantee that the actors' demands would be heard, and often satisfied, in one form or another, sooner or later. The *function* of these institutions, as with the Guidance Committee, was not to aggregate the interests and demands of the business community for the purpose of formulating positive-sum policies that might benefit both business actors and the economy as a whole. Instead, their function was to circumscribe decision-making by limiting it to a small set of actors and, subsequently, to manage the demands and preferences of these actors, not in accordance with what serves the economy but rather in accordance with what serves whom (that is, what demands and policies must be adopted because of the weight of the actors and their partners pressing for them).

Finally, these are essentially *top-down* institutions that are governed primarily by regime, not by business rules. The implications are immense. First, these institutions represent a few business actors rather than sectors, industries, or the business community at large. Furthermore, these institutions consider the interests of said actors as broadly representative of the interests of entire sectors. This myopia creates a short circuit vis-à-vis information gathering and exchange (the information loop) and undercuts the credibility of even the most mundane policies because such policies serve particular interests: thus, independent business actors do not support them and in some cases elect not to take advantage of them for fear of losing their independence or injuring their reputation among their allies and partners.[79]

Moreover, the manner in which board members of the Chambers of Commerce and Industry are elected further diminishes the credibility of these institutions. For instance, through the 1990s in the Chamber of Industry in Damascus, as is the case with other influential Chambers of both Commerce and Industry elsewhere, the distribution of proregime and independent board members was predetermined by the regime. In that Chamber, which seems to be the case across the board, "six out of the eighteen board members are appointed by the government. The election for the remaining twelve is real and clean."[80] Nonetheless, according to a number of independent board members in Damascus and Aleppo, where the Chambers are most powerful, the pressure that is exercised by regime officials and their protégés within the Chambers has invariably been more than sufficient to ensure that Chamber presidents are either "men of the regime" (*rijaal al-nithaam*) or men beholden to the regime. It is thus important to continue to examine the process of (s)election of the Chambers' board members, since they are the ones who elect the Chambers' presidents, while the presidents of Chambers are represented on the Guidance Committee and are able to weigh in on its decisions with their own and their allies' demands—hence, the connection between ostensibly representative business institutions such as the Chambers, on the one hand, and the Guidance Committee, which purportedly links state with business interests, on the other. In reality, not only are such "representative" institutions and "linking" institutions engineered to serve the interests of exclusionary state-business networks; they are often used to maintain high barriers to entry for "outsiders," lest rent opportunities become further divided or, worse still, erode. Interestingly, this is the scenario that unfolded in the late 1990s and early 2000s, leading to the regime's effort to further circumscribe the circle of beneficiaries of new large-scale subsectors in telecommunications and transportation.

Trust and Institutional Gridlock

Lack of trust between the regime and the business community (based on political as well as social antagonism) produced exclusionary business institutions that were neither representative of the business community nor responsive to the interests of independent businessmen. Instead, they reflected the interests of the increasingly influential networks of capitalists and bureaucrats, networks that served as the launching grounds for rejuvenating old institutions and creating new ones. Furthermore, the intranetwork dynamics within these institutions produced unintended consequences, such as an undermined ability of the state to steer the economy, notwithstanding retrospective sanctioning and ex post facto disciplinary actions whereby the state cracked down on economic players as a result of their illegal "past" practices.

This pattern of exclusionary institutions has sustained the lack of trust between the regime and the business community even while producing what can be called calculative or encapsulated trust between the regime and select business actors. Calculative or encapsulated trust emerges between parties that share short-term interests, and thus their cooperation is delimited by short-term goals. Even though calculative trust is not unique to state-business relations, it is important to note that the social antagonism that exists in Syria has played an additionally constraining role, even for investors within the networks who feared an ultimate crackdown on their business ventures. The San-qar family, discussed earlier in this chapter, is an example, and for good reason, as they suffered an encroachment on their business ventures by regime insid-ers. For an economy to grow in a sustained manner, long-term investment schemes, for instance the production of capital goods, are necessary to bring about the kind of added value that provides collective benefits (to capital, labor, and the state), even if disproportionately distributed. In the continued absence of trust between the state and the business community, as well as the mun-dane calculative trust that emerges between bureaucrats and select capitalists, the time horizons of investors and their partners are severely shortened, re-sulting in splitting investment between the local and the international and in the promotion of short-term or nonproductive ventures that produce little if any added value. This benefits a few parties immensely at the expense of pro-viding collective benefits; for example, by protecting inefficient manufactur-ers or monopoly traders, prices of respective products and commodities rise beyond their local, regional, and international market value. In this context, institution-building and development hit a dead end of sorts at the turn of the century and stagnated until 2005, when we began to see new political-eco-nomic formulas emerge, most likely as a result of this institutional stasis. In the meantime, the succession struggle was a more pressing preoccupation, which further prolonged economic inertia. More strategically important, however, were the unintended consequences of mistrust. On the one hand, the portion of the economy controlled by members outside the state elite was shrinking as a result of economic transactions set in place to maintain the regime's control. On the other hand, and as a consequence, the regime's leverage within and out-side the networks was decreasing as the structural power of accumulated capi-tal (dependent *and* independent) was increasing.

Unintended Consequences of Mistrust

While the literature focuses on the effect of institutions on trust between actors, Syria is a case that tells us what happens when mistrust informs institutional development. The question of trust has been dominated by analysts who em-phasize its political-cultural dimensions more than its strategic dimensions. However, when conceptualizing organizational trust, it is crucial to understand calculative behavior as inherent to the fundamental "arithmetic" of trust, and how it articulates the way in which social and situational factors influence the salience and relative weight afforded to various instrumental and noninstrumental concerns in such calculations.[81] This book applies a "rational choice new institutionalism" approach to explain the unintended institutional and economic outcomes of mistrust between the regime and the larger business community, manifested through the effect of economic networks.

The exclusionary networks that were formed are conditioned by this mistrust and produce what is called "calculative trust." This short-term trust between regime officials and select business actors produces two outcomes: first, it produces excessively tailored economic policies that help bring the economy to a halt; second, it empowers private sector partners (through rent-seeking) beyond the initial expectation of the regime elite, who conceptualize power primarily in political terms and initially neglect the encroaching power of capital.

The unintended consequences of mistrust for institution-building can be summarized as follows. Assume two parties A and B, both representing a group of individuals within a larger network. Party A represents a broad array of individuals within the regime who are willing to cooperate with private partners, and party B represents private individuals willing to cooperate with the regime. Assume that both parties generally cooperate because they need each other, not because they trust each other, hence the strategic characteristic of the networks. Party A seeks capital and entrepreneurship that it does not possess, and B seeks the opportunities and protection that are selectively available to individuals willing to cooperate with party A. A third assumption is that ultimately the top elites within party A must also act collectively to achieve its highest goal (regime security), while party B can achieve its highest goal (profit) either as individual actors or as a collective. The question is, at what point do institutions that are based on calculative mistrust between bargaining partners produce unintended outcomes for the parties involved, especially for the stronger party? In other words, when will negative economic effects of networks—which include the political and economic elite—begin to endanger regime security, a concern for all regime loyalists but a preoccupation of the top leadership in particular?

Mistrust between parties within institutions at the point of their inception is likely to be an outcome of bargaining processes that predate their emergence. Depending on changes in the conditions under which prior bargaining took place, mistrust within institutions is either increased or reduced. If mistrust between parties predates the emergence of institutions—understood here as a set of rules—the rules are likely to reflect the interests of the more powerful parties. Power differentials are one key factor in determining the dynamics of network relations as well as individual behavior of actors within institutions.[82]

Even when trust is not an issue between two parties that are asymmetric in terms of their respective forms of power, the stronger party is likely to have more leverage and thus be able to exact higher distributional gains from cooperation, at least initially. Hence, the regime initially benefits disproportionately from the development of informal economic networks.

Power differentials can be defined as a function of breakdown values; that is, the party that has a greater set of alternatives available to it in case of noncooperation is invariably the one with greater power and greater leverage. Since some parties would be more affected by noncooperation, they are likely to seek cooperation in the short and medium run even if their gains are reduced in the process. Thus, the weaker parties (here, private businessmen) cooperate not because they trust the rules of the game or their more powerful partners (among the political elite). Rather, they cooperate because they are able to exact higher distributional gains through cooperation than they would in the case of noncooperation. This calculus holds irrespective of the fact that the more powerful party is disproportionately benefiting. When mistrust between parties is an issue, what changes is not so much the behavior of individual actors—since all actors will continue to serve their own interests—but the type of cooperation that takes place: cooperation in a low-trust system of networks does not involve the kind of open information exchange and reciprocity that is necessary for formulating productive, long-term economic policies. For instance, the occasional hoarding of information by the regime, and the selective withholding of information by private actors, lead to the evasion of long-term productive investment. Instead, intranetwork cooperation produces short-term, tailored policies that benefit both parties immediately as individuals but at the expense of state coffers, the business community as a whole, the consumer, and the development of the productive forces of the economy, including labor. The entire economy suffers.

Furthermore, unintended consequences related to the increase in business power in general end up delimiting the regime's choices for an exit that sustains its security. Economic networks and ties within the networks remain intact, and continue to act as an agency that influences decision-making and benefits from rent-seeking. In Syria, however, at the turn of the century, as the balance of power within networks began to change, the top tier of the regime elite, who otherwise benefited as individuals from this dynamic, began to consider the structural pitfalls of a downward-spiraling economy. But this realization took some time as other, more pressing economic security purposes had been attended to in the wake of near economic collapse in the mid-1980s.

Practical Implications of Institutional Gridlock

The interplay between the two levels of analysis—ordinary intranetwork trans-actions and the broader political-economic context—reveals contradictions that are sooner or later attended to by the top regime leadership (in Syria, the president and his aides—primarily, Asad senior, his son Bashar, his other son Maher, and his son-in-law Asef Shawkat). The contradictions begin to arise when the weaker parties (B) accumulate distributional gains and broaden their alternatives, thus changing breakdown values. At that point, cooperation be-comes somewhat strained, especially if compounded by political crises, such as that of the impending succession in the late 1990s. However, while changes in breakdown values are not sufficient to terminate cooperation, they do affect the bargaining that takes place between both parties and the extent to which each party, especially the weaker one, is able to press for advantageous cooperative formulas. In Syria, the improved bargaining power of the private members of economic networks was a result of tailored policies that were formulated in the late 1980s and early 1990s.

By 1995, the cumulative effects of tailored policies and decreasing local and foreign investor confidence in Law No. 10 had brought the economy to a halt. Be-cause of their increasing wealth and thus their decreasing vulnerability to unfa-vorable cooperation, the mistrusted capitalists stood to benefit from bargaining with the regime. At the same time, the regime was seeking an exit from economic stagnation and decline that had reduced economic growth to negative figures for consecutive years. But the choices of the top regime leadership were rather lim-ited: they were neither able to give more concessions to network members, be-cause they would be doing so at a higher risk, nor able to broaden the political game to involve hitherto excluded actors, both domestic and international, since that would have undermined further their decisional autonomy.

The most secure exit from the perspective of the regime elite, then, was to crack down on the networks, reorganize them to the extent possible, and fur-ther restrict the largest distributional gains to smaller circles of regime loyalists. This process halted the development of exclusionary institutions and led to the reorganization of latent interests in the business community, the kind that after 2005 spurred the establishment of the first independent, though not all-inclu-sive, business associations. Crises of power succession and consolidation in such contexts—such as Syria witnessed from the late 1990s to the early 2000s—can accelerate the process by creating a split between those who stand to gain from the impending succession and those whose fortunes are yet to be determined under the new power formula. In Syria, this was manifest in the split between the regime's old guard and the supporters of Bashar al-Asad. As the old guard benefited disproportionately from existing networks, the succession crisis pit relative reformers (the new leadership) against the regime's old guard, which included figures like Vice President Halim Khaddam and Chief of Staff Hikmat Shihabi. In Syria, the regime's old guard aligned themselves with the private network members having stronger ties to the business community, including the Sanqar family. The soft-liners (the new leadership) opted for diverting the most lucrative rent opportunities to a small number of individuals with high proximity to the family of the president, most prominently Rami Makhlouf, while making most other economic opportunities more open to a larger segment of the business community. The new leadership had been securing various posts within the government and the military and security apparatuses since 1998. Furthermore, it had been recruiting new, younger, and more dynamic cadres who were previously not affiliated with the dominant economic networks. These changes culminated in the power reshuffling and consolidation that took place in the 2005 Ba'th Regional Conference, where Bashar firmly established himself at the helm. The networks ultimately persisted, but they shrunk as new forms of economic governance emerged and competed with them.

The result by 2005 was an institutional gridlock that put on hold many of the plans for economic opening because of the risks involved even in further reorganizing rent-seeking networks. The institutional dead end was a creation of the regime, which had boxed itself in since the 1980s when it helped consolidate informal economic networks that monopolized most distributional gains from subsequent processes and policies of economic change. It is noteworthy that even within exclusionary networks, private sector members were deprived of the instruments and information they needed to lend more credibility to their alliance with the state economic elite. Once more, the social mistrust between the regime and the business community as a whole permeated the regime's own networks. However, this did not occur at the expense of the alliance between the state elite and the select business actors within: it occurred at the expense of the health of the economy.

NETWORK DYNAMICS: TRUST AND ECONOMIC PERFORMANCE

This book argues that economic networks formed an important intervening factor in the economic performance of Syria. To be sure, the collusive informal relations between state officials and businessmen in a low-trust system have shortened time horizons of investors and policy-makers, leading to a decade of economic decline and attendant developmental distortions. Before delving into the pattern of economic liberalization that ensued, we must identify the relational dynamics within the networks, which produced tailored and often counterproductive economic policies and investments.

Literature on the political economy of economic reform suggests that types of economic networks are correlated with particular performance outcomes.[83] The state-business networks that enjoy higher levels of trust, transparency, information exchange, credibility, and reciprocity are believed to promote successful reform outcomes and undercut the possibility of collusive (crony) arrangements, in which privileged actors capture the benefits of reform. Conversely, a lack of trust between the state and the business community as a whole exacerbates other aspects of the relationship, especially transparency and information exchange. This latter case of a low-trust system depicts the situation between state and business in Syria, which led to the dominance of selective informal ties between them at first, and then to poor economic performance. Combined with the fact that Syria's economic reform path after 1986 was homegrown and relatively insulated from direct external interference,[84] this distinctive lack of trust encouraged the kind of rent-seeking that was marked by commercial and nonproductive business ventures, which provided little or no added value to the economy.[85] As a result, employment, productivity, and efficiency suffered tremendously by the late 1990s. Furthermore, this low-trust system has had a huge effect on the style of reform, not least fiscal reform. In the continuing absence of trust, especially after 1986 (as the following chapters indicate), fiscal issues and policy-making were manipulated in an extralegal manner both to raise the barriers to entry into the domain of beneficiaries and to protect the beneficiaries themselves: fiscal policy regulations stipulate one thing that applies to the entire population, while network members freely transgress these regulations because of their connections or because they *are* the "connection." This accounts for the severe lack of transparency and information exchange in relation to budgetary and fiscal matters, which emanates from the absence of trust between the state and the business community at large. Finally, although this is not peculiar to Syria, the historically marked lack of trust between state and business actors compelled an unusually large segment of the elite (in the military, security services, party, and bureaucracy) to go into business shortly after the 1970 coup, and to occupy the top rungs within the entire business community. I term this process "fusion," indicating the combination of decisional power and capital in the hands of one person: the state official. Thus, reform policies and (re)regulations were no longer simply produced by policy-makers to be consumed by policy-takers (private business actors); most of the powerful policy-makers before 2005 were heavily involved in private business ventures, starting with the former Syrian prime minister Mahmood al-Zu'bi and his deputy for economic affairs. This factor, the fusion of the role of bureaucrat and capitalist, accompanied by increasing familial ties through marriages between the state elite and the old bourgeoisie, has contributed to the gradual easing of social dissonance, and therefore mistrust, between the state elite and the business community a few years into Bashar's rule, although it has by no means created a fundamental shift in trust relations.

In assessing the quality and form of relations between state and business as well as performance outcomes, the issue of trust occupies center stage. Trust between bureaucrats and the business community is said to "reduce transaction and monitoring costs, diminish uncertainty, lengthen time horizons, and thereby increase investment (and policy fulfillment generally) above normal levels."[86] Thus, in the presence of trust between state and business, information is exchanged more generously; reciprocal relations can develop with minimal monitoring costs; decision-making processes become more transparent; and investors assume the credibility of policies in terms of formulation and implementation. Hence, uncertainty decreases, investors' risk-aversion diminishes, and commitment to both short- and long-term investment becomes a matter of economic, not political, calculation.

However, in the absence of trust between state and business, as is the case in Syria, an underlying safety net is removed and all aspects of the relationship suffer.[87] Individual bureaucrats and capitalists, or networks thereof, are left to their own devices. They can develop a more narrow relation of trust, what can be called calculative, strategic, or circumscribed trust.[88] Strategic trust has a temporary nature: it therefore shortens time horizons for investors involved. The task for network members, both state-related and private, becomes the maximization of rent-seeking in the shortest possible time span. Unsound economic policies—whether tailored to individuals or to groups—proliferate, as will be examined in the following chapter. The consequences of economically unsound policies that could have been averted or mitigated through trusting relations, become severely exacerbated. In addition to the credible contention that unsound policies cause more damage than sound policies provide benefits, the absence of trust becomes an important contributing factor to economic failure such as we have witnessed in Syria after 1994–95. Conversely, sound economic policies fail to yield the expected investment rush when trust is in short supply. Ironically, lack of trust between the state and the business community has led to the creation of tighter relations among individuals and groups on either side. And although trust within networks has been largely of the strategic variety, it has proved enduring in the medium run in various LDCs (late-developing countries).[89] In practice, as with the case of Law No. 10, this leads to the temporary co-opting of reform measures by network members who, in any case, have had a significant impact on formulating such "laws."[90]

Using Syria as a case of a low-trust system between state and business, we are able to identify the institutional and social conditions that gave rise to economic networks between bureaucrats and capitalists, and trace the impact of these conditions on the intranetwork dynamics. However, while it is apparent that the alliance among network members is rather tenuous, it remains comparatively durable when the relationship between the regime and the entire business community is considered. The best indication of the relatively homogeneous, even if temporary, interests within these networks is the manner in which they influenced the pattern of economic liberalization in general, and fiscal as well as regulatory change in particular, at least between 1986 and 2005. Economic networks, representing neither the corporate interests of the state nor the private sector proper, have been decisive in both pushing for certain kinds of reforms and prejudicing against others. This occurred informally, as well as through the type of exclusionary economic institutions that were rejuvenated in the late 1980s, producing what can be called circumscribed liberalization, that is, a pattern of economic change that primarily benefits the winners in prereform arrangements.

5 THE POLITICAL DYNAMICS OF ECONOMIC LIBERALIZATION

THE POLITICAL DYNAMICS of the liberalization process in Syria reflect both the broad strategic priorities of the regime and the ability of economic networks to capture the most significant benefits of liberalization at the expense of the economy, the state's corporatist interest, and the private sector. The regime's calculations involved a risk assessment of two related processes: the gradual dismantling of a centralized economy and the reshuffling of social alliances. So long as the regime preserved its own security through its continuing domination of the public sector and its prevention of collective action among the dominant forces in the private sector, economic failure would be tolerated, even if unintended. If the public sector had to be compromised, it would happen only in the context of a broad migration of regime loyalists into the private sector.

I shall begin with a quote from a Syrian industrialist that provides a cross section of the prevailing contradictions in Syria's liberalization experience.

Suppose you want to start a factory in Syria today [April 1999]: first, you will not be able to get a legal permit to do so, because we have no designated industrial zones. So, secondly, you must find an agricultural land on which to erect an illegal industrial factory, and register it as *mustawda'aat ziraa'iyyah* [agricultural depot]. Thirdly, almost everything you need to build the factory you either have to smuggle in, buy illegally on the black market, or pay more than three times its market price in competing industries in neighboring countries. By the time you arrange for a power generator and plumbing, and before you import machines, parts, and raw materials, you've increased your production cost by 30 to 50 percent. You have to pay bribes constantly and continuously, and this is just the beginning of the ensuing chaos, treachery, and *forced* illegal activity. For beginners . . . all over the world, factory machines are tax-free, being means of production. Not only does it take six months to a year for machines to get to us, but also we keep paying taxes on them even after they become useless! You have to smuggle parts into Syria because we can't use DHL. Our raw materials are often more expensive than finished imports. How, then, can we compete? . . . If the Syrian industrialist wants to avoid all illegal operations, he should close shop and send his employees home. But if you want to work, to survive, then you have to engage in illegal operations. This is why our shadow economy constitutes the largest portion of our real economy. . . . What happened to Investment Law [No. 10] and where are our laws [citing the gap]? What happened to encouraging industrial projects, exports, and the private sector?[1]

This series of complaints by an industrialist in the late 1990s is imbued with indicators of change in the policy environment of the Syrian political economy. Since the 1990s, and to an even greater extent since 2000, Syria has become far more exposed to the outside world in many respects, and the "private sector" has been permitted to move into various areas of production and trade that were previously dominated or monopolized by the public sector. Underlying such indicators of change, however, is a set of ossified institutional, legal, and ideological structures that undergird business transactions. The contrast is striking,[2] for the new freedom of movement the regime granted the private sector was, in the final analysis, often technically illegal.

On the one hand, a process of homegrown liberalization has officially taken off in Syria under the title "economic pluralism" (*al-ta'addudiyyah al-iqtisaadiyyah*),[3] the official development strategy rejuvenated in 1991 to legitimate the private sector's compromised role. Beginning effectively in 1986 at an informal level, this liberalization process was the state's response to a severe foreign exchange crisis prompted by a dramatic decline in aid from the Arab Gulf states and compounded by the public sector's inefficiency in substituting for imported goods. Since then, under Bashar's guidance, the regime has continued to insist on gradualism as the guiding principle behind economic reform, but it has grudgingly acknowledged and created a larger role for private sector business in the Syrian economy. Economic liberalization has opened various sectors of the Syrian economy to private investment and has had a tremendous impact on Syria's overall development, particularly its social structure and corporatist system of interest representation.

On the other hand, the Syrian economy has not undergone any significant "reform" at the structural, institutional, and legal levels.[4] Empirically, the state retreated and the private sector advanced—public sector business activity dropped and private sector business activity soared. However, while the economy was privatized, it was not rationalized. Policy-making inputs from the private sector increased, but policy-making mechanisms and institutions were not changed to reflect that. New laws and decrees were passed, but older and constraining ones remained. Hence, the peculiar situation of "liberalization without reform"[5] that exists in Syria today. Though matters changed after 2003, it remains true that after more than a decade of liberalization since 1991, Syria remained without a private or efficient banking system, without a financial market, without officially delineated industrial zones, and without officially sanctioned institutional mechanisms associated with free(r) market development.

Although liberalization without fundamental reform is not specific to the experience of Syria, it acquires an extreme form there due to the institutions, legal structures, and networks that predated liberalization, persisted, and in some respects, flourished. Most notable is the concentration of wealth and power within maturing economic networks which long predated official liberalization initiatives in 1991. The influence of these networks on governing institutions, wealth redistribution, and the productive base of the economy is evident in the developmental consequences of liberalization in Syria, most of which are still felt at the end of Bashar's first decade as president.

What explains this pattern of economic liberalization? What are the components, dynamics, and mechanisms of such a strategy? And what are its developmental outcomes? Though aspects of these questions may be causally related, the questions themselves point to three distinct research areas and, initially, must be taken up separately to avoid turning correlations into causalities.[6] First, I shall turn to the literature on the Syrian case.

THE SYRIAN CASE

In the late 1980s and early 1990s, Syria political economy analysts tapped into the macrolevel variables that provide indicators for trends and relationships between various political economic processes.[7] Much of the literature dealt with the broader processes of "reform" and the constraints imposed by prior populist legacies. Researchers examined the private sector as a whole, and examined the state in more or less the same manner. But often, for good reason, researchers have not yet tapped into the muddy network of public-private ties to uncover a host of factors and relationships that would help us explain or clarify the source of particular liberalization patterns and developmental outcomes. Prior to 1996–97, field research regarding such specific and sensitive issues as the particular beneficiaries, dynamics, and problems of the government's liberalization strategy was far more difficult, and far less rewarding, considering the state of constrained discourse. After 1997, such issues began to emerge more conspicuously in public discourse[8] and in the print media that were permitted to operate in Syria.[9] This study has benefited from the healthier research environment in Syria that emerged since the late 1990s.

In the early and mid-1990s—when much of the literature on Syria's reform experience emerged—much of the general political economy literature focused excessively on numeric data, whether official or otherwise, pointing in a particular direction, namely, the numerical growth of the private sector as an important indicator of economic reform success.[10] It is this growing private sector that is putatively going to push for further economic, if not political, reform. The Syrian case tells us otherwise: namely, that it is more important to examine the particular social, institutional, and legal dynamics of economic change to discern particular relationships between patterns of liberalization and possibilities for structural economic reforms.

To bring the illustration closer to cases such as Syria, it is said that economic reform in authoritarian-populist regimes is a highly risky affair, most significantly because it involves a transfer of wealth from the public to the private sector, disrupting the interests of those who benefited from the old arrangements. Furthermore, economic reform involves the gradual introduction of the rule of law, increased participation, a high social cost generally for those with limited income, and potential sociopolitical unrest. However, with the exception of the misdistribution of wealth, which so far has had no mobilizationary effects, Syria seems to have been able to weather virtually all politically disruptive side effects of economic "reform." One could argue that this is because there has not been much genuine economic reform there. This is only partly true, for despite the dearth of economic liberalization policies after Investment Law No. 10, economic change in the 1990s was quite evident. This, more than any other single fact, is where the specific nature of the Syrian case becomes apparent.

With respect to the argument that credits private sector growth for economic improvement during the 1990s, the Syrian case ostensibly provides positive evidence. However, closer inspection compels us to dig further, or elsewhere, for reform indicators. As discussed in Chapter 3, between 1986 and 1994 Syria witnessed a remarkable growth in the size, capital, and activity of the private sector, whose share of fixed capital formation rose from 34 percent in 1985 to 65 percent in 1993.[11] Although subsequent years saw a decline in private sector output as the initial consumer boom, fuelled by new oil discoveries, deflated, since 2003 the private sector has reclaimed more than half of all fixed capital formation, reaching 54 percent in 2005.[12] Similarly, private domestic investment reached over 60 percent in the mid-1990s, then decreased throughout the latter part of the decade, but reemerged as the majority share of gross domestic investment after 2000 (see Figure 5.1).

However, these substantial numerical increases in the private sector's fortunes, at the expense of the public sector, occurred without any structural economic reform, let alone substantive liberalization in the political sphere. More significantly, there has been virtually no change in the style of policymaking, nor in the irrational nature of economic, financial, and monetary policies. Worse still, the number of notorious laws and decrees that in practice prevented or derailed private initiative in the mid-1980s increased during the 1990s. The same goes for the degree and kind of bureaucratic and systemic obstacles that hampered investments, especially in the industrial sector.[13]

But how could the private sector in the mid-1990s come to constitute more than half of the Syrian economy without concomitant change in its political power, or in the proclaimed socialist identity of the economy, or in the accountability of government, or in the central-command nature and processing of economic policies? The tenor of these questions has two faces: How could the regime afford the dramatic reduction in public sector assets and still retain its economic decision-making power? Alternatively, how was the new private

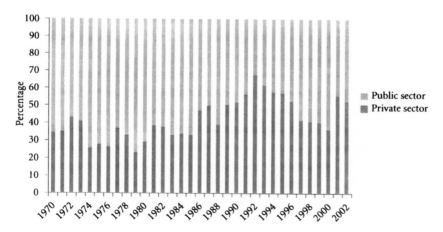

Figure 5.1. Gross domestic investment expenditure. Data from Central Bank of Syria Quarterly Bulletins, 1970–2002.

wealth prevented from being transformed into political power? These questions address the political-economic dimension of this research. The expense at which the Syrian regime took these actions addresses the developmental dimension. Both dimensions will be examined in this chapter.

THE STATE OF THE SYRIAN ECONOMY:
ECONOMIC CRISIS AS CAUSE *AND* EFFECT OF LIBERALIZATION

The starting point of systematic economic liberalization in Syria was the immediate government response to the economic crisis that hit the country in 1986.[14] During that year, and as a result of the gradual drying up of external capital inflows in the form of aid, political rent, and workers' remittances, the Syrian treasury was in dire need of hard currency "to meet its foreign exchange obligations."[15] Furthermore, after years of slow decline in the post-boom period of the 1970s, the inefficiency and lack of productivity of Syria's heavily subsidized public sector was completely exposed. The 1986 crisis set in motion the liberalization process that we have been witnessing in Syria for nearly a quarter century.

The period between 1986 and 1991 was of critical importance for the liberalization period that is, ostensibly, still in effect. First, it was the period in which the regime finally surrendered its commitment to the public sector as the sole engine of economic development. This acknowledgment, evident through policies, deregulation, and finally, proclamations in 1991, was accompanied by the rapid rise of the private sector's share of investments, capital formation, and employment generation. Furthermore, this was the period in which the economic networks combining private individuals and public officials (and their relatives) were consolidated, both formally and informally, through guaranteed membership in the Chambers of Commerce and Industry, participation in parliamentary elections, and inclusion in the ministerial Guidance Committee—an ostensible substitute during a period where five-year plans had become nearly defunct.[16]

That period also marks the end of an era of proclaimed ideological economic development. Until 2005, the most recent five-year plan had been drafted in 1985, although incompletely so, and was never published or implemented. Likewise, no Regional Command Conferences were held during the subsequent fifteen years. Both of these facts are of importance for understanding how much the regime was willing to publicize the gradual, if hesitant, abandonment of central-command economic administration and the lowering of the Ba'th party's profile.[17] In 2004 the State Planning Commission stated that it would begin incorporating market principles into its economic policy-making by the end of the decade, a statement that was only mildly amended at the most recent Regional Command Conference, held in 2005, where it was decided that Syria would adopt a "social market economy."[18]

Though incomplete, the economic measures that the government implemented before 1991 set the economy on a course of temporary recovery. At the time, the regime was defensively preoccupied with the processes of perestroika and glasnost that were sweeping the socialist world. Until 1991 the leadership had followed a narrow, statist logic of stability, ignoring similar reform calls from both capital and labor.[19] In the post–Gulf War period, the Syrian economy enjoyed steady growth. Aid from Gulf countries resumed; a new investment law went into effect; and oil finds and exports increased. Public spending for various infrastructural projects and social services resumed; more jobs and foreign exchange were generated; the Syrian pound was relatively stable; and the private sector's share of capital formation, production, and exports grew to levels not seen since 1963.[20] Reports claiming an economic growth rate of 6 to 7 percent proliferated in local and international publications.[21] Much of that growth turned out to be temporary and numeric, not structural and enduring. As the economy grew in the early 1990s, corruption and back-door deals between public officials and members of Syria's business community grew even faster, turning developmental opportunities into rent-seeking. Consequently, economic "growth" peaked in the first half of the 1990s and started to decline thereafter.[22]

Today's deteriorating economic conditions reveal the illusory nature of economic "growth,"[23] which dramatically declined to 1.3 percent in 1997, judging from relatively optimistic Syrian government statistics. However, figures calculating the net domestic product at factor cost show a negative economic growth rate of 4.4 percent for the same period. The decline continued in 1999; oil prices, the source of 60 percent of Syria's foreign exchange and exports, had dropped in 1998. Scant rainfall in the late 1990s directly affected the agricultural sector, which accounts for more than 30 percent of the Syrian economy as well as workers' livelihood, and continues to comprise roughly 20 percent of GDP.

OFFICIAL AND UNOFFICIAL ECONOMIC LIBERALIZATION

Beginning in 1986, the Syrian regime embarked conspicuously on a home-grown[24] ad hoc and heterodox process of economic liberalization that aimed to remedy macroeconomic imbalances, and ultimately to skirt any type of fundamental restructuring of the economy. The year 1986 marked Syria's most pressing economic crisis since 1970, manifested in severe shortages of foreign exchange. Immediately, Syria upgraded its liberalization measures targeting foreign trade, exchange rate, and investment regimes. Such measures, however, were far from programmatic and thus remained un- or underinstitutionalized. At the same time, the government unmistakably started to acknowledge the validity of adopting measures that signaled movement away from a central command economy, if not toward a market-oriented economy. First, the government acknowledged its inability to provide sufficient foreign exchange to finance a variety of basic consumer goods, as well as agricultural and industrial supplies, and made the move to privatize "parts of the public-sector foreign trade monopolies."[25] By 1987, under a new cabinet, the government acknowledged "for the first time . . . the validity of the free-market rate as an indicator of the value of the Syrian currency," and by 1991 had likewise acknowledged the validity of the "neighboring country rate," which approximated the market value of the Syrian currency.[26]

Two specific developments marked significant liberalization measures in the area of investment. First, in 1986 the government permitted—under Legislative Decree No. 10—the establishment of mixed public-private ventures in the agricultural sector, primarily for export-promotion purposes.[27] In industry, liberalization policies were fewer and farther between. Before 1991, they were limited to the gradual expansion of the list of products that the private sector was permitted to produce.[28] A more significant (albeit hasty) shift came in 1991 with the introduction of Investment Law No. 10, which was intended to mobilize domestic and expatriate capital in the form of inward domestic investments.[29] Notwithstanding some additional, minor policy changes—including amendments made to Law No. 10 in 2000—the rate at which liberalization measures were introduced slowed down considerably in the mid- to late 1990s, and such measures were largely limited to increasing the scope of existing measures rather than expanding the domain of economic sectors targeted for liberalization.

Since taking power, however, Bashar has overseen a wave of new legislation addressing the Syrian economy. Most notably, tax laws have been reformed; trade has been liberalized with the signing of both the Greater Arab Free Trade Agreement (GAFTA) in 2005 and a bilateral free trade agreement with Turkey in 2004; private financial services (including banking and currency exchange) have been legalized; the commercial code has been updated; and Investment Law No. 10 has for the first time been amended, and then replaced entirely with a new decree. However, these reforms have not yet created much positive economic growth. In part this is due, as in previous periods of liberalization, to the piecemeal nature of their implementation. In its 2005 Investment Climate Assessment, the World Bank summarized the following failings of such legislation:

> The recent and substantial lowering of tariffs has not yielded its full impact on trade and investment in part because non-tariff barriers remain substantial. . . . The benefits of a lower corporate tax rate were reportedly mitigated by the absence of accompanying reforms in tax administration. . . . The impact of opening banking to private participation has been muted by the lack of simultaneous institutional, regulatory and structural changes in the banking sector. Substantial investments in electricity generation were not matched by simultaneous improvements in distribution, meaning that service, as experienced by firms, remained unreliable in many locations.[30]

In many ways, however, the content of the legislation is not to blame, as the roots of the current economic stagnation go much deeper. Shana Marshall characterizes the whole effort to date as a "hollow reform process," which "fundamentally alters legislation but whose enforcement often falls victim to political realities."[31] Whereas Syria's ranking in the World Bank's "Doing Business" index has risen over past years, its ranking on Transparency International's "Perceptions of Corruption" index has fallen. Most independent economic analysis points to extralegislative factors such as corruption, political risk, and isolationist foreign policy choices as the chief deterrents to doing business in Syria.[32] Highlighting this, Syria's ranking in the United Nations Development Programme's (UNDP) "Diversion of Public Funds" index fell from 43 (out of 128) in 2006 to 114 in 2007.[33]

The Official Record of Economic Liberalization

The official record of economic liberalization and privatization in Syria since 1986 reveals four major categories of liberalization measures, all of which have been determined to a large extent by the Guidance Committee.[34] These categories are trade, currency exchange, investment, and foreign investor rights. I summarize all four here, then discuss trade and investment reregulation in more detail, because of their magnitude and because the principal beneficiaries have been members of state-business networks who dominate the Guidance Committee meetings.

Trade deregulation measures came largely in the form of lifting existing restrictions, primarily on imports. Alternatively, they "sanctioned the *de facto* abolition of effective state control over foreign trade through increased smuggling" in the early to mid-1980s.[35] *Exchange rate liberalization* began in 1987, stabilized in the early 1990s, and ended in a unification of exchange rates in 2002. In 2003 the government lifted the ban on dealing with foreign exchange, and with it the hefty prison sentence for violators. *Investment laws and decrees that offer special privileges and tax incentives for new enterprises* included: the Higher Council for Tourism Decision No. 186 (dating back to 1977 but with periodic revisions); Decree No. 10 of 1986, allowing for the creation of mixed-sector ventures in the agriculture sector (75% private ownership, 25% public ownership, privately managed); the notorious Investment Law No. 10 of 1991, which was intended to encourage foreign direct investments and, later, domestic investments in industry—and even later in the transport sector; the establishment of enterprises in industries or services that were largely reserved for the public sector (for example, pharmaceuticals, textiles); the establishment of new enterprises in new domains, or the expansion of existing enterprises into these new domains (for example, car rental agencies); and finally, in 2000, an amendment to Investment Law No. 10 of 1991—Law No. 7—granting foreign investors the right to own their investment properties, and relaxing restrictions on repatriation of profits.[36] This and other measures ultimately led to the 2007 overhaul of Law No. 10 introduced by Legislative Decree No. 8, which increased the range of mobility for foreign capital invested in Syria. The decree authorized investors to repatriate benefits gained on capital invested in Syrian banks; provided exemptions for customs taxes on manufacturing and industrial supplies and equipment ("the means of production"); proposed the creation of an investment promotion organization, which was then established by Legislative Decree No. 7; and extended the sectors accessible to foreign investment to agriculture and land reclamation (including enterprises in industry, transport, information and communication technologies (ICTs), environmental projects, services, electricity, oil and mineral wealth, and any other areas the Supreme Council for Investment might deem appropriate in the future).[37] However, as the text of the decree specifies, the enjoyment of these privileges is at the pleasure of the council: "The Supreme Council shall have the right to decide granting the investment facilitations, guarantees and advantages stipulated in this Legislative Decree, as well as any other additional advantages and guarantees, to any other enterprise." The fourth category of official liberalization measures, *foreign investor rights*, included the following: the establishment of enterprises by direct foreign investments (until 1999, Nestlé was among the very few such ventures); the establishment of agencies for foreign companies (primarily in the auto and clothing industries, mainstays of the elite's offspring for whom contracts began to surface in the late 1990s); and finally, in 2003, the broadened scope of investment allowed in the free trade zones established around the country, allowing greater scope for domestic and foreign investors, with minor restrictions.

Trade Deregulation   The state allowed the private sector to import various goods, but complex conditions were attached, such as quotas, commissions, special bank credit, restricting imports to foreign nationals, and importing through the export dollar. The regime and its allies, as well as public officials' offspring in the private sector retain the "keys" (forms of permits and licensing) to all these conditions. They therefore are the primary beneficiaries of freer trade policies. The resultant hike in the cost of imports is shifted onto the consumer. "Independent" or vulnerable merchants would absorb the cost of the conditionality, whereas connected merchants would avoid it and split the untaxed additional margin of profit with their connection—unless, of course, they *are* the connection. Members of economic networks have therefore benefited quite disproportionately from freer trade policies. They continue, however, to press for tailored free trade policies that support their own business ventures.[38] As the World Bank has assessed (cited earlier), "substantial lowering of tariffs has not yielded its full impact on trade and investment in part because non-tariff barriers remain substantial."[39]

Investment   Investment Law No. 10 of 1991[40] serves as an illustrative example of laws that purport to promote investments that bring added value.[41] The ill-prepared orphan law and its accompanying bureaucratic obstacles (especially for industrialists), as well as its direct contradiction with existing laws, including ones that prohibit dealing with foreign currency,[42] have pushed most potential investors away and attracted those with political connections and who are in search of quick profits. The "keys" to Law No. 10 projects are handled by the Higher Council for Investments, a body that routinely submits to what is called in Syria a "subsidized contract" (*mashru' mad'uum*), that is, politically subsidized. According to a Syrian businessman and former economist,

> you cannot establish a project under Law #10 unless an "anonymous" name [regime official] shares 10–20% of the profits, not of the capital . . . and they'll make you sign a contract. . . . [I]f you want to avoid this silent partnership, you

would go through administrative hell later on—that is, if the Higher Council [of Investments] approves your application.[43]

According to a prominent businessman who reiterates the prevalent critique of Law No. 10:

Law #10 was created with bad intentions that aim at benefiting specific individuals and cliques. Take for example the Rent-a-Car type of companies established under this so-called investment law. These represent the intentions and the aim of the much-celebrated Law #10. Essentially, these are companies that take advantage of the tax and custom duty breaks and import foreign luxury cars which are intended for rent but end up being leased, and effectively sold, in the local market. Where is the productive investment in such establishments? Where is the contribution to our GDP? Where are the employment opportunities that have been created? And finally, what is their export value that is supposed to generate foreign exchange? Most of the companies established under Law #10 have not met even half its requirements in practice. . . . Only 10–20% of projects proposed under Law #10 are carried out/realized. The remaining projects never make it but their number do on government statistics.[44]

Hence, more than 60 percent of investments under Law No. 10 did not go to manufacturing but went to the nonproductive and environmentally disastrous transport sector,[45] where microbuses were imported by the thousands and where luxury cars were sold under the guise of rent-a-car enterprises. As stated in the previous chapter, more recently tourism has become the main attraction for investment rather than manufacturing or infrastructure projects. Until the end of 1998, only 196 manufacturing projects were launched with a total capital of 24.5 billion Syrian pounds. These projects have created only 8,180 jobs. Thus, the proportion of projects in manufacturing established under Law No. 10 (itself designed to attract manufacturing projects in the first degree) is a mere 21 percent, with only 6.5 percent of the total capital invested under the same law, the rest being in less productive sectors. The labor share of manufacturing projects was only 10 percent.[46] On all counts, these figures represent the failure of Investment Law No. 10 in promoting manufacturing and employment (see Table 5.1).

In any case, the largest new enterprises in industries or services that were reserved for the public sector or in new domains were dominated by the very same category of people who, through Law No. 10, nearly monopolized these sectors or domains, enjoying a form of import or quality protection. These individuals

Table 5.1. Summary of Investment Law No. 10 of 1991

Rationale

The main rationale of this law is to attract direct inward investment on a large scale, especially in manufacturing. Project applications have to be in line with the government's economic plan.

Project requirements

- Generate growth and create jobs
- Be export-oriented or promote import substitution
- Contribute to the transfer of technology, managerial know-how, and expertise
- Generate jobs

Project returns

Fiscal and regulatory exemptions (i'fa'aat), incentives, and privileges

- Free transfer of profits and capital employed
- Tax- and duty-free imports and tax exemptions on profits for up to seven years (the last two are granted if 50% of earnings are from exports)
- Exemption from Foreign Exchange Law No. 24 (1986)
- Permission to open foreign exchange accounts and retain 75% of revenues from exports

Institutional setup

Applications are processed (within one month after submission) by the Investment Bureau (Maktab al-Istithmaar), which is attached to the ministerial Higher Council of Investment (al-Majlis al-Wizari al-A'la lil-Istithmaar). The Bureau then monitors performance. If projects have not been started within one year, the license is withdrawn.

Summary of general points of contention

Concerns of expatriate "investors"

- Doubts about commitment of regime to liberalization
- Conflicting legislation: Law No. 10 exempts investors from already enforced laws (for example, Law No. 24)
- Endurance of political stability
- Restrictive and arbitrary legislation, especially in real estate

Necessity of more market reforms

Further market reforms are required to underpin private sector involvement in the economy. The following is a list of suggested reform measures:

- Unification of the multitier exchange rate
- Overhaul of the financial and banking sectors (that is, services: credit allocation, interest rate policy, interbank funding); but private banking would end the state's monopoly over foreign exchange, and therefore the state's firm hold on the economy, and would lead to the devaluation of the Syrian pound
- Reform of labor law (for example, job security, terms of employment, entitlement to social services)
- Creation of a Damascus Stock Exchange: this, however, would be largely futile without large-scale privatization of state enterprises and assets or the expansion of private sector investments and entry into sectors hitherto monopolized by the state
- Consultancy services (for example, market research, feasibility studies, and management, accounting, and audit services)

Prerequisites for direct foreign investments and larger private sector role

- Political stability
- Confidence in the economy
- Rule of law: the establishment of a legal framework for efficient operations and for the provision of legal protection and commercial arbitration without state interference

Other infrastructural handicaps

- Outmoded and inefficient power plants
- Outmoded and inefficient telecommunications system
- Lack of international communications and access through the internet

are well known in Syria and are invariably members of state-business net-works.[47] The sectors in which monopolies and tailored protection proliferate include textiles, pharmaceuticals, and food processing, and some finishing and converting industries. Especially protected and monopolized products include jeans fabric, synthetic threads, luncheon meat, ceramics, cheese, and virtually all home appliances (except stereo systems and VCRs).

The list goes on. The import of these illustrations is that all of these benefi-ciaries have all along been familiar powerful figures, either in the state or in the private sector. Furthermore, in the words of a prominent businessman-turned-politician: "Law #10 is effectively a process of transferring protection and mo-nopolies from the public sector to individuals in the private sector. . . . We need customs protection, not individual protection."[48] One must add that in nearly all instances, protection of specific private industries is based on economically irrational grounds, where even in the best case, protection does not take into account Syria's comparative advantage in production, including cheap labor and the availability of raw materials in agriculture.[49]

Perhaps the most recurring critique of Investment Law No. 10 of 1991 is that it was not complemented by basic changes in the overall investment climate. Until Bashar took power, Law No. 10 was a "loner" law: it was unaccompa-nied by complementary laws and regulations, let alone the cancellation of ob-structive ones, all of which would facilitate the process of investment. Thus, the law remained underutilized and was thoroughly abused. Not all private sector members supported the promulgation of other supportive rules and regula-tions. In fact, there were numerous instances in which powerful "sharks" were more interested in raising the barriers to investment rather than either lower-ing them or facilitating investment. Such a stance derived from the fact that investments under Law No. 10 were hampered by a variety of legal and bureau-cratic obstacles. In turn, only a few private sector moguls, invariably belonging to regime-business networks, were either able to transcend such obstacles be-cause of their connections or capable of withstanding the risks of government crackdowns.

Finally, what seemed to be the wave of the future in Syria in the 1990s was the establishment of agencies for foreign companies, especially in the booming auto industry and the telecommunications sector. This domain is completely monopolized by the most powerful individuals in Syria, whether public of-ficials and their offspring or a few individuals in the private sector. Telecom-munications deals regarding cellular telephone contracts and systems were captured early on by the Makhlouf family (that of the late president's wife)—and their ostensible private sector partners—a group that already ran the duty-free zones and a dozen other gigantic operations[50] (although the stage of capital concentration around the turn of the century was creating strong rivalries between the elite's offspring and the traditional private economic elite).

At the level of big capital, if we examine the various ways in which ownership was transferred, sources of services changed hands informally, or licenses were granted to both old and newly established businessmen, we find that such transactions moved strictly within an already established network of public-private ties.

The Unofficial Record of Economic Liberalization

The unofficial record of economic liberalization and privatization includes new forms of activities that coexist with old laws and regulations. These activities constitute the largest portion of Syria's shadow economy. For the most part, they are neither included in the general budget nor taxed. The following paragraphs outline instances of unofficial liberalization or privatization within the economy. These activities illustrate more clearly the circumscribed manner in which property changes hands or new opportunities can be exploited.

The unofficial privatization of services traditionally rendered by the state and the public sector. These include various vegetable, fruit, and meat companies, postal and telephone services, public construction, and alternative forms of banking, domestically and abroad, through private agents (for example, the infamous investment scandals).[51] Most of this privatization went to or is administered strictly by public officials and their offspring.[52] Another source of such privatization had its roots in the 1980s. Beginning at that time, public sector managers and various private sector businessmen established well-rooted relations that went beyond those established in the late 1970s. This occurred as a result of the state's economic policy of giving primacy to those establishments in the public sector that could generate foreign exchange through exports. As a consequence, public sector firms had to earn their own hard currency through their own transactions and activities, which henceforth invariably included cooperation with the private sector. Either the public sector would sell their products directly to private firms or to the public in return for hard currency, or per Decree Nos. 158 and 160 of 1989, the private sector "was allowed to import certain raw materials for public-sector industries and let these establishments work for their account against a certain percentage of the material or hard-currency payment."[53] In practice, this translated in the 1990s into privatization of public sector operations by well-connected individuals and their partners. The web of private-public relations created by such arrangements persisted long after they expired or diminished in importance. Such webs survive today and secure for select members of the private sector various lucrative deals with state firms, under the auspices of state firms, or with foreign companies via state firms.

Maneuvering around established customs duties. Syria has one of the highest rates of customs duties, but its revenues were one-fourth those of the Lebanese customs revenues on nearly the same amount of imports throughout the 1990s. The ratio of customs duties to total imports in Syria does not exceed 5 or 6 percent, whereas it reaches an average of 7 percent in the Arab Gulf countries, where such duties are among the lowest in the world. The ratio in Lebanon is between 15 and 20 percent.[54] This translates essentially to free trade for a select group, or a transfer of wealth to customs officers, who take over these public services by creating duplicate private sector firms.

Maneuvering around established basic food subsidies and pricing policies. The government reduced the amount and quality of imported and subsidized foods such as sugar, rice, and tea and domestic subsidized bread, forcing consumers to seek unsubsidized alternatives, imported or domestically produced by particular private sector individuals. This is another way to slowly liberalize prices and for price hikes to seep through the pricing policy.[55]

Maneuvering around established laws prohibiting mediation between the state and foreign companies. Legislative Decree No. 51, issued in 1979, pushed sanctioned mediators underground, where their profits soared and where they avoided paying taxes.[56] This was the prelude to what we saw in Egypt around the turn of the century, when foreign companies established firms in that country through foreign mediation. The import of this category in Syria is that *only* those with sufficient power could dare to commit such transgressions.

Temporary reversal of the foreign trade and balance of payments deficit through debt repayment agreements with the Soviet Union.[57] The export surplus that Syria witnessed in 1989–90 was actually a disguised and latent balance of payments deficit. The Central Bank used to pay inflated sums in Syrian pounds to well-connected local exporters, who then converted the local currency to dollars and stashed them in foreign banks. In essence, therefore, the 70 billion Syrian pounds in business and trade over a period of five years came out of Syria's treasury and was saved in foreign banks as hard currency—as though the public sector were financing imports.[58] There was thus a transfer of wealth from the public and state sector to individuals in the private sector, most of whom are quite familiar to Syrians.

Maneuvering around established Law No. 24, which prohibited dealing with foreign currency before 2003. This is the "export dollar" phenomenon: to reduce the foreign trade deficit, the government decided to tie imports to exports across all sectors. Merchants and others who wished to import either had to export (sometimes they practiced dumping products outside Syrian borders) or had to buy the export dollar for 56 or 58 Syrian pounds on the black market, that is, 10 percent higher than the neighboring country rate. This is also related to what are called "illusionary exports," which were intended to circumvent Law No. 24, among other things.[59] In any case, the beneficiaries are the same individuals who ran the vast black market network in hard currency in the 1980s, along with their middlemen in the private sector, some of whom sat on the Chambers' boards of directors in Aleppo and Damascus throughout the 1990s and beyond.

The systematic promotion of smuggling through the Lebanese gate. This occurred in the following manner: a product that enjoyed high demand (for example, Marlboro cigarettes, particular medicines) was placed on the list of banned imports, presumably to protect local production. At the same time, authoritative individuals oversaw the smuggling and sale of that very product into Syria. This practice was intensified in the 1980s and tapered off after the 2000 succession, until it virtually ended in 2005 when Syrian troops withdrew from Lebanon.

Official Liberalization Policies Versus Actual Measures

Liberalization measures in Syria cannot be discerned simply by examining the official policy record. Unofficial or informal liberalization and privatization measures constitute a significant part of economic change on the ground. Whereas this situation is not particular to Syria, it is more pervasive there than in cases such as Egypt or Jordan. In fact, it was this unofficial set of liberalization measures, outlined above, that was responsible for the creation of the larger part of what is called "the new wealth" (*al-tharwa al-jadida*) as well as the new economic elite. Syrian laws that prohibited dealing with foreign exchange, and the near absence of market mechanisms, created a large underground sphere of economic interaction and exchange in which business must be conducted. For instance, judging from the 1998 official figures on imports and exports, nearly two-thirds of the foreign exchange used to finance *documented* imports was not accounted for officially.[60] Other examples abound, but the importance of these observations to the project at hand is that these realities are directly responsible for a significant part of the distorted developmental consequences of economic liberalization in Syria.[61]

CIRCUMSCRIBED LIBERALIZATION

The capital that was accumulated in various ways in the 1970s and 1980s by individuals in both the public and the private sector was augmented in the 1990s and, as is said in Syria, "whitened" or cleaned (*tabyeed*). This is true to the extent that the aforementioned practices are viewed as more legitimate than the smuggling, black marketeering, and trade in narcotics that marked preferred methods of capital accumulation for most of the beneficiaries in the pre-1991 period. Politically speaking, the beneficiaries from official and nonofficial economic liberalization and privatization are drawn from the same group of primary beneficiaries under Syria's centralized economy.

This leads to the phrase "circumscribed liberalization," for which I offer a preliminary definition: circumscribed liberalization refers to a pattern of economic liberalization, including privatization, that is embedded in and largely limited to an already established informal network of public-private ties, whereby the beneficiaries of the old and the new arrangements are essentially the same. In other words, circumscribed liberalization describes the effort of a regime to change things in such a way that everything still operates as it did before. This pattern of "liberalization" also helps explain the lack of symmetry between the numerical expansion of the private sector and its impact on official economic policy-making. The legal forms of capital ownership have changed hands, but the beneficiaries, and in many cases the hands, remain the same. There is another important function of circumscribed liberalization which had a tremendous effect until 2005,[62] and that was to disguise the contradiction between a growing capitalist economic base and a socialist-nationalist superstructure, still lingering with its laws and institutions. In other words, that function lets market practices, however corrupt, creep into a rhetorically socialist system. It is significant that this pattern of liberalization could take hold only as the public-private ties or economic networks became mature, stable, and more or less consolidated. It also reflects what can be called state-business collusion, which can occur only when the business community as a whole has acquired a certain modicum of power.

The web of public-private ties that is woven around state-business relations has provided the social basis for circumscribed liberalization. There are two primary avenues of transferring wealth within this pattern of economic liberalization or, ultimately, within these networks:

1. A formal, not substantive, transfer of property and rights from the public to the "private" sector via selected individuals who are already part of the economic networks that have historically benefited from the property transferred.

2. An informal transfer of public property usage rights from the state to specific individuals working in the state and/or private sector (that is, public sector firms operating through private capital and management, with returns accruing primarily to private individuals).

In both instances, as discussed above, the social content of wealth and rights transfer remains the same, that is, floating within the same economic networks that predated liberalization. Furthermore, because of their circumscribed nature, both of these types of economic transfer have had insignificant reverberations by way of actual economic restructuring. The first variety, formal transfer of ownership, which is evident numerically in the growing size of the private sector, has not changed the way the concerned capital is invested and accumulated (or smuggled outside the country); nor have the "new" social carriers of this capital been interested in converting their economic wealth to political power, or in directly opposing the state in any way, shape, or form. The second variety, informal transfer of ownership or rights, has led to the fragmentation of the state's bureaucracy and public sector (through personalization), diminishing further the state's administrative capacity (regulatory and extractive) and infrastructural power. Circumscribed liberalization/privatization and its detrimental social, economic, administrative, and infrastructural correlates were the price for preserving the regime's decisional and coercive power.

In the Syrian case, the institutional legacy of populist-authoritarianism left the regime with a narrow set of options regarding inclusion of social forces.[63] The need for capital investments from domestic social forces and the fear of abandoning all semblance of populism have imposed a particular pattern of responses to persisting economic crises. In dealing with these needs and fears, the regime embarked, largely informally, on selective economic deregulation and trade liberalization in the 1980s while carefully preserving the formal legal, structural, and ideological frameworks of the economy. This strategy produced two outcomes. First, it translated into economic liberalization without structural reform, an ad hoc and heterodox liberalization process that is largely reversible in the short run at the microeconomic level. Second, it allowed the state to control the winners and to prevent them from acting collectively. The social content of economic liberalization without reform is illustrated by the circumscribed pattern of liberalization delineated earlier, whereby informal economic networks that predate official liberalization continue to benefit from official liberalization measures after 1991. Through this dual strategy of minimalist populism and circumscribed liberalization in the late 1980s and 1990s, the regime satisfied demands for "liberalization" and contained populist discontent—in the short run, and notwithstanding developmental consequences (see "The Developmental Consequences of Economic Liberalization" later in this chapter).

Political Dynamics

The Syrian regime attempted to achieve its strategic goals by establishing various instruments of political and economic control that constitute barriers to entry into the network of "beneficiaries." Such instruments included the manipulation of laws and regulations, investment and import licensing, licensing for new industrial projects, macroeconomic monopolies, and other more directly coercive means. Most notably, at the macroeconomic level, the regime exercised strict control of its currency and money supply, a practice since 1970. This opened the door to numerous other types of "legitimate" sanctioning at the microeconomic level. Along with the authority to legislate and issue licenses and permits, such macroeconomic control afforded the "government" a most opportune tool: the chaining of liberalization measures and policies. Nearly every liberalizing measure—then and since—has been accompanied by a safety valve of sorts that protects the state's ability *and* right to control the short- to medium-term consequences at the microeconomic level. For example, until 2003, the right of entrepreneurs to deal in foreign exchange in purchasing factors of production was coupled with a bar to freely or legally converting profits into hard currency; also, the right to invest in new industries is complicated by zoning permits and various other legal constraints on importing goods and factors of production.

At the sociopolitical level, the barriers to entry into the network of beneficiaries were determined by the leadership's perceived threat of the consequences of inclusion. Depending on such perceptions, "reformers" are more or less risk-averse. For good reasons the top regime leadership has been notorious for being risk-averse.[64] Initially, the perceived threat of inclusion determined the red lines that circumscribe the reform domain (sectors) and scope (issues).

Extending from 1986 to 1990–91, this initial process of circumscribing "reform" spawned various regulations and policies that set the incentive structure for engaging in economic activity. This incentive structure served as a mechanism for political learning, while catalyzing the cohesion of winners within established economic networks,[65] which were undergoing an informal process of consolidation that had started in the mid-1970s.

As discussed earlier, shortly before 1990 and once these economic networks were largely consolidated, they spawned official and formal institutions that aimed at lending stability and legitimacy to liberalization processes while expanding their rent-seeking opportunities. The formalization reflected these networks' or winners' interest[66] in engineering and rejuvenating institutions to protect, legitimize, monitor, and concentrate new wealth. Essentially, the Chambers of Commerce and Industry, as well as successful parliamentary election bids in the late 1980s and early 1990s, were top-down initiatives that nonetheless reflected the hitherto modest ambitions of junior partners within economic networks.

Cloaked in the regime's language of "economic pluralism"—the ideological grounding of political-economic change—official liberalization in 1991, coupled with oil finds and renewed Arab aid, began to reduce the regime's perception of threat, allowing for a less risk-averse approach to liberalization at the middle level of economic policy and measures. The barriers to entry thus were lowered, principally through a freer atmosphere of import licensing[67] and a more favorable taxation policy.[68] Henceforth, barriers to entry and the scope of liberalization were determined through various forms of bargaining and negotiations within the public-private economic networks themselves, and not solely by the "government." The newfound power in particular segments of the business community extended the interest in circumscribed reform to various elements within its top rungs.[69] This is made evident by the continuing deliberate absence of avenues for small and medium capital investments, which pertain to 90–95 percent of capital holders in Syria. The post-1991 formula of circumscribed liberalization persisted until the late 1990s, when in the absence of centralized and autonomous administrative agencies, fiscal and economic policy manipulation had produced unintended outcomes. The most significant of such outcomes were the creeping liquidity crisis and the sharp drops in investments in the mid-1990s. In 1995 the government began to hit the brakes on circumscribed liberalization by raising the barriers to entry, but by then it lacked the administrative capacity to monitor the rippling effects of its consequences. The result was the pausing of liberalization at the high policy level, leaving the economic networks to free-play at the middle policy level. Between 1995 and 1999, a remarkable process of capital concentration was under way. This process coincided with a dramatic decrease in consumers' purchasing power as a result of growing inflation in 1994–96 and stagnant wages from the early 1990s through the early 2000s.

The mid-1990s also marked the coming of age of a number of sons of officials who went into business only to find their fathers' protégés quite entrenched economically. By the late 1990s, the economy, including rents, had shrunk sufficiently to create a crowded pool of rentiers without many business opportunities, let alone rents. As a result, these networks at present are undergoing significant internal competition, or latent political conflict, which is played out against the backdrop of the succession struggle. Furthermore, the so-called "sharks and dinosaurs"[70] in Syria—well-connected business tycoons and their official protectors, respectively, the former being the creation of the latter, if not their actual offspring—are beginning to realize the potential of their fundamental long-term differences.[71] This situation seems ripe both for making new vertical alliances (between factions of the regime elite and particular business interests) and for realignment (within the business community, along social, sectoral, or corporatist lines). Calls for more profound economic reforms began to be heard at the turn of the century.[72] The cabinet that was formed prior to the death of Hafiz al-Asad in March 2000 was poised to undertake the initial steps in that direction, now clad in the language of "modernization." However, judging from the ministers who were left in place, the horizon did not seem promising.[73] Only a number of years into Bashar's presidency did we begin to witness the inclusion of professional technocrats in the economic bureaucracy, including Isaam al-Za'im (the former minister of industry, who ended up resigning in 2003) and Abdallah al-Dardari (previously the deputy prime minister for economic affairs, whose position was removed in March/April 2011).

Corporatist Reshuffling and the Growing Influence of Private Wealth

Since its tilt toward the business community in 1970, the regime has been keen to keep that group under control—a goal that became increasingly difficult as the private sector grew. The response of the regime has always been to keep private sector transactions in a gray legal area.[74] Both the manner in which the private sector was incorporated by the state and the legal environment that was furnished have consistently reminded individual members of the private sector of their vulnerability, even as private sector growth outstripped that of the public sector in the early 1990s. However, this private sector vulnerability was accompanied by near-fatal blows to labor, by way of demobilization, constraining laws, and by the early 1980s, the complete co-optation of the labor leadership as an independent force.[75] Furthermore, the vulnerability of private sector individuals is felt less in the strictly economic sphere. There, capital and, less often, skills substitute for political vulnerability and constitute a much-needed bargaining chip in collaborations with state officials.

Despite official proclamations to the contrary, by 1991 various groups and members in the private sector had a more privileged standing within the regime than did labor as a corporate interest. Whether one examines the record of policy formulation, the privileges doled out to private sector members, or the disparate eventual fortunes of capital and labor, it is evident that the regime had begun to adjust its corporatist formula to accommodate its changing political needs. It would be a mistake, however, to overlook the growing, if not organized, influence of private sector members on the course of economic liberalization. In fact, the formation and development of economic networks combining state officials and individuals in the business community has been a key factor in framing developmental measures and policies after 1986, but especially since 1990.

Public-private economic networks that operated informally in Syria in the 1970s and 1980s became formally exposed in the early 1990s through various processes of institutionalization. These processes include the rejuvenation of the role of the Chambers of Commerce and Industry in the late 1980s and the expansion of the role, and presence, of the private sector in parliament and in the official "economic pluralism" strategy heralded by President Hafiz al-Asad in the early 1990s. After the enactment of Investment Law No. 10, economic and fiscal policy changes in favor of private wealth became apparent primarily through statistics, if not always through official announcement of policy shifts. These changes are most evident in the areas of wages, taxes, investment, and lending patterns in state-owned banks.[76] Large portions of the state's yearly expenditures were diverted from public to private targets, and larger proportions of the state's revenue began to be drawn from the middle and working classes. As recently as 2007, and as noted earlier, Syria's ranking in the UNDP's index "Diversion of Public Funds" fell to 114 (out of 128).[77] Public sector wages were frozen for roughly a decade—from 1994 through 2004—until the regime's need to reduce subsidies and avoid outrage at rising prices led it to increase public sector wages in 2004.[78] Despite these increases for a large portion of the population, poverty remains high and subsidies will have to be reduced further as oil revenues decrease. Tax collection in most forms has been ruthless, targeting the less advantaged or connected economic sectors since 1991, and investment patterns shifted from being predominantly public in nature to becoming predominantly private in the mid-1990s, benefiting privileged economic networks disproportionately.[79]

The "Role" of Law Versus the Rule of Law

The picture is at once simple and complex, as described in the quote from Riad Saif at the outset of the chapter: the contradictory legal environment in Syria—let alone the notorious category of verbal decrees and decisions issued and reversed regularly by the minister of the economy and foreign trade and through the prime minister's office—made virtually all major business transactions both legal and illegal at the same time. In other words, the rule of law was replaced by the role of law in sustaining a particular form of economic activity with its attendant winners. The best way to explain this situation is to borrow an example, again from industrialist Riad Saif:

> Our situation is like being in a room with one open door that has a "no exit" sign on it and a guard standing by. If you get out, which you must do to survive, you have violated the law. It is up to the "officials" [al-mas'ulin] to apply the law or not.[80]

This legal context was made possible by the accumulation of laws and regulations, some of which extend to Ottoman times. It creates a situation in which, for all intents and purposes, the law becomes an arbitrary tool controlled by the regime in its definition and enforcement of barriers to entry into the network of beneficiaries. In this regard, the contrast between Syria and neighboring countries—which themselves suffer from a similar type of constrained business environment—is telling (see Figures 5.2 and 5.3).

The Media

Given the state-owned status of the media and its proximity to the Ba'th party and the political leadership, it has functioned as an obedient tool of the regime. Despite the prevalence of this fact in Syrian society, the role of the media should not be underestimated, as it often is by many in the local and Western press. The

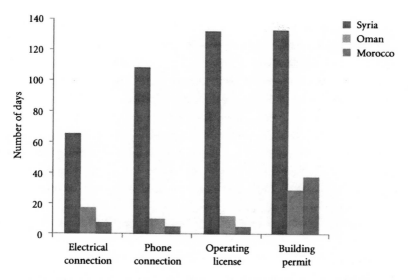

Figure 5.2. Delays in obtaining business services. Data from World Bank, "Syrian Investment Climate Assessment," figure 2.2.

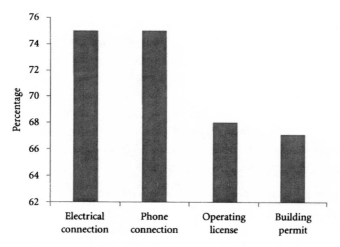

Figure 5.3. Percentage use of informal means for business services in Syria. Data from World Bank, "Syrian Investment Climate Assessment," figure 2.2.

media in Syria serves as the most consistently reliable source of signaling because of its direct relation to the press offices of the president and various ministries, notably the Ministry of Information. In the absence of other avenues in which sensitive matters could be discussed openly, the media provides the signals for social actors, whether businessmen, laypeople, academics, or in some cases even politicians, all of whom know the source of extraordinary news or green lights which they encounter only in print. Finally, anyone who has visited Syria since 2001 has observed a different role for the media. Since the new press law was issued in September 2001, guaranteeing the "freedom of the press,"[81] a number of important publications have emerged, many with an unprecedented critical edge. Such publications are beginning to point out some of the excesses of the *shabakaat* (networks).[82]

THE DEVELOPMENTAL CONSEQUENCES OF ECONOMIC LIBERALIZATION

The Stagnation of the Economy

The Syrian economy grew, as the figures show, between 1987 and 1994 but gradually fell into a deep slump afterward because of the nonproductive and artificial nature of this growth (nonproductive sectors, and therefore consumption, grew at faster rates than production). The surplus of the economic growth, much celebrated by officials, private rentierdom, and some Arab and Western academics, was not reflected in the incomes of average individuals, precisely due to its rentierist origins, which do not contribute added value. Eschewing economic reform or restructuring came at the expense of all of the state's noncoercive capacities, leaving Syria at the threshold of the twenty-first century with a disabled administrative and public sector system, the rehabilitation of which requires much more than financial resources, empty public sector reform policies, or rhetoric about generic civic responsibility.

Macroeconomics of Syria's Liberalization Patterns

Syria's economic stagnation is rooted in official as well as informal economic and fiscal policies and decisions that have undergirded incentives for liberalizing the national market since the early 1990s.[83] On the one hand, this includes shifts in government spending[84] and investments that benefited a growing rentier stratum interested in making short-term commercial investments; on the other hand, austerity measures in the 1990s aimed at controlling inflation and stabilizing the Syrian pound by raising taxes and keeping wages down. Such policies have been detrimental to the working and lower middle classes, as well as to job seekers. Today, more than 60 percent of new jobs require low-skilled labor and offer low wages,[85] a sign of an increasingly service- and commerce-oriented economy that has become less productive.

If the social victim was the lower classes, the economic victim was Syria's productive sectors. Hindered by bureaucratic red tape, contradictory laws and regulations,[86] and antagonistic commercial interests, Syria's productive sectors experienced an even sharper drop in activity. Throughout the second half of the 1990s, public and private investments (as a percentage of GDP) fell steadily;[87] low oil prices pushed the trade balance into the red repeatedly; and the overall balance of payments was continuously on the verge of deficit until 1999.[88]

Social Consequences and Challenges

The most striking consequence of economic liberalization in Syria today is the steady decline of wages vis-à-vis prices, especially public sector wages. Public sector employees' purchasing power is increasingly dismal. While prices continue to rise, wages remain constant—and insufficient. Syria's economic liberalization, though painfully slow and closely controlled, has widened this gap. In contrast to the 1980s, virtually every imaginable consumer item became available in Syrian stores after the early 1990s. But on the basis of public sector wages, most of these items were beyond the reach of the average civil servant, who earned a paltry 3,000–4,000 Syrian pounds each month at the turn of the century (the equivalent of $60–$80)—not enough to cover the most basic living expenses.[89] Wages did continue to increase steadily, but they did not keep pace with inflation and soaring prices in the new century.

Unemployment and Labor   Until 1995–96, public sector employees could manage by finding a second, part-time job because the private sector was employing an increasingly larger share of the labor force. Between 1970 and 1984 the number of individuals employed in the private industrial sector jumped nearly 60 percent, and consistently employed upwards of 60 percent of Syria's industrial workforce.[90] Over two decades the private sector had greatly benefited from the foreign exchange crisis, *infitah* economic liberalization policies, and the preference of the political leadership for a private industry that would be "confined to small and artisan converting industries which bring forward quick profits . . . and demand low investment sums."[91] As a result, the private sector was able to offer higher wages to qualified labor, causing a vast rate of turnover in the public sector.

As economic slowdowns continued after 1995, however, the private sector could not absorb so many new workers. In fact, many private sector firms have downsized their workforces in order to offset losses and position themselves in a time of uncertainty. Private sector wages, considered relatively high in the early 1990s, fell in the late 1990s relative to prices of imported consumer goods.

Unemployment remained high when Bashar took over the presidency,[92] and it is not likely to shrink in the near future, as 220,000–300,000 people enter Syria's labor market every year. Heightening the unemployment problem is the continuous return of increasing numbers of laborers from both the Arab Gulf and Lebanon. Legal reforms in Lebanon have made it harder for several hundred thousand Syrians to find convenient employment next door. The withdrawal of Syrian troops from Lebanon and the diminished influence of Syria there after 2005 reduced the possibility of any substantial employment in that country—a trend that started after 2000. The job-generation problem continued to intensify under Syria's high rate of population growth and its relatively young population. The high number of entrants into the workforce per year at the turn of the century placed unprecedented pressure on the government to generate employment.

Where did these dependents and the growing army of unemployed workers turn to? Most have looked to their nuclear or extended families for assistance, but such support systems cannot endure these hard times. Others have chosen the outlet of protest, such as during the December 1998 demonstrations against the US/UK military strikes on Iraq, during the US invasion of Iraq in 2003, and later in response to the notorious Danish cartoons in 2005 depicting Prophet Muhammad. The unprecedented magnitude of these demonstrations not only reflected public anger about double standards and foreign aggression against another Arab country, or Muslim sentiment toward the denigration of its most significant symbol, but also bespoke widespread social frustrations in the absence of nongovernmental channels through which to express discontent.[93] The uprisings in 2011 reflect further disappointments that have been brewing ever since, not least because of the gradual withdrawing of subsidies on basic goods and the stagnation of the labor market.

The Effects of the "Shadow Economy" on the Distribution of Wealth The shadow economy is a sphere that is beyond regulation, not least because it is itself crawling with "regulators" or their protégés. It is a sphere that by definition and in practice cannot be legally regulated. The enormous size of the shadow economy before 2005 reflected informal processes of transferring wealth from the public economy to the private economy. A concurrent shift occurred in the social content of investment and allocation: once the wealth was transferred in such an informal manner to private hands, it could neither be taxed nor allocated for public purposes. Thus, a large proportion of the labor force that has depended on public investments and services is forced to live without them and to pay more for alternatives, in terms of products (for example, various textiles) and services that are unsubsidized and priced higher than the domestic as well as global market value.

Coupled with rapidly rising inflation in the mid-1990s and the constant income levels of most workers during that decade,[94] the effects of the growing shadow economy and economic liberalization in general have been financial impoverishment for workers and strict tightening of belts for the lower middle classes—hence, the growing social polarization that has characterized Syrian society since the mid-1990s.

The Informal Sector A correlate of the shadow economy is the informal sector, which grew tremendously in the early 1990s. The activities of the informal sector are not part of the government's accounts and are thus not included in its calculation of the comparative growth of the public and private sectors. The informal sector is considered part of the private, not public, realm and thus reflects patterns of growth therein. It is comparatively quite large. Whereas the average contribution of the informal sector in least developed countries ranges between 5 and 35 percent of GDP, it was more than 40 percent in Syria at the turn of the century.[95]

In 1999, the informal sector accounted for 42.9 percent of the total labor force in Syria, while the public and private sectors constituted 26.8 and 29.8 percent, respectively.[96] Most of those employed in the informal sector worked in the agricultural (41.8%), construction (24.1%), and commercial (14.2%) sectors (see Table 5.2).[97] What is significant about the development of the informal sector in Syria is that its size doubled following economic liberalization measures. While in 1987 informal sector labor accounted for 20 percent of economic activity—this being shortly after the start of the economic crisis—its proportion reached upwards of 40 percent in 1999.[98] It is noteworthy that more than 50 percent of informal sector workers were between the ages of 15 and 29, revealing the decreasing opportunities available for Syrian youth during liberalization

Table 5.2. Breakdown of Syrian formal and informal sectors, by economic sector, 2003 (percentage)

	Total	Informal sector	Formal sector		Mixed/ cooperative sector	Percentage of survey
			Public	Private		
Agriculture, hunting, fishing	100	82.0	1.6	16.3	0.1	26.1
Mining, manufacturing, electricity, gas, water	100	7.6	16.1	75.9	0.4	13.6
Building and construction	100	58.1	8.9	32.3	0.6	11.2
Wholesale and retail trade, hotels, restaurants	100	22.1	1.9	75.6	0.4	15.1
Transportation, storage, communications	100	62.1	15.7	21.6	0.7	6.0
Finance, insurance, real estate	100	16.5	16.2	66.0	1.3	2.0
Collective, social, personal services	100	4.4	85.3	9.9	0.3	25.9

SOURCE: Syrian Central Bureau of Statistics, Labor Force Survey, 2003.

Table 5.3. Breakdown of Syrian formal and informal sectors, by age, 2003 (percentage)

	Total	Informal sector	Formal sector		Mixed/ cooperative sector	Percentage of survey
			Public	Private		
15–19	100	46.6	5.6	47.4	0.3	11.9
20–24	100	38.4	21.3	40.0	0.3	15.1
25–29	100	37.4	26.4	35.7	0.4	13.2
30–34	100	32.6	33.8	33.3	0.4	12.7
35–39	100	32.9	37.2	29.5	0.4	12.2
40–44	100	30.8	39.1	29.7	0.5	10.4
45–49	100	33.2	37.2	29.2	0.4	8.0
50–54	100	34.9	35.5	29.1	0.5	6.8
55–59	100	38.9	32.5	28.5	0.1	3.8
60–64	100	53.9	9.2	36.1	0.8	2.5
65+	100	60.3	2.9	36.7	0.1	3.3

SOURCE: Syrian Central Bureau of Statistics, Labor Force Survey, 2003.

periods. However, government statistics do not sufficiently account for changes in the informal sector, especially when they undermine purported outcomes of economic liberalization (see Table 5.3).

Since most informal sector laborers are illiterate or can barely read and write (70.7%), the statistics also reveal the decreasing emphasis on education, in general—leading to a high rate of dropping out—and the lack of demand for skilled labor in the "new" Syrian economy, in particular (see Table 5.4).[99] Service, construction, and commercial sectors demand largely unskilled labor, while manufacturing and other sectors that provide added value demand a skilled and literate labor force (see Table 5.2). The decline of productive sectors after 1987—a fact not readily discernible in official statistics because mining and manufacturing figures are jointly categorized—is most evident in the growth of demand for unskilled labor, most of which is supplied by the informal labor sector. These figures also reflect negative economic growth since 1985 (see Table 5.5). Economic growth between 1973 and 1985 was at an average of 6 percent; it dipped to negative 1.3 percent between 1985 and 1990 and then rose again to an average of 8 percent between 1990 and 1995; between 1995 and 2000, official statistics report a 1–3 percent growth rate,[100] with less than 1 percent growth in 2000,[101] while independent economists argue that the growth rate during that period was closer to the negative average of the late 1980s.

Table 5.4. Breakdown of Syrian formal and informal sectors, by education, 2003 (percentage)

	Total	Informal sector	Formal sector		Mixed/ cooperative sector	Percentage of survey
			Public	Private		
Illiterate	100	70.7	6.0	23.1	0.2	12.5
Read and write	100	54.7	10.9	34.0	0.4	11.0
Elementary school	100	41.4	15.4	42.9	0.3	42.7
Middle school	100	26.9	33.6	39.2	0.3	12.3
High school	100	14.2	54.9	30.1	0.7	7.8
Secondary institute	100	4.1	82.2	13.1	0.5	7.2
University	100	5.5	65.7	28.1	0.7	6.6

SOURCE: Syrian Central Bureau of Statistics, Labor Force Survey, 2003.

Table 5.5. Syria's GDP growth

Year	IMF (percentage)	World Bank (percentage)	Year	IMF (percentage)	World Bank (percentage)
1970	−5.91	−3.81	1988	12.72	13.27
1971	10.98	9.92	1989	−6.07	−8.96
1972	21.58	25.03	1990	10.36	7.64
1973	−2.98	−8.55	1991	10.73	7.90
1974	19.25	24.13	1992	13.25	13.47
1975	21.14	19.52	1993	7.41	5.18
1976	8.93	10.96	1994	5.53	7.65
1977	−1.40	−1.27	1995	5.42	5.75
1978	8.30	8.73	1996	2.97	4.40
1979	3.60	3.63	1997	−1.09	1.80
1980	10.49	11.98	1998	5.55	6.34
1981	8.46	9.51	1999	−3.12	−3.55
1982	2.58	2.12	2000	2.30	2.74
1983	1.61	1.43	2001	3.68	5.20
1984	−6.50	−4.07	2002	5.90	3.96
1985	7.30	6.12	2003	−2.14	1.64
1986	−4.76	−4.95	2004	6.72	5.83
1987	1.25	1.91	2005	4.50	4.50

SOURCE: IMF, World Economic Outlook; and World Bank, World Development Indicators Database.

COMPROMISING THE INSTITUTIONAL AUTHORITY AND SOCIAL BASIS OF THE STATE

The fact that fundamental economic reform has neither accompanied nor followed economic liberalization in Syria, not even with a considerable amount of time by 2005, has to do with a gradual trade-off that the regime—governed by its narrowing social base—intensified since 1986. The trade-off consists in compromising further the state's infrastructural and administrative power for the sake of preserving its decisional and coercive power through the proliferation of collusive relations with the rising rentierist segment of the business community. The aggregate effect of extrainstitutional deals and unofficial liberalization measures eroded further the legitimacy and capacity of governing institutions, at least until the first decade of the new century. Administrative corruption, that is, the use of public resources and office for private purposes, was extended within the state domain from the regime elite down to lower-level bureaucrats, and within the private domain to the upper stratum of the new business elite, which survived on various forms of state-sanctioned rent income. Other secondary beneficiaries included the rest of the new business elite (though decreasingly so) and those employed by the private sector in the first part of the 1990s. An indication of this regime-rentierdom alliance and its nature can be found in the unchanging figures of per capita income since the early 1980s, when the economic crisis began to fester and when the regime stepped up the kind of activities that have compromised the integrity of its institutions.[102]

The structurally detrimental consequence of this trade-off or compromise is the further fragmentation of the state's institutional structures. The state's capacity to administer a central command economy in Syria has steadily diminished since the mid-1970s.[103] Despite an attempt during the early 1980s to centralize the administrative apparatus, this capacity reached an all-time low by the end of the decade. The central command administration gave way to an alternative form of economic administration marked by fragmented decentralization.[104] Over the mid- to late 1990s and into the first three or four years of Bashar's presidency, this fragmentation led to a near paralysis, a distortion, and destructive unintended outcomes in policy implementation and bureaucratic routine. This new and largely unintentional by-product of Syria's pattern of economic development served neither as a transition to a more market-oriented economy nor as the maintenance of tight control over the process of liberalization. In fact, fragmented decentralization served as a vehicle or catalyst for a de facto privatization of various public sector services, trade transactions, and industry (see "The Unofficial Record of Liberalization" earlier in this chapter). Furthermore, fragmented decentralization has led to various extrapolitical outcomes,[105] namely, an unintentional disjunction between policy formulation and policy implementation. Once policies are formulated, they submit to various unmonitored and corrupt micropractices outside the domain of the government. These practices not only empty the policies of much of their content by virtue of gearing them to private beneficiaries,[106] but also skew implementation to the point where the policies and their effects are completely disjointed or disconnected. Hence, we observed the ineffectiveness of a number of policies beginning in the mid-1990s, and the accompanying unintended consequences that require further policies, regulations, legislation, and decrees. By the late 1990s and early 2000s, this had created a vicious cycle of policies, decrees, and unintended outcomes that seriously hampered economic activity. Even the state-owned press (*Tishreen, Al-Thawra,* and *Al-Ba'th*) became replete in 1999 with complaints and near-comic anecdotes about the ensuing chaos.[107] It was not until 2005 that the disjunction was addressed with the emergence of a new team of technocrats who were handpicked by Bashar to oversee the continuation of economic reforms in Syria.

CONCLUSION

The institutional trajectory of populist development, as well as the strategic decisions of political actors which included privileging particular economic ties, were among the most important factors in framing reform sequence and outcomes in Syria. To the extent that institutional arrangements bound the state and society in a zero-sum relation, the strategic choices of political actors became limited either to stagnation or to a narrow set of high-risk options in an authoritarian context of risk aversion. Economic networks seemed to be an interim solution for safe "economic change," but the unintended consequences were greater than anticipated and called for a rethinking of the breadth of the circle of beneficiaries. The institutional outcomes of economic reform, and its attendant sociopolitical changes, consisted in a trade-off whereby the state's infrastructural and administrative power was severely compromised for the sake of preserving its decisional and coercive power, that is, its security. This compromise involved the reshuffling of alliances in favor of big business and at the expense of labor unions and labor, in general, and the public sector, in particular (especially trade, transportation, and nonstrategic industrial sectors). The social consequences of corporatist reshuffling were further polarization and the rapid shrinking of the middle class.

The political victim of such corporatist reshuffling and attendant economic policy measures has been the coherence of the state's bureaucratic agencies and consequently the state's overall administrative capacity. The infiltration and subsequent division of spoils of various state agencies—a process that began in the early 1970s—by both officials and burgeoning economic networks reached monumental proportions in the early 1990s. Liberalization policies were tailored according to the interests of those who controlled different agencies and ministries and their associates. As these largely separate networks matured and their hold over rejuvenated public and private institutions grew stronger in the mid-1990s, policies began to reflect the contradictory interests of various bureaucratic agencies and their heads. The macro- and microeconomic consequences have been detrimental to the health of the Syrian economy, a fact that became obvious only after 1996, when investments and growth plummeted dramatically, with no reversal in sight.

The larger economic victims of Syria's pattern of liberalization until 2005 are its productive sectors, whose deterioration has occurred at the expense of the growth of the largely nonproductive trade, transportation, telecommunications, and service sectors. Furthermore, the absence after 1991 of a clear identity for the Syrian economy has eliminated any semblance of political-economic priorities and created what local economists have called a "gray" economy, where all kinds of policies, laws, and regulations can be rationalized if not justified.[108] The introduction of the Social Market Economy in 2005 is supposed to remedy the identity problem, but Syria's economic woes run deeper.

For years after Hafiz al-Asad's death, high-level political actors had their hands tied institutionally: they could no longer rely on labor and labor unions (which they had discredited throughout three decades), nor could they manipulate the largely Islamist opposition to their favor. Cracking down on pervasive networks—their own creation—in any meaningful way could be a highly risky affair.[109] As a result, the regime opted for circumscribing further the circle of beneficiaries. Stagnation or stasis, often conflated locally and internationally with political stability, remained the outcome until 2005. The answer to how long the Syrian regime can endure this erratic pattern of economic fluctuation depends on the strategic choices that political leaders will have to make in the short to medium run. Judging from the institutional predicament the regime found itself in during the first five years after the death of Asad senior, the set of plausible options has not spoken of positive-sum outcomes vis-à-vis society. However, there is some evidence that the second five years of Bashar's presidency have heralded a new style of governance in the economic realm, one that has the potential of initiating a move toward more positive-sum outcomes between state and society. But the gains will not be automatic; they will always collide with the glass ceiling absent a modicum of political reform. The following chapter will examine fiscal policy change as a focused case study of network influence.

6 THE IMPACT OF ECONOMIC NETWORKS ON FISCAL CHANGE

FISCAL CHANGE is part of the general economic change Syria has witnessed since 1986. But fiscal change and change in fiscal policy are not necessarily the same thing, and certainly not in Syria: general fiscal policy need not change to accommodate the interests of powerful networks. Members of these networks are able to benefit from tax and other exemptions tacked onto other reform measures. In a country where tax evasion (50 billion Syrian pounds' worth) amounted to three times the tax revenue collected, official fiscal policy is hardly a measure of any influence.[1] Thus, it is more important to examine actual changes to the extraction and allocation of state revenue than changes to policies governing the extraction and allocation of state revenue.

The impact of economic networks on economic and fiscal policies in Syria between 1986 and 2005 is evident both in the economic statistics and in the decline in living standards of the majority of Syrians.[2] The focus here on fiscal policy is not meant to deflect attention from other areas. On the contrary, it is meant to demonstrate how the influence of economic networks has decisively crept into the crucial developmental areas of budgeting, tax laws, and associated regulations. The outcome of a state's expenditure policy in any given society is a window into what is considered socially and politically important to decision-makers, and what the medium- to long-term economic future of that society is likely to be. Though the examination of fiscal policy ought not be isolated from the examination of other areas that impinge on the economy, it is here considered as an indicator that reveals the priorities of the government and how these priorities are formed and executed.

THE EMPIRICAL RECORD OF FISCAL CHANGE IN SYRIA, 1986–2005: THE GENERAL BUDGET

The budget is prepared in such a manner as to avoid pointing out explicitly the beneficiaries or holding any particular party accountable, except of course the state in the abstract. A number of cautionary points on how the budget is prepared and what it represents guide this research effort. The budget is released six or seven months into the year in which it should take effect. By that time,[3] its effectiveness is dramatically diminished, especially with regard to investment spending. Most crucial budgetary decisions are handled by the Ba'th party leadership and not the government officials entrusted with preparing the budget—hence, the prevalence of the mysterious categories of "other expenditures" and "various expenditures" that amount to 25 percent of the budget.[4] In effect, administrative officials in the economic institutions, that is, those who are supposed to prepare the budget, "have become administrative employees that execute ministerial and *non*-ministerial orders."[5] The administrative nature of setting exchange rates prior to 2002 allowed for selecting different exchange rates for different purposes (for example, imports, central bank loans, customs duties, exports).[6] This led to severe economic distortions and rendered much of the data in the budget misleading, especially with regard to what are referred to as "achievements" in the Ministry of Finance. Although the budget takes into account the regional distribution of the Syrian population, it does so in an unscientific manner: allocations do not reflect year-to-year changes in the regions and populations concerned.[7] The reason is the near-total absence of studies that would calculate the effects of previous budgets on the various regions and population groups and segments (for example, by region, cost of living, income, age, and sex).

The above cautionary points indicate why the figures of the general budget in Syria either are unreliable on a number of issues or must undergo an informed filtering process before they begin to approximate reality.[8] Nonetheless, these reasons for caution reveal two important points: first, the lack of budgetary credibility demonstrates why it is important in most cases to look elsewhere for indicators on public spending and wealth distribution; and second, they begin to tell us where to look. The deliberate obfuscation of budgetary matters tells us to look for those benefiting from the manner in which the budget is prepared. Invariably, these are the private sector beneficiaries of vast tax exemptions and their associates in government.

Hence, when examining the government's accounts of revenues and expenditures, it is important to note the difference between the nominal conception of budget deficits or surpluses on the one hand, and the real social and economic outcomes and effects on the other. According to most critical economists (that is, not the "state intellectuals" beholden to the regime's rhetoric), the methods by which the budget is drafted, and by which the process itself is politicized, tell us much more than the surpluses and deficits listed on the government's balance sheet,[9] as well as allowing us to better assess the source of shifts in the allocation of public resources.

Shifts in Extraction and Allocation of Resources

In the Syrian case, it is prudent to start with general figures that reveal the broad and readily ascertainable shifts in the distribution of wealth, starting in the 1970s but more clearly since 1986. For instance, increases in gross domestic product (GDP) have been met with a lower rate of increase in per capita income (see Table 6.1).[10]

Rapid population growth accounts for some of this discrepancy, but not all of it, as the very poor distribution of wealth makes clear. In fact, even according to official Syrian statistics, per capita income at the end of the 1990s was much lower than that of the early 1980s, when Arab aid dried up after the 1970s oil boom and the Syrian economy suffered sharp downturns.[11] Moreover, the distribution of the actual per capita income reveals that less than half of that amount was getting to the average Syrian citizen, as evident in the dramatic drop in living standards of most Syrians in the 1990s.[12] The question is, where did the money go?

Table 6.1. Increases in GDP relative to increases in national income per capita

	GDP Syrian pounds, millions (current prices)	National income per capita Syrian pounds (current prices)
1980	51,270	5,702
1985	83,225	7,803
1990	268,328	20,699
1995	570,975	39,227
2000	903,944	50,329
2005	1,493,766	74,454
Percentage change		
1980–2005	2,813.53	1,205.75
1990–2005	456.69	259.70
2000–2005	65.25	47.93

SOURCE: Central Bureau of Statistics, Statistical Abstract 2008.

In response to economic crisis pressures and the growing influence of crony relations in the mid-1980s, the government started to reduce the quantity of goods and services that were subsidized,[13] and increased the prices of various subsidized products to "turn governmental institutions from a state of loss to a state of profit."[14] The ways in which the government went about doing so had devastating long-term consequences in both social and macroeconomic terms. Most significantly, for instance, hiking up the price of formerly subsidized crops, especially wheat, in the late 1980s caused the government to borrow from the central bank to cover the costs.[15] Such borrowing served to increase inflation and impose an indirect tax on the Syrian population, which was then faced with higher prices all around for the same products. Noteworthy here is that the hike in prices was not accompanied by a proportional hike in salaries, forcing most Syrians to borrow, work more, or in most cases, reduce their already decreasing living standards.[16] More recent subsidy reductions enacted after 2005 were accompanied by a hike in public sector salaries in an effort to stem any discontent from the rising prices of fuel and food products. However, this provides no benefit to state revenues and risks inflation.[17] Table 6.2 illustrates the near-steady reduction in government subsidies.[18]

It is evident that the numeric figure representing the sum of indirect taxes minus public subsidies rose dramatically from 1986 through the mid-1990s, after being in the negative in 1985 (when the amount of subsidies was larger

Table 6.2. Indirect taxes and reduction in government subsidies

Year	Indirect taxes—public subsidies (Syrian pounds, millions)	Year	Indirect taxes—public subsidies (Syrian pounds, millions)
1985	(−919)	1996	51,413
1986	190	1997	54,961
1987	5,359	1998	n/a
1988	9,149	1999	−12,300
1989	13,961	2000	−19,500
1990	13,745	2001	−12,000
1991	20,532	2002	−2,200
1992	29,405	2003	7,100
1993	40,811	2004	25,200
1994	53,047	2005	36,700
1995	61,004		

SOURCE: Dalila, "General Budget Deficit," 279; International Monetary Fund, "Syrian Arab Republic: Statistical Appendix," 28; International Monetary Fund, "2009 Article IV Consultation—Staff Report," 18.

than that of indirect taxes);[19] that is, the general public was being taxed more and the products they purchased were subsidized less. This situation was caused primarily by keeping wages down while strengthening the mechanisms of tax collection, especially vis-à-vis public sector and lower-income salaried workers.[20] Almost yearly throughout the 1990s, the Ministry of Finance announced budget surpluses[21] drawn from a 30 percent increase in tax collection over projected figures. It failed to announce that at the same time, government spending on public investment was slashed 25–40 percent, while current account spending on matters such as personal luxury commodities exceeded projected figures.[22] As the stagnation of the late 1990s set in, however, and subsidies began to be cut in order to preserve government revenue, this calculation dived back into the negative, and only in the mid-2000s began to regain the levels of the early 1990s.

Simultaneously, tax exemptions for a plethora of new commercial activities after 1991 denied the treasury a substantial increase in tax revenue while only benefiting a select few who were poised to take advantage of tax loopholes and exemptions.[23] A larger discrepancy lies in the unusual correlation between dramatic increases in domestic public revenues and a dramatic decline in overall economic growth after 1994. According to conventional economic principles, increases in domestic public revenues usually accompany positive, not negative, economic growth rates. In the Syrian case, and on the basis of other statistics on taxation surveyed later, this also means that a substantial amount of the accumulated wealth in Syria was (and continues to be) neither taxed nor recorded. Because there is no effective tax collection system in place, by 2004 nearly 90 percent (9.2 billion Syrian pounds) of the income tax revenue in Syria was paid by government employees through automatic withdrawal.[24] Thus, the wealthy accumulate more untaxed wealth while the government cuts subsidies, leaving the middle and working classes to pick up the tab by way of strict tax collection measures and rampant inflation caused by central bank loans that finance deficit spending on administratively hiked prices. Further, segments of the population on the lower rungs of the economic ladder are being taxed on subsistence income and not surplus income, contrary to conventional economic principles. In Syria, wages continue to be far lower than the value of labor power, or far lower than the cost of living.[25]

While the tax burden in Syria continues to be less than half of what it is in most other countries—that is, 13–15 percent as opposed to 20–30 percent[26]—this does not represent the actual tax burden across the board. As demonstrated, the actual patterns of tax extraction from rich and poor differ tremendously. The budget, however, does not reveal such imbalance. The reason is not simply administrative; it is political through and through, and can be traced to the increasing power of economic networks beginning in 1986, when the budget replaced the five-year plans as the government's principal mechanism of central planning.[27]

Other Measures of Fiscal Change: Lending and Foreign Exchange

The effectiveness of fiscal policy is intimately related to lending and currency exchange policies. However, there is no such thing as an official lending policy in Syria. As late as 2000, banks were not providing even basic banking functions necessary to facilitate investments and loans, let alone capable of supporting the total overhaul of which the Syrian financial services sector was in desperate need.[28] As discussed earlier, private banks did not begin opening for business until 2005, and prior to then, all lending decisions or policies were usually exegetically administered by officials in various ministries, particularly the Ministry of the Economy and Foreign Trade and the Ministry of Finance. Until the regime unified the currency exchange rate in 2002, the most recent law regarding exchange policy had been drafted in 1981,[29] and both lending and foreign exchange policies were subject to administrative orders and other ill-defined "necessities." Exchange policies have increasingly reflected the interests of big business since the mid-1980s but in a more visible way since 1991, when Syria began to unravel its central command economy. Ultimately, the stasis in currency exchange policy served as a powerful barrier against entry into big business for the unconnected, while the potential illegality of currency exchange served as a powerful tool for the top regime leadership against existing members of economic networks who might develop dissident views.

The new business elite were increasingly the beneficiaries of changes in bank lending patterns. From 1991 through the early 2000s, state banks across the board—from the central bank to the agricultural, commercial, public lending, and real estate banks—increasingly shifted their lending away from developmental investments and toward short-term commercial activity. The Industrial Bank was effectively frozen by virtue of its limited financial resources, but even these were borrowed by sources that were "exempt" from paying their loans by virtue of the political weight of their associates.[30] According to bank officers, such unpaid loans did not appear as delinquent in the bank's reports once the loans were made.

Although less ascertainable via statistics, a more general illustration of net-works' influence on economic and fiscal decisions, if not policies, is the actual lending procedures of the Central Bank of Syria and its sectoral branches. Ana-lysts looking for official mechanisms governing loan processing would come up empty-handed. As the central bank and its sectoral branches are subject to state control, with the cabinet ministers and the prime minister acting as silent busi-ness partners, lending decisions can be implemented by administrative fiat once a sum of money is earmarked for certain investment projects.[31] What is also crucial to note here is that fiscal policy-making involves the vocal business part-ners of officials who have access to pivotal state-business linking institutions such as the boards of Chambers of Commerce and Industry or the Guidance Committee (see the section in Chapter 4 titled "Networks and Institutions").

Nonetheless, much can be deduced through cross-referencing and informed inference regarding lending practices intimately related to the general budget. Between 1991 and 1998, the sum of money borrowed from the Agricultural Co-Operative Bank and the Commercial Bank of Syria doubled, while the sum of borrowed money remained largely unchanged during that period in the indus-trial and other sectors (for the public *and* private sectors). Between December 1991 and June 1998, the amount of money borrowed from the commercial, agri-cultural, and industrial branches changed respectively in the following manner: 71.4 to 156.7 billion; 12 to 28 billion, and 5.9 to 5.07 billion Syrian pounds.[32] Even on the basis of the government's own estimates (depicted in Figure 6.1), the amount of money invested by specialized banks in commercial activities dwarfs that invested in industry or agriculture, starting in the mid-1980s and continu-ing through the mid-2000s (although to a lesser extent after 2000).

The import of this lending pattern for the matter at hand is twofold. First, the state-owned and -controlled banks were lending more money (on easy terms, with no guarantees or collateral) to the less productive and no-toriously more corrupt commercial sectors, where rent-seeking networks are lodged. Second, though these figures apply to both public and private sectors, it is evident that the commercial *private* sector, in both agriculture and trade, was the primary beneficiary. The vast majority (98%) of the agricultural sec-tor has been historically in private hands, and since 1987 the commercial sector has been predominantly private, becoming even more so after 1991 when the private sector began encroaching heavily on external trade. These two sectors were dominant in the private sector in the prereform period of the 1970s and 1980s, when economic networks were formed; hence, the decisional and policy

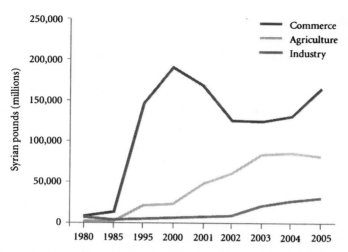

Figure 6.1. Distribution of specialized bank credit by economic activity. Data from Central Bureau of Statistics, *Statistical Abstract 2007*, table 10/15. (Inconsistencies in reporting period are intentional as these are the only years information was provided for by the Syrian Central Bureau of Statistics.)

influence of prereform economic networks on these sectors specifically. Evidence of the preferential treatment accorded to private business in the commercial sectors reinforces the contention that not only have these networks survived and benefited from economic reform, but they have played a significant role in shaping the process, through both formal and informal avenues.

Also related to the general budget is the issue of administratively set exchange rates, which represents another area from which economic networks have benefited and even worked to perpetuate, as other areas of the economy were undergoing measures of piecemeal liberalization. The 1986 foreign exchange crisis created among leading policy-makers and prominent businesspeople an obsession with accumulating foreign currency, irrespective of the means, the source, or developmental consequences of controlling foreign exchange. For instance, by the end of 1998, the commercial bank had a frozen account of more than $5.5 billion in Swiss banks, presumably a reflection of the deep sense of insecurity created by the 1986 crisis.[33] This sum has effectively been denied for domestic investment purposes. The government continued to sell various public sector products in exchange for hard currency, while at the same time, private dealings with hard currency carried a penalty of up to fifteen years in prison, according to the letter of Decree No. 24 governing currency. However, these penalties naturally existed alongside a myriad of intricate regulations that provided small legal loopholes for well-connected people to participate in some limited dealing in hard currency.[34] Thus, various public-private economic networks benefited from their obsession,[35] while the government, including members of the most powerful of these networks, satisfied its security concerns by reserving the legal right to crack down on those who had to engage in unlawful currency exchange in order to do business. As a seasoned Syrian economist noted, "only the government has the right to violate the law or force citizens to violate the law so it can selectively persecute them for the violation according to the law!"[36] This observation was particularly applicable to currency exchange.

To avoid the regulatory mess and the consequent perils, most investors have refrained from investments that would require extensive foreign exchange dealings, and most Syrians had their foreign exchange accounts in neighboring countries[37] or in Europe and the United States. Before 2003, free trade zones and whole cities in both Egypt and the UAE were replete with Syrian investors who were not willing to risk doing business inside Syria because of the restrictions on dealing with foreign exchange, let alone other monumental bureaucratic hurdles.[38] In the late 1990s, the Economist Intelligence Unit estimated the total amount of Syrian capital held abroad at $35 billion.[39] More recently, Syrian minister of finance Mohamed al-Hussein placed the figure at closer to $60 or $70 billion.[40] In sum, lending and foreign exchange policies or "decisions" have led to capital flight and provided a disincentive to productive investments, thereby denying the treasury the benefit of taxes and interest rates. This situation, which could be slowly reversed by the authorities, is sustained because of the rent-seeking benefits that accrue to members of powerful economic networks, including those who have not yet (at the time of this writing) repaid their loans from the central bank's sectoral branches.

Development and the General Budget: Sectoral and Class Bias

The percentage of actual development spending in the budget throughout the 1990s was quite low, at 20–40 percent lower than what was allocated. There are two main reasons for this: first, as noted above, the budget takes effect six months into the respective year; and second, development projects that are not completed in a given budget year are rebudgeted in the next year. In effect, this means that the same amounts of money are earmarked for many of the same unfinished projects every year, leading to massive unproductive dumping of public money, which ends up partly in the hands of the same economic networks that invest in maintaining this mode of budgeting. The remaining surpluses are saved in foreign banks, presumably as a reserve to be used by the top regime leadership in times of profound economic crisis.[41]

Furthermore, even the official figures show that beginning in the mid-1980s, there was a substantial drop in investment expenditures. Even during the boom years of the early 1990s, the temporary increase in investment did not come close to matching the investment expenditure figures of the early 1980s.[42] Moreover, when investment expenditures from the early 1990s are broken down into sectors, we find, for example, that a disproportionate part went to the electricity sector, which is essentially nonproductive in and of itself and has not contributed to any increase in production in the manufacturing sector[43]—hence, the demise of the development of production in the greater part of the 1990s in favor of developing the nonproductive service, commercial, tourism, and transportation sectors. Those who dominate these sectors are the same individuals and networks who lobbied for, and benefited from, new investment and tax laws in 1991.[44] It is true, as Volker Perthes notes, that "private-sector representatives, particularly industrialists, had . . . long demanded that tax laws be reformed," but it was not the industrialists who benefited the most, as the record of investments under Law No. 10 shows;[45] instead, it was the commercial and transport sectors, whose big tycoons began to influence the decisions of new and revived economic institutions and associations, notably the ministerial Guidance Committee and the Chambers of Commerce, respectively.

Finally, on the basis of the earlier distinction between the class implications of direct and indirect taxes under the Syrian regime, the same bias applies to the distribution of the tax burden. The approximate figure for "indirect taxes"[46] is much higher than that for direct taxes. According to Dalila, to calculate the real figures for direct and indirect taxes, we must first take out the category of oil from direct taxes and add on price differentials to indirect taxes. Only then would we find that the total amount for indirect taxes is two or three times that of direct taxes.[47] This reflects the influence of those with higher incomes, since indirect taxes affect most if not all of the population equally while direct taxes affect tax brackets differentially (see the following section on tax exemptions). Moreover, the growth rate of tax revenues in the 1990s was consistently two to four times the growth rate of the national income at the same time that most new "big" business ventures were largely tax-exempt for at least the first five to seven years.[48] In 1996 and 1997, for instance, the growth rate of tax revenues was four times that of the national income.[49] This trend continued into the 2000s: the growth rate of tax revenues between 2000 and 2005 was 1.2 times that of national income.[50] Where was the tax revenue coming from? Similarly, this reflects class bias in tax extraction against the middle and working classes in Syria, since most new businesses were untaxed as the economy slumped in the mid-1990s. This is not simple functional reasoning, as the sections below will demonstrate. The dominance by big commerce of institutional arenas, where bargaining for tax exemptions takes place, has left its imprint on various economic and fiscal measures.

TAX POLICY: THE SIGNIFICANCE OF TAX EXEMPTIONS

A marked impact of economic change during the 1980s and 1990s in Syria was the redistribution of wealth from lower-income groups to higher-income groups. The redistribution did not occur solely as a result of business pressure, nor was it a reflection of dirigisme. In fact, this is where the analytical utility of the notion of economic networks becomes evident: for neither is the regime interested in polarizing society (no established regime resting on even a modicum of populist legitimacy would have this as its explicit goal), nor is the business community as a whole interested or able to act collectively, much less to do so for the benefit of some sectors at the expense of others. Economic networks of capitalists and bureaucrats (often fused) in LDCs help explain the particularist turn away from both the state and the business community as corporate interests. Notably, this diversion of resources has at times undermined the regime as a social force, leading, for example, to the freezing of reform measures vis-à-vis high-range economic policies after the commercial boom of the early 1990s. The area of tax law reform and tax exemptions is instructive. The fiscally consequential record of tax and customs duties exemptions will be discussed before analyzing the mechanisms through which economic networks influence the implementation and interpretation of tax regulations, if not reform.[51] Though we are interested in changes that occurred between 1986 and 2005, there are also some regulatory changes that had their roots in legislation prior to this period: (1) The 1972 legislative Decree No. 84 regarding duty-free areas exempted all foreign products from all kinds of taxes and customs duties.[52] (2) The 1985 Decision No. 186 exempted projects in the tourism sector (providing first- or world-class service) from all kinds of taxes and customs duties for seven years, and eternally exempted 50 percent of profits from taxation (this included all necessary imports). The decision was extended to restaurants and bars. It is an example of an illegal tax exemption. Because it was issued by the executive branch rather than the legislative branch, this decision was a clear and recurring violation of Section 81 of the Syrian constitution, which forbids the modification or creation of a tax except through legislative authority.[53] (3) The 1986 legislative Decree No. 10 exempted stockholding companies in the agricultural sector from all kinds of taxation and customs duties provided that products were not sold on the local market. This included all factors of production and vehicles imported for "business" purposes.[54] (4) The 1991 Law No. 10 exempted projects in manufacturing, agriculture, and transportation (and other sectors) from paying income tax for seven years, including taxes and customs duties on all related imports.[55]

Most of the above exemptions are associated with essentially nonproductive ventures and do not distinguish between a cement factory and a nightclub. This is a result of the increasing pressures of economic networks immersed in legal as well as under-the-table trade transactions, and at the same time reflects the type of economic operations that the state is willing to cede to the private sector. In other words, it is not a reflection of the preferences of the broad-based business community, but a response to the lobbying of privileged networks in the Guidance Committee, networks that stand to benefit from the ability to circumvent or ignore the letter of the law.[56] This explains their satisfaction after 1991 and the marked reduction by powerful beneficiaries in efforts and heavy demands to open up the economy.[57] The situation changed in the late 1990s, of course, when privileges became less and less economically rewarding as a result of economic downturns and fierce competition from the maturing offspring of entrenched officials.

The empirical record of change in tax policies and decisions supports two conclusions: first, as Syrian economist Rislan Khaddour put it, "tax exemptions became a tool for the distribution of poverty instead of being a tool for the distribution of wealth,"[58] since the mid-1980s. Second, tax exemptions are essentially methods for administratively sanctioned tax evasion brought about by deliberately vague tax law regulations and modifications. These regulations, which became more explicitly pro–big business as the 1980s came to a close, are the outcome of various forms of "bargaining" or collusion, either informally or in the institutions that link state and business.[59]

ECONOMIC NETWORKS: DOMAINS OF INFLUENCE

A principal mechanism by which wealth is redistributed from lower-income groups to higher-income groups in Syria is thus found in the realm of taxation, which in most LDCs should be examined as two separate processes: the formulation of the actual laws and regulations, and their implementation. The reason for distinguishing between the formulation and implementation of tax policy is simply that in the absence of the rule of law, the letter of the law becomes a tool that is subject to exegetical use by the powers-that-be.[60] More specifically, to the extent that the powers-that-be are able to selectively set aside, or overstep, the rule of law, it becomes more pressing for researchers to focus on implementation rather than on actual tax policies—the latter, in any case, are themselves socially and economically problematic. The lack of separation of powers becomes a crucial factor here. Syria is an instructive case in this regard, where we find the near-literal fusion of the legislative and the judicial branches into that of the executive, and where monitoring and "accountability committees" are firmly under the control of the prime minister.[61] Under such conditions, which have their own causes of emergence,[62] tax policy formulation and implementation are subject to various systemic and social pressures.

In the Syrian case, where the core of the tax law that was passed in 1949 was not modified until 2003, implementation processes for both the original letter of the law and the myriad of added regulations, of the legal and illegal variety,[63] become more important than the actual tax laws or broader policies. This is evident in the areas of direct taxes and customs duties, where the actual state revenue from these categories is but a fraction of what it is supposed to be according to both imports figures and even declared incomes that have already been partly exempted from taxation.[64] In 1992, for instance, the ratio of taxes to GDP was 6.53 percent, by far the lowest among Arab and most other countries.[65] Yet, lower-income groups pay their taxes fully, almost to the last penny in the case of public sector workers. By contrast, in 1992 the government collected only $300 million in taxes from the private sector, while that sector contributed 60 percent of GDP. This translates into an average tax burden of 3 percent of the declared income of the private sector in 1992.[66] By 2004 the fraction of GDP contributed by the private sector had reached 87 percent, while its contribution to the tax burden had increased to only 10 percent.[67]

It would be a mistake to dismiss the influence of economic networks when we are not able to ascertain all links in the tracing of the causal chain between networks and "policy reform." In fact, the impact of economic networks on economic policy reform understates their influence simply because, comparatively, there were virtually no reform policies to speak of in Syria. But members of these networks are handsomely, some say "criminally,"[68] enriching themselves. Members of these networks have not been keenly interested in policy reform as such, because the policy environment has not constituted a barrier for them. Moreover, many members of these networks have accumulated a large portion of their capital by transgressing laws and regulations that no one else can without incurring a high risk under current policy conditions. Why change the rules when you are the only one who can bend them to your benefit, and why make long-term investments when rent-seeking in quick-profit commercial activity brings more capital?

Equally important is the assertion that economic networks are not the sole reason for such infringements and their economic and developmental outcomes. The larger institutional context in which the networks are lodged is the starting point of other scenarios, where economic and collective concerns are subordinated to political, and perhaps unaccountable, concerns. Networks are simply one empirical manifestation that is bounded in space and time in its impact on economic change, at least until 2005. Fiscal policy is one case where such influence is detected.

CONCLUDING COMMENTS

The tenor of this case study is simple, and it applies to both fiscal and regulatory change: whereas the Syrian regime is able to control what can be termed guiding or high-range economic policies and decisions, on which economic networks have little effect, it is unable[69] or unwilling[70] to meddle with most middle- and lower-range policies and decisions that are indeed subject to ample pressure and veto power from powerful economic networks, especially in commerce and tourism.[71] Exceptions occur, especially when the top regime leadership recognizes the perils of unfettered network influence on policy, as was the case in the late 1990s and early 2000s. But such exceptions do not cover all instances of influence that have become part and parcel of how policy is formulated and implemented in the absence of relatively autonomous economic decision-making institutions. The realm of total regime control over economic matters continues to be restricted to high-range economic policy. Here such policies refer to general matters such as the actual tax law and divisions into income brackets, while middle-range policies refer to the numerous regulations and exemptions that are tacked onto existing laws. Lower-range policies refer to areas that are pertinent to specific activities or commodities and are usually subject to change without explicit referral to, or approval by, institutional authorities: for example, whether importing particular metals, threads, or machinery is exempted from customs duties according to existing regulations and modifications of tax laws. In an economy dominated by small-scale ventures, even if run by "big business," and where manufacturing is restricted to consumer, not capital, goods, influence over middle- and lower-range policies is what most business sectors—particularly those in dominant economic networks—are interested in, not least when it comes to tax laws. Hence, we have seen the increasing importance in Syria of middle-range economic institutions such as the Guidance Committee (officially titled the Committee for the Guidance of Imports, Exports, and Consumption) at the expense of the more traditional and centralized Economic Committee. Often labeled the "Tailoring Committee," the Guidance Committee became the sole economic institution in which the private sector was represented until 2005. While the Chambers of Commerce were considered the institutional expression of the private sector as a whole in the 1990s, the Guidance Committee became the institutional expression of privileged economic networks, despite its stated function as the institution that aggregates and responds to the interests of the private sector, the public sector, the General Federation of Trade Unions, and the Ba'th party.

Because of the factor of mistrust, the relational dynamics within these institutions have produced unintended consequences that are detrimental to the health of the economy. This continues to occur well beyond the realm of fiscal policy, although other areas, such as the oil sector, are even more difficult to research. The price the Syrian economy has paid for transgressions and unintended consequences is extremely high but has remained within bounds that can be tolerated by the regime, notwithstanding its downsizing of the networks during and after the succession crisis in 2000. It is questionable how long the top Syrian leadership can afford to subordinate the interests of the state to the security of the regime. All indicators since Hafiz al-Asad's death—including the further circumscription of reform benefits—point to a more appropriate question: we should ask whether the Syrian regime is able to get out of the social and institutional deadlock in which it has been lodged for nearly four decades. Under the leadership of Bashar in the second five years of his rule, steps toward breaking out of this deadlock are being taken. How far these steps go will depend on how committed the current leadership is to fundamental change domestically as well as on regional and international variables that impinge on domestic policy preferences.

CONCLUSION
State, Business, and Networks

They [rent-seeking networks] are still around, and they are powerful, but they are undergoing a change. . . . They used to set the rules, we admit that, but now they no longer do so. It is the WTA [World Trade Organization] that they have to keep up with. So far, they have been feeding on government projects. Now they have to start competing.

There has been a paradigm shift after the President's speech [at the tenth Ba'th Regional Command Conference in 2005]. They [rent-seekers] have to adapt to us, and not the other way around. . . . Everyone is preparing for a new era.

"Social Market Economy" does not mean the retreat of the state, but a change in its role. . . . Today, technocrats are technocrats. Before, technocrats were politicians.

—Abdallah al-Dardari,
former deputy prime minister for economic affairs

THIS BOOK IS A MODEST ATTEMPT at understanding the causes and consequences of network influence on the economic sphere, and a delineation of the implications of this form of agency for economic change and development in Syria and beyond. Economic change serves as an indicator, a pattern that reflects the influence of structures and agencies as they interact and often shape one another. Thus, this study is not concerned solely with economic change. It is also about social and political-economic change, processes that are often separated.

Methodologically, the question of causality may seem more elusive than desired. The dialectics of mistrust, informal relations, exclusionary institutions, and economic outcomes are difficult to disentangle. The argument in this book does not lay the responsibility for economic change in Syria squarely on the influence of networks. Rather, it highlights their disproportional influence and traces their deleterious effects, which exacerbated existing modes of economic governance for nearly two decades.

The broader causal narrative involves tracing the impact of this history of social conflict to the pattern of state intervention and the economic and developmental effects it bore from 1986 to 2005. Along the way, historically and causally, a number of factors intervened; chief among them was the nature of cooperation between the state and the business community, or between power and capital. State-business relations after the 1963 Ba'thist coup were colored by profound mistrust. Prompted by domestic and regional changes, the subsequent form of state-business cooperation was characterized by informal and exclusionary economic networks bringing together state officials and select business actors. This form of cooperation was dictated largely by the regime's security concerns, which dissuaded it from more official, and therefore potentially threatening, collaboration with the business community as a whole. To be sure, the deep sociocommunal mistrust between the holders of power and the holders of capital exacerbated the regime's security concerns; it did not create them. What ensued with regard to the formation and development of these networks tells a different analytical narrative, one that is informed by the methodological tools of network and institutional analysis, and within the same context that the old social conflicts molded, with one significant alteration: massive inflow of external capital and rent to state coffers.

The factor of continuous external rent through the early 2000s, notwithstanding temporary dips in the mid-1980s, strengthened the political autonomy of the Syrian regime at the expense of its administrative functions of regulation, extraction, and monitoring. It also afforded the regime the ability to pursue a two-pronged strategy of maintaining its distributive commitments while engaging in selective economic liberalization until 2005, when new forms of economic governance started to emerge, in part as a response to the imminent drying up of known oil and gas reserves.

Economic networks, combining an increasingly powerful and "enterprising" state elite and newly created business elite, flourished in the 1980s, when the public sector was failing miserably, and were consolidated in the 1990s, when the private sector experienced a surge in (nonproductive) investments. By the late 1980s, these informal networks combining capitalists and bureaucrats had molded existing economic institutions that preserved and promoted their own exclusionary interests in expanding rent-seeking opportunities. Through the exclusionary institutions and continued informal relations, these public-private ties exercised a disproportional influence on the commanding heights of the Syrian economy and helped shape the parameters for a reform process from which they emerged as the primary beneficiaries. By exercising leverage over the instruments of the reform process (economic institutions, sanctioning power, and legislative mechanisms), members of these economic networks were able to sway the pattern of state intervention in the economy according to their temporary common interests, which invariably superseded those of the state and the business community as a whole. The resultant pattern of circumscribed liberalization produced few new winners but significantly empowered the same old winners. By empowering its private partners with whom it shared temporary interests, and by alienating the remaining social forces, the regime severely limited its room for institutional maneuver as well as its ability to reshuffle social alliances through existing or new institutions. In effect, the top regime leadership could not provide the legal, institutional, and social environment that would make the pursuit of self-interest less detrimental to the development of Syria's society and economy. In the process, the regime's security at least was preserved. To be sure, Syria was lodged in a tough regional environment and, for the most part, a hostile international one; this placed even more pressure on maintaining regime security.[1]

Economic stagnation and poor developmental outcomes were unintended by-products. They were in large measure the price of maintaining regime security, a price that became too high in the late 1990s, causing a reorganization and narrowing of the networks themselves thereafter, and opening the door to the introduction of alternative forms of governance. With the introduction of the Social Market Economy in 2005, resilient networks of privilege coexisted alongside emerging forms of economic governance.

FINDINGS: A STARTING POINT FOR FURTHER RESEARCH

This research has a conceptual and an empirical objective. Conceptually, it aims at demonstrating the analytical import of examining the origins, nature, and impact of economic networks. Empirically, it aims at tracing the influence of economic networks on economic reform and outcomes, particularly regulatory and fiscal policy change and their developmental correlates. The case of Syria compels researchers to probe the concept of networks in order to understand political-economic outcomes that cannot be explained entirely by state-centered or society-centered approaches, which focus on statist logic, class, or particular corporatist interests.

Three research areas have been covered: first, the question of the origins of these state-business networks; second, how their conditions of emergence largely determined the ensuing relationship between networks and institutions; and third, the influence of these networks on regulatory and fiscal policy decisions after 1986. This last factor is the missing variable that can help explain the outcomes—including unintended and contradictory ones—of the reform process more generally. While the impetus for weaving these networks stems from the state's security concerns, their sustenance and consolidation were also self-propelled, according to a strategic logic internal to the relational dynamics of these networks and the context with which they were dialectically related. Economic actors within the networks were not acting solely on the basis of their class status or official position within government. Network analysis provides insights and explanations of behavior that are not readily available from an analysis of actors' attributes (such as class, community, positionality). In fact, particular kinds of relations can be used to overcome or override real or perceived constraints of attributes such as class or status: "Relations reflect emergent dimensions of complex social systems that cannot be captured by simply summing or averaging its members' attributes. . . . The strong inference is that exclusively focusing on actor attributes loses many important explanatory insights provided by network perspectives on social behavior."[2] The utility of network analysis in this study does not derive from eliminating other influences on behavior. Rather, it derives from identifying how network relations mediate interests and attributes of actors in ways that do not comport with traditional expectations derived primarily from rational choice or class position. Though the network is molded by its environment, the relational form and content among network members constitutes an independent variable that helps us understand outcomes that are not adequately explained otherwise.

Factors Sustaining Economic Networks, 1986–2005

If lack of trust is conducive to the emergence or exacerbation of informal networking between bureaucrats and capitalists, what then accounts for their sustenance? Surely, if particular security concerns discourage official and widespread state-business collaboration, it is likely that similar concerns would give rise to similar associative preferences under similar conditions.

But some of these conditions—such as communal dissonance, at least within the business community—have been changing with no corresponding change in the manner in which the state relates to business. The business community in Syria is no longer dominated by the traditional urban-Sunni bourgeoisie, the historical culprit. Nonetheless, not only were the networks able to survive; they also became stronger. This book has identified some institutional and relational conditions that sustained robust rent-seeking networks until 2005. These networks acquired a life of their own, making networks themselves a rewarding object of study. From the examination of network formation, dynamics, and influence we can discern a set of factors that has contributed either to the sustenance of collusive relations between state and business or to the prevention of broader collaboration within the business community at large.

The factors sustaining economic networks can be divided into institutional, relational, and resource-related factors. The first among the *institutional* factors is the right to arbitrary intervention by the prime ministry in nearly all economic affairs, which makes that institution a locus for rent-seeking formulation and disempowering other economic institutions.[3] Second is the top-down state-business linking institutions with government power over selection, election, and demand formulation, which diminishes the power of the larger business community qua community. Third is bureaucratic fragmentation across economic and administrative institutions, which leads to multiple centers of authority for arbitrary economic decision-making or transgression regarding low- to medium-level policy. Fourth is the contradictory legal context, which is ripe with tailored regulations. This type of "regulation" is caused by arbitrary administrative decrees that bypass the legislature (through the Guidance Committee, for example). The contradiction is exacerbated by the not-so-unintentional persistence of outdated laws as a tool for arbitrary recrimination.

Relational factors that sustain economic networks include first the continued lack of trust between the state and the business community at large, which is caused by continuing patterns of communally guided recruitment and promotion at the level of the top regime elite. As the decades have rolled, the ruling elite has become increasingly homogeneous, not heterogeneous. A second factor is the fusion of the role of capitalist and bureaucrat in the person of the top official: the decision-maker and the most powerful investor are often the same person (or belong to the same family). Third is the government hoarding of various policy-formulating tools (for example, information) and the resulting absence of credible information exchange channels between the government and the general pool of investors, including many of the government's own partners. Such formulas discourage going into (big) business if one is not connected to the networks.

Finally, paramount among the *resource-related* factors is the continuous inflow of external rent to the tune of 40–65 percent of foreign exchange generation. This allowed the regime to eschew fundamental reforms until shortly before 2005, when it moved to prepare for a future in which this income is expected to be indeed finite.

Changes with respect to these factors have begun to signal the twilight of economic networks, at least in their virile form. A few years into Bashar's presidency, the top regime leadership was not simply looking for a complementary economic engine: it began to develop an interest in a true economic partner that would be capable of high levels of efficiency and productivity to offset declines in state revenue and state provisions (not to mention public sector inefficiency), declines that do not bode well for economic or regime security. The networks had to be further constrained to make room for other forms of governance that are more apt for this purpose. This is a research task for another endeavor.

Implications for Further Research on Networks

Although we can discern the principal factors that sustain state-business networks, there are some conspicuous limitations in the Syrian case to further developing network analysis at this time. Unlike the case of Russia, for instance, the kind of emerging network research that taps into the attitudes and orientations of network members is *still* nearly impossible to conduct in Syria for security reasons.[4] Network members rarely speak openly about who their partners are or were, their role in networks, and their attitudes about them. More research needs to be conducted to further unpack the specific dynamics of network relations during the 1990s. A good deal of what can be obtained remains in need of further corroboration to specify linkages and names (although the structure is unmistakable). This is the other principal reason—besides the promises of anonymity given by this author to interviewees—why it was difficult to disclose names and connections fully herein.

But existing research conditions do not mean that we must wait. On the contrary, research during such times is crucial for any cumulative effect to emerge in the future. Numerous observations can be gleaned from the current state of economic networks in Syria. It is a fact, for instance, that certain individuals are "members" of economic networks in which they serve as fronts for business partners who belong to the political elite. These relationships are, naturally, undocumented, but they are as real as any other relationship. Though they are obscure, they carry within them the potential to answer questions on the causes of reform outcomes, questions that so far have been inadequately answered in the literature that restricts research to the realm of official documentation. Thus, cross-referencing and analysis of current and historical factors is necessary, and has contributed to the length of footnotes in this book.

One other variable that is conspicuous by its absence throughout this study and, empirically, in the Syrian experience is that of international financial institutions (IFIs). The IFI conditionalities that can be observed elsewhere in the region, such as in Egypt and Jordan, have often had a significant, though not necessarily productive, impact. The absence of such conditionalities has stripped from the state the opportunity to lay blame on external factors for the failure of economic reforms. However, the lack of embeddedness of Syria in the global economy at least until 2005 has also stripped from the business community the ability to establish alternative alliances or even enduring business relations with outside actors. This limitation has weakened the leverage of the business community with the state and strengthened the impact of privileged economic networks on policy-making, even if, as discussed above, their influence is indirect and waning. It is also noteworthy that IFI interference does not necessarily diminish the power of networks, as evidenced by the case of Egypt. It simply makes it more difficult for the regime to make unilateral policy decisions across the board, whatever the content. In both countries, it seems, the larger population is not benefiting; for instance, the distribution of wealth in both Syria and Egypt has been inequitable since the early 1990s as the privileged sectors' wealth increased without corresponding increases for other social groups.[5] Fiscal policy, discussed in Chapter 6, is central to this dynamic in both cases.

The Syrian case clearly supports the contention that a dialectical approach to network analysis is crucial for understanding the formation and development of networks. Specifically, the Syrian case confirms two assumptions posited by David Marsh and Martin Smith, authors of the dialectical model:[6] first, that the "broader structural context affects both the network structure and the resources that actors have to utilize within the network"; and second, that "network interaction and bargaining reflects a combination of the actor's resources, the actor's skill, the network structure and the policy interaction."[7] This accounts for the ability of politically impotent private business partners to wield significant influence within economic networks. From afar it seems that private sector members of privileged networks are powerless: upon closer inspection, one observes a subtle shift in power relations in their favor, and in the favor of capital more broadly, as time goes by.

Another analytical contribution of the Syrian case is the importance of security as an additional incentive for intranetwork cooperation, which often rises over and above short-term individual economic interest. Whereas network members collaborate to increase profits in the case that Marsh and Smith discuss,[8] network members in Syria cooperate also to survive, either in the political sense from the perspective of the political elite, or in the economic *and* political sense from the perspective of their private business partners. The alliance between the Damascene business elite and the state against the rising militant Islamist opposition in the late 1980s and early 1990s is a clear and trend-setting case in point. The retrenchment of the remaining network members in the face of the short-lived reemerging civil society's calls for fundamental economic reforms after 2000 is another testament.

Unintended outcomes as a product of network interaction is yet another insight derived from the Syrian case. Neither the state qua state nor the business community as such has been wholly responsible for economic change in the period under study. Rather, it is the intermediary realm of public-private networks that has disproportionately guided economic change. And though networks benefit from rent-seeking, a constellation of unintended policy outcomes spun the economy into a downward spiral between 1994 and 2005. According to Marsh and Smith, "policy outcomes are the product of the interaction between agents and structures, not merely the sum of the effect of structure and agents."[9] Thus, the less coordination there is within and between institutions, and the less actors are constrained by institutional authority, as is the case in Syria, the more unintended the outcomes. As discussed in Chapter 4, with time, calculative trust between regime officials and the private business elite leads to changes in "breakdown values": the more private sector actors accumulate capital, the less dependent on the state they become. This dynamic continues under the rule of Bashar and is continuously reinforced by generational change. Not only are private sector network members growing more independent as the dispersion of resources proceeds away from the state. Just as important is the fact that many of the offspring of state officials who have gone into business are not as wedded to the state or to the regime as such. They benefit today from proximity to the state via familial relations, but at the same time they can envision for themselves a future where another source of their power will be privileged positions in the growing market. The more that capital is accumulated by increasing numbers of individuals, the less necessary it is to join or be connected to privileged networks, especially when these networks are not viewed as being as vital to the regime as they were earlier.

Another potentially fruitful area for further network analysis is the array of linkages that are developing between this burgeoning cohort of offspring of regime officials and powerful yet independent private sector actors. Both are finding common cause in pushing for a more predictable regulatory framework and investment environment. The changes in the financial sector since 2005 have been quite substantial relative to the prior stagnant environment, making such demands resonate with the broader universe of potential investors, locally and internationally.

WHAT NEXT FOR SYRIA? "MORE CHANGE, LESS CONTINUITY?"

Finally, one might wonder if informal networking, the subject of this study, actually helped the Syrian regime in addressing and dealing with its security concerns *until* 2005. On the surface, it seems as though it did, judging from the kind of political control of which the same elite is still capable. Furthermore, it is true that the two decades of liberalization bred new and powerful stakeholders who have an interest in maintaining the status quo, or at least social order, both of which are in any regime's interest. However, in economic terms, one again may wonder whether by 2005 the levers of the Syrian economy were still under the same kind of regime control that characterized the 1970s and 1980s, or even the 1990s. The empirical evidence suggests that state-business networks had become so entrenched that they endangered not only the economic future of Syria, by discouraging productive investment, but also the future of the current regime itself. Here, al-Dardari's words at the outset of this chapter resonate insofar as it is no longer tolerable for the regime to allow rent-seeking to go unchecked. Regime technocrats *and* politicians recognize the perils of too much continuity and too little change: al-Dardari states clearly and soberly, "[O]ur slogan is 'change within continuity,' but the dangers of persistence [continuity] have become greater than our ability to manage them."[10] This seems to be common knowledge at the very top of the Syrian leadership, but unintended consequences of prior legacies might get in the way. Environmental factors such as the debilitating waves of drought during Bashar's rule have also added fuel to the fire. Unlike during the Hafiz al-Asad era, there is an increasingly higher cost to disciplining economic actors in general, and economic networks in particular, despite their waning influence. By the same token, maintaining the status quo is proving more and more untenable, as the uprisings of 2011 demonstrate.

From 2005 until 2010, the new leadership under Bashar had been far more likely to push the economy in more legal-rational directions. Specifically, if the leadership continues to embrace the expansion of independent financial markets after the establishment of the Damascus Stock Exchange in March 2009, and continues to support the institutionalization of private interests as it did with the Syrian Business Council in 2007, the importance of the networks will naturally subside over time. Emerging business associations, as a function of a government decision to grant such licenses across the board in February 2010, is another step in that direction. But the move is not automatic: one challenge for the Syrian leadership is to prevent the capture of policy-making by the formal-institutional economic elite (over and beyond the networks), an outcome that was evident in the Egyptian case prior to 2011.

In the meantime, networks would still operate, as they do across the business world everywhere. However, they would no longer be the only avenue for safely entering into the big business environment. Clearly, most of the above scenarios are not devoid of political risks for the regime, nor do they necessarily improve the lot of all Syrians—who will continue to suffer so long as their political empowerment is not in sight. But under a more rule-oriented environment that is more inclusive of hitherto absent labor and other populist voices, some of these scenarios would improve the productivity of the Syrian economy and restore developmental progress in some sectors. Such scenarios, however, run counter to the dominant neoliberal trends, locally and globally.

The question of "what next?" for Syria is layered, then, and remains one of intertwined thresholds, not to mention the spring 2011 uprisings, whose outcome is not yet clear. Assuming the regime will persevere, at what point will the push for economic rationality collide anew with the regime's political logic? And if or when this happens, at what point will hardliners within the regime step in to reassert regime security at all costs? In a region ripe with unsavory actors and (persistent threats of) war, and a world dominated by the unprincipled foreign policies of superpowers such as the United States, these important questions might be eclipsed by existential ones that invariably benefit the domestic status quo, not least the unprecedented challenge that Bashar is facing today. The Syrian predicament is difficult: because of the relatively positive nationalist credentials of the regime in the region, most of Syria's citizens, who would otherwise prefer a more democratic order, will not hesitate in supporting the regime against any external aggression, thereby unintentionally reproducing the status quo. Moreover, it seems that many Syrians have yet to take to the streets to join the protesters, which above all else reflects a fear of the unknown consequences of abrupt regime breakdown. This, however, may change as regime brutality escalates

The current Syrian leadership has a rare opportunity to challenge both rent-seeking networks and aggressive external powers legitimately, as well as neutralize its own hardliners, if it can risk granting bold and collective political and civil rights that hitherto have been curtailed. But that train may have passed. Syria is an immensely resource-rich country, especially in its human capital. I have written this book in the hope that in the future, the Syrian people will encounter fewer social, political, and economic constraints and be freer to realize the full potential of modern Syria.

REFERENCE MATTER

NOTES

Introduction

1. Interview with an official at the Ministry of Industry, Damascus, June 1, 1999. The italics denote a saying of sorts that the interviewee was repeating.

2. See Central Bureau of Statistics, "National Accounts," in *Statistical Abstract 2007.*

3. Net inflow of foreign direct investment (FDI) to Syria in 2000 was around $270 million. Compare this to FDI inflows to Jordan ($815 million), Tunisia ($725 million), and Egypt ($1.25 billion) in the same year. World Bank, World Development Indicators Database.

4. Populist rule, connected in cases like Syria with populist authoritarianism, describes a coalition that at least initially embraces labor, the peasantry, middle-class professionals associated with the public sector, the nationalist bourgeoisie, and all coercive apparatuses. Hinnebusch defines a populist authoritarian regime as one which "seeks to establish the authority of a strong state autonomous of the dominant classes and external powers and to launch national economy development aimed at easing dependence and subordinating capitalist forces to populist goals." See Hinnebusch, *Authoritarian Power and State Formation in Ba'thist Syria*, 2.

5. See Waterbury, "State Bourgeoisie and Its Allies."

6. Tailored policies refer to policies that are made to fit those who formulate them or have a hand in doing so, irrespective of the impact on the economy as a whole.

7. Such declarations were made in 2004 by the state planning commissioner and at the Tenth Regional Conference of the Syrian Ba'th party in 2005, when the regime officially unveiled the term "social market economy." See Haddad, "Syria's Curious Dilemma."

8. In a June 2006 interview, Abdullah al-Dardari, then deputy prime minister for economic affairs, clarified that 7 percent is the target growth rate for 2010. Also see Andrew Tabler, "Squaring the Circle: Deputy Prime Minister for Economic Affairs Abdullah Dardari on Syria's 10th Five Year Plan," *Syria Today*, no. 16 (June 2006); State Planning Commission, "10th Five Year Plan."

9. See Syrian Enterprise and Business Center, "Syria's GDP Rose by 7% in 2008."

10. See Economist Intelligence Unit, "Syria Country Report," April 2010, 19.

11. See Figure 1.2 on GDP growth.

12. See World Bank, "Syrian Investment Climate Assessment," 8. Also see Central Bureau of Statistics, "National Accounts," in *Statistical Abstract 2007*.

13. See Evans, *Embedded Autonomy*.

14. On economic or policy networks or, alternatively, on distributional coalitions, see, for instance, Buck, "Networks of Governance and Privatization"; and Schamis, "Distributional Coalitions and the Politics of Economic Reform in Latin America."

15. See, for instance, Lorenz, "Neither Friends nor Strangers"; and Schmitter and Streeck, "Community, Market, State and Associations?"

16. For an introduction to the basic concepts of network analysis, see Knoke and Kuklinski, "Network Analysis." For empirically grounded research on network analysis, see Dimaggio, "Nadel's Paradox Revisited"; and Emirbayer and Goodwin, "Network Analysis, Culture, and the Problem of Agency."

17. This refers to the potential tendency to reduce all outcomes to the impact of economic networks, which is a slippery slope, especially when the focus is on informal networks.

18. See Schneider and Maxfield, *Business and the State in Developing Countries*; and Heydemann, *Networks of Privilege in the Middle East*.

19. Economic networks in Syria refer to what generically could be called big business. Although one might find wealthy Syrians who are not associated with these networks, seldom can one find powerful *and* continuously active businessmen who are not part of these networks.

20. Middle- and lower-range policies are distinguished from high economic policy. The latter refers to the broad contours of the economy as defined by the regime leadership; for example, whether or not to open certain economic sectors or subsectors to private business. Middle- and lower-range policies refer to what happens to such decisions in practice: for instance, who is given privileges, and on what conditions.

21. Signs of economic stagnation beginning in the mid-1990s include an overall drop in production; a rise of unemployment to unprecedented levels; the shrinking of foreign investments; a drop in real wages, purchasing power, and aggregate demand; the shutting of some enterprises established under Law No. 10; and finally, the stockpiling of goods in factories and at retail stores. See Central Bureau of Statistics, "National Accounts," in *Statistical Abstract 1998*. For more information on indicators regarding Syria's economic stagnation in the late 1990s, see Economist Intelligence Unit, *Syria: Country Profile 1998, 1999*, and *2000*.

22. To be sure, economic networks did not cause economic decline but exacerbated inefficiency in an economy with a declining productivity since the early 1980s, despite its numeric growth in the late 1980s. For more on the causes of economic decline in the 1980s and 1990s and on the artificial growth in the late 1980s, see Haddad, "Political Dynamics of Economic Liberalization in Populist-Authoritarian Regimes."

23. See Heydemann, "Upgrading Authoritarianism in the Arab World."

24. See Hirschman, *Exit, Voice, and Loyalty*; and Evans, *Embedded Autonomy*.

25. See Wade, *Governing the Market* and "East Asia's Economic Success"; and Johnson, "Political Institutions and Economic Performance."

26. See Evans, "State as Problem and Solution"; and Skocpol, "Bringing the State Back In," 16.

27. See Rueschemyer and Putterman, *State and Market in Development*, 255.

28. See Haggard and Kaufman, *Political Economy of Democratic Transitions*; and Brumberg, "Authoritarian Legacies and Reform Strategies in the Arab World."

29. See Geddes, "Challenging the Conventional Wisdom," in *Fragile Coalitions*; Heydemann, "Political Logic of Economic Rationality"; and Haggard and Kaufman, *Politics of Economic Adjustment*.

30. See Farsoun and Zacharia, "Class, Economic Change, and Political Liberalization in the Arab World."

31. A partial treatment of the topic appears in Lawson, "Private Capital and the State in Contemporary Syria."

32. See Musacchio and Read, "Bankers, Industrialists, and Their Cliques."

33. See Geddes, "Challenging the Conventional Wisdom," in *Journal of Democracy*, and "Heart of the Matter?"

34. See Perthes, *Political Economy of Syria Under Asad*.

35. Within this literature, this work on Syria presents a crucial case where the pattern of economic liberalization did not lead to any significant economic restructuring, even when compared to cases such as Egypt, Tunisia, Jordan, and Morocco. These cases are presented as IMF "success stories" in the 1990s. See Pfeifer, "How Tunisia, Morocco, Jordan and Even Egypt Became IMF 'Success Stories' in the 1990s."

36. See Krueger, "Political Economy of the Rent-Seeking Society"; Olson, *Rise and Decline of Nations*; Bhagwati, "Directly Unproductive Profit-Seeking (DUP) Activities"; and Reynolds, "Political Economy of Interdependence in the Americas."

37. See Schneider and Maxfield, *Business and the State in Developing Countries*.

38. See Heydemann, *Networks of Privilege in the Middle East*, 1–34.

39. See Lucas, "Politics of Business Associations in the Developing World."

40. See Snyder, "After Neoliberalism"; and Heydemann's introduction in *Networks of Privilege in the Middle East*, 1–34.

41. See Knoke, *Changing Organizations*; and Egbert, "Business Success Through Social Networks?"

42. For a discussion on the question of agency, see Emirbayer and Goodwin, "Network Analysis, Culture, and the Problem of Agency."

43. See, for instance, Schamis, "Distributional Coalitions and the Politics of Economic Reform in Latin America."

44. See Schneider and Maxfield, *Business and the State in Developing Countries*, chapters 1, 7. The authors provide a review and a commentary about various argu-

ments and theories on state-business relations. Furthermore, chapter 2, on theories of state-business relations, and Peter Evans's chapter ("State Structures, Government-Business Relations, and Economic Transformation"), both in the same book, provide a theoretical framework that potentially guides research on the subject. For a nuanced version of business-state relations, see Kim, "State and Business in the Developmental Process."

45. See Schneider, *Business Politics and the State in Twentieth-Century Latin America*; Hamilton, *Asian Business Networks*; and Richer, *Business Networks in Asia Promises Doubts and Perspectives*.

46. See Simon, "Development Reconsidered."

47. It is important to note that we are concerned here with cases where populist-authoritarian institutions persisted, as opposed to several Latin American cases where an abrupt change occurred from populist- to bureaucratic-authoritarianism; see O'Donnell and Schmitter, *Transitions from Authoritarian Rule*; and O'Donnell, *Modernization and Bureaucratic Authoritarianism*.

48. See Lucas, "Politics of Business Associations in the Developing World," 73.

49. In his "Politics of Business Associations in the Developing World," Lucas suggests "in the absence of business associations, entrepreneurs will respond to collective problems with adaptive and avoidance techniques such as bribery and clientelism" (74).

50. See Knight and Sened, *Explaining Social Institutions*; Levi, "State of Trust"; Williamson, "Calculativeness, Trust, and Economic Organization"; and *Markets and Hierarchies*.

51. See Granovetter and Swedberg, "Introduction."

52. See Wasserman and Galaskiewicz, *Advances in Social Network Analysis*, xii (emphasis mine).

53. See Knoke and Yang, *Social Network Analysis*, 8.

54. See Granovetter and Swedberg, "Introduction," 9.

55. Ibid.

56. See Lomnitz and Sheinbaum, "Trust, Social Networks and the Informal Economy."

57. Ibid., 6.

58. See Putnam, *Making Democracy Work*; and Fukuyama, *Trust*. For a critique of the concept of social capital from a rational choice perspective, see Levi, "Social and Unsocial Capital."

59. See the following chapters in Heydemann's *Networks of Privilege in the Middle East*: Haddad, "Formation and Development of Economic Networks in Syria"; Sfakianakis, "Whales of the Nile"; Wurzel, "Patterns of Resistance."

60. See Heydemann's introduction in his *Networks of Privilege in the Middle East*.

61. The field research was facilitated by an SSRC fellowship in 1998–99, and biyearly visits henceforth.

62. Regime tolerance of public discourse on economic issues in Syria underwent a

significant increase after 1997, as the heir-apparent, Bashar al-Asad, was being groomed for eventual succession.

63. See Perthes, *Political Economy of Syria Under Asad*, "Introduction," 13–14.

Chapter 1

1. See Shafer, *Winners and Losers* for more on the conceptualization of business, and chapters 1 and 2 in Maxfield and Schneider, *Business and the State in Developing Countries*. In late-developing countries, it is highly unlikely to find the core of business in the form of large corporations and firms, a form that characterizes business in more advanced economies. Moreover, the business-as-sector conceptualization is more likely to be found not only in more diversified economies but also in ones where economic sectors determine policy, and not vice versa; see Shafer, *Winners and Losers*. For surely even the least developed countries have sectoral divisions in their economies, but the allocation of resources remains politically controlled, not sectorally driven; see Shafer, *Winners and Losers*. Thus, it is unlikely to find many instances of sectorally driven economies in less democratic and economically rationalized late-developing countries. Finally, business as capital and business as network pervade all cases in which one can speak of state-business relations, including the more populist-authoritarian and less rationalized economies.

2. See World Bank, "Syrian Investment Climate Assessment," 8. Also see Central Bureau of Statistics, "National Accounts," in *Statistical Abstract 2007*.

3. *Subsidized* is a widely used word in Syria. It denotes that someone or something (for example, a business contract) is politically supported from "above," or by the regime elite. Such vocabulary became ubiquitous simply because of the ubiquity of transgressions in politics, business, and social life since the early 1970s.

4. See "What Happened with the Mercedes Dealership? The Former Minister of the Economy and an Automobile Company Stop a Judicial Order That Licenses a Dealership," *al-Iqtisadiyya*, December 30, 2001, 8.

5. A similar argument, though with a different explanatory purpose, was posited in Heydemann, "Political Logic of Economic Rationality." Heydemann argued that economic reforms in Syria were driven by a political logic that constrained economic rationality. A decade later, however, as rent-seeking networks became more prevalent and consolidated, economic stagnation became potentially destabilizing. Though still driven by a similar political logic, the cost of constraining economic rationality has become much greater and, some argue, unsustainable.

6. The use of the phrase "lack of 'ability to discipline'" refers primarily to the inability of the state to discipline the private sector as a whole, particularly the economic networks that include the biggest investors. Although the state could crack down on the private sector, even on network members, it is not able to guide their investments in the direction of productive ventures that contribute added value to the economy. Alternatively, the state can only open the door for investors to invest in lucrative deals that

are usually of a commercial nature. This inability stems from the unwillingness of the top leadership to exercise the rule of law—that is, to undermine its arbitrary power—across the board, which requires the extension of guaranteed civil and political rights. At a minimum, disciplining the business sector in a particular productive direction that brings added value to the whole economy requires the provision of appropriate and predictable administrative and legal environments. The weakness of such environments deters most domestic and foreign investors interested in long-term development with long-term payoffs.

7. Collective gains are defined in this chapter as gains that potentially benefit all sectors of society and—as with public goods—from which no sector can be excluded by administrative fiat, for example, providing a legally and bureaucratically secure and hospitable environment for investments.

8. See the weekly *al-Wasat* 437, June 12–18, 2000, 12.

9. On lucrative deals in the communications sector, see Saif, "Cellular Telephone Contracts," a controversial paper presented by MP Riad Saif to the Syrian Parliament on August 14, 2001. The paper exposes the scandal of the lucrative and not cost-effective cellular telephone contracts between the government and individuals affiliated with the state but acting as private businessmen.

10. Banque Audi, "Syria Economic Report," August 2008, 7. http://www.banqueaudi.com/geteconomy/syria/SyriaEconomicReport.pdf (accessed September 2009).

11. Author interview with Haytham Joud, principal founding member, guiding member, and chairman of Syria Holding, in Damascus, July 24, 2007.

12. Ibid.

13. The legacy of regime-business (or, alternatively, urban-rural) antagonism is well documented in nearly all research on Syrian politics in the 1950s, 1960s, and 1970s. Particularly, see Hinnebusch, *Authoritarian Power and State Formation in Ba'thist Syria*; Heydemann, *Authoritarianism in Syria*; and Batatu, *Syria's Peasantry, the Descendants of Its Lesser Rural Notables, and Their Politics*.

14. These emerging economic networks were instrumental in stemming the tide of the Muslim Brotherhood in Damascus in the late 1970s because business elites there did not lend their support to the Islamists. Around the same time, especially in the early 1980s, the state began to lose the active, though often passive, support of its peasant-labor constituency amidst economic decline. This loss of support was compensated by the support of rising business elements and, more broadly, members of the middle classes who had seen their fortunes slashed in the radical pre-Asad years of the 1960s. On the Muslim Brotherhood, see Batatu, *Syria's Peasantry, the Descendants of Its Lesser Rural Notables, and Their Politics*, 108. On the shifting social basis of regime support, see Perthes, *Political Economy of Syria Under Asad*, Ch. 3, 120–22.

15. See Dalila, "*'Ajz al-Muwaazanah al-'Aamah wa Subul Mu'aalajatuhu*" [The general budget deficit and ways for its treatment].

16. Eighteen percent of the Syrian workforce is employed by the government, which is a higher percentage than the Middle East and North Africa (MENA) region average of 17.5 percent—already the highest average of any world region. In 2002, civilians employed in public administration numbered 872,500; this figure is considered conservative by most independent Syrian economists. Nonetheless, in a country with a population under 17 million, the number of people Syria employs in the public and governmental sectors is similar to that in Egypt, a country with a population exceeding 62 million. On Egypt, see Pratt, "Maintaining the Moral Economy." On Syria, author interview of Syrian economist Saʿid Nabulsi, Damascus, February 15, 1999; and see International Monetary Fund, "Syrian Arab Republic: Statistical Appendix." Also see Central Bureau of Statistics, "National Accounts," in *Statistical Abstract 1998*, "The Staff in the Government by Departments and Type of Work," 87; and International Monetary Fund, "Syrian Arab Republic: Article IV Consultation—Staff Report 2005."

17. This language pervades all presidential speeches after the private sector was rejuvenated in the late 1980s. Bashar's inaugural speech in August 2000, one that reputedly ushered in an era of "modernization" and "reform," emphasized the primacy of the public sector; and the tenth Five-Year Plan, issued in 2005, likewise focused on the need for public sector reform rather than its privatization or gradual subordination to the private sector.

18. These figures are available in various reports, such as the *World Development Report*; however, the actual amount of aid is invariably underreported, according to officials who dealt with such transfers and who were able to compare actual versus official figures. The transfers that did not make it into the official figures were not ultimately deposited in the Syrian Central Bank. As will be discussed at the end of this chapter, accurate statistical information on Syria—particularly concerning sensitive economic sectors—is difficult to come by. However, this difficulty is indicative of the importance of rent to the regime. Interview with a former official at the Commercial Bank of Syria, Damascus, March 8, 1999; and Perthes, *Political Economy of Syria Under Asad*, 35.

19. External assistance fluctuated in the 1980s in terms of sums and donor party. While Arab aid decreased dramatically in the 1980s, aid in various forms (for example, oil concessions) from Iran accrued steadily in the 1980s, totaling nearly one billion dollars a year. Interview with a former official at the Commercial Bank of Syria, Damascus, March 8, 1999. Also see Perthes, *Political Economy of Syria Under Asad*, 34; and (cited by Perthes) Economist Intelligence Unit, *Syria: Country Profile 1993* and *1994*, 53.

20. See the semiofficial figures in the Syrian weekly *al-Iqtisadiyyah* (ʿIzz al-Din Juni, "Oil, the Lifeblood of Development and Industrialization in Syria: World Prices Substantially Influence Oil Exports," December 2001, 27, 30). These figures, supplied by the Institute of Planning in Damascus, are therefore conservative, since the official figures for oil income are not publicly available. Nevertheless, these semiofficial figures and percentages regarding oil production and exports have hitherto been used by nearly all

Syria researchers to date. The author's interviews with former bureaucrats in the Syrian state-banking sector and with high-level employees of foreign companies operating in Syria under government contracts—for example, Dutch Shell—reveal the conservative nature of these estimates.

21. See International Monetary Fund, "Syrian Arab Republic: Article IV Consultation—Staff Report 2005."

22. See British Petroleum, "Statistical Review of World Energy."

23. See International Monetary Fund, "Syrian Arab Republic: Article IV Consultation—Staff Report 2005."

24. See Perthes, "Syria Under Bashar al-Asad," 30.

25. "Syria—Raising Levels of Expectation," *Shell in the Middle East* no. 21 (April 2003): 6; "Syria—Oil, Gas and Utilities Report," *Business Intelligence—Middle East*, December 21, 2004. http://www.bi-me.com/main.php?id=186&t=1 (accessed October 2009).

26. See Economist Intelligence Unit, "Syria Country Report," 8; International Monetary Fund, "Syrian Arab Republic: IMF Article IV Consultation Staff Report," February 2009, 7.

27. Interview with former deputy prime minister for economic affairs Abdallah al-Dardari, Damascus, July 25, 2007.

28. World Bank, World Development Indicators Database, 2007.

29. United Nations Conference on Trade and Development, World Investment Report 2009, 290–95.

30. See Perthes, *Political Economy of Syria Under Asad*, 203.

31. Ibid.

32. Ibid., 204.

33. See Niblock, "International and Domestic Factors," 58.

34. For full data on Syria's national debt numbers, see the World Bank's World Development Indicators Database. For the Syrian government's analysis of its debt situation, see the tenth Five-Year Plan, at http://www.planning.gov.sy/files/file/FypChapter1 En.pdf (accessed September 2009).

35. See Niblock, "International and Domestic Factors," 58. Also see Stallings, "International Influence on Economic Policy"; Pool, "Links Between Economic and Political Liberalization"; and Waterbury, "Coalition Management."

36. This situation has changed somewhat, particularly immediately following the death of Hafiz al-Asad, when at least two semi-independent publications emerged after Bashar's proclamation of new media legislation. See Sami Moubayed's article in the Lebanese *The Daily Star* ("Syria Heralds Entrance of a Freer Press: Assad Authorizes New Media Law," September 24, 2001). However, after signaling his intentions to allow further freedom of expression, Bashar balked in the face of the outpouring of civil society organizations and public discussions that were forming. Dozens of activists were arrested; many still remain in prison at the time of this writing, nearly ten years later.

The rollback of free speech liberties in Syria has spread to the internet: in August 2007, the Ministry of Telecommunications issued a binding cabinet law requiring that all articles and comments published online be accompanied by the full name of the author, or else the website would be shut down. See al-Safir, "Syria: Ministry Introduce Website Censorship Measure," August 3, 2007.

Chapter 2

1. For the burst of consumption, see Perthes, *Political Economy of Syria Under Asad*, Ch. 2; on the downward decline, see Economist Intelligence Unit, "Syria Country Report," 1998 and 1999.

2. For a review of the arguments, see Geddes, "Challenging the Conventional Wisdom," in *Journal of Democracy*.

3. See Evans, *Embedded Autonomy*.

4. Hinnebusch, *Authoritarian Power and State Formation in Ba'thist Syria*, defines a populist-authoritarian regime as one that "seeks to establish the authority of a strong state autonomous of the dominant classes and external powers and to launch national economy development aimed at easing dependence and subordinating capitalist forces to populist goals" (2). Brumberg states that populist regimes embrace a coalition that includes hitherto excluded sectors (for example, workers, peasants, radical intelligentsia) and excludes the largest segments of the business community, apart from what is often called the nationalist bourgeoisie; see Brumberg, "Authoritarian Legacies and Reform Strategies in the Arab World."

5. See Schneider and Maxfield, "Business, the State, and Economic Performance in Developing Countries."

6. Ibid.

7. See Williamson "Calculativeness, Trust, and Economic Organization."

8. See Schneider and Maxfield, *Business and the State in Developing Countries*, Ch. 1.

9. For a discussion of the concept of collusion and its implications for economic relations, see Alexeev and Leitzel, "Collusion and Rent-Seeking."

10. *Random House Webster's College Dictionary* (New York: Random House, 1997), 259.

11. *Webster's Third New International Dictionary, Unabridged* (Philippines: Merriam-Webster, 1981), 446. The definition also includes: "agreement between parties considered adversaries at the law" and "a secret agreement considered illegal for any reason."

12. See Dillman, *State and Private Sector in Algeria*, 11–15.

13. The majority of the Syrian population is Sunni. For a discussion of the demographics of Syria, see Van Dam, *Struggle for Power in Syria*.

14. See Batatu, *Syria's Peasantry, the Descendants of Its Lesser Rural Notables, and Their Politics*.

15. See Brumberg, "Authoritarian Legacies and Reform Strategies in the Arab World."

16. See Hinnebusch, *Authoritarian Power and State Formation in Ba'thist Syria*, 1–7; and Heydemann, *Authoritarianism in Syria*, 12–16. Heydemann provides a nuanced analysis of shifting alliances in the early periods of populism, in which capitalists and oligarchs are at odds (14–15).

17. See Brumberg.

18. See Heydemann, *Authoritarianism in Syria*, 181–92.

19. See Waterbury, "Private Sector: Out of the Shadows."

20. See Heydemann, *Authoritarianism in Syria*, 19.

21. See Batatu, *Syria's Peasantry, the Descendants of Its Lesser Rural Notables, and Their Politics*, Ch. 22; and Hinnebusch, *Authoritarian Power and State Formation in Ba'thist Syria*, Ch. 9, for the best accounts of the confrontation between the Syrian regime and the Islamists, and its causes.

22. See Hinnebusch, *Authoritarian Power and State Formation in Ba'thist Syria*, 130. Also see Batatu, *Syria's Peasantry, the Descendants of Its Lesser Rural Notables, and Their Politics*. Even within the party, Batatu attests, "[t]he internal party discords were never purely sectarian or purely regional in character" (171).

23. See Hinnebusch, *Authoritarian Power and State Formation in Ba'thist Syria*, 130.

24. According to Nasir Nasir, a public sector economist, the regime at the time faced a dilemma: it needed the party to broaden its rule, but without its politics. "[T]here was a need after 1970 to find a mobilizational alternative to the Ba'th because it was the tool of the leftist wing of the party at that time. The rise of the military and the security apparatuses is related to this dilemma"; interview, Damascus, April 20, 1999.

25. See Hinnebusch, *Authoritarian Power and State Formation in Ba'thist Syria*, 137–39.

26. See Waldner, *State Building and Late Development*, Ch. 1.

27. Ibid.

28. See Chaudhry, "Middle East and the Political Economy of Development"; and Heydemann, "Upgrading Authoritarianism in the Arab World."

29. See Waterbury, *Political Economy of Two Regimes*.

30. See Heydemann, *Authoritarianism in Syria*, 19.

31. See Waterbury, *Political Economy of Two Regimes*, 17–20; and Heydemann, *Authoritarianism in Syria*, 18–19.

32. See Waterbury, *Political Economy of Two Regimes*, 20. According to Heydemann's reading of Waterbury, Nasir was not prepared to wield an iron fist and risk class conflict. See Heydemann, *Authoritarianism in Syria*, 18.

33. See Ehteshami and Hinnebusch, *Syria and Iran*, 71.

34. In no small part this occurred because of the class interests of middle peasants who supported the triumphant Ba'th faction and feared further land reforms. See Hinnebusch, *Authoritarian Power and State Formation in Ba'thist Syria*, 138–39.

35. This understanding is prevalent in Syrian academic circles; however, it is not

discussed in the open. Those who do discuss such matters in the company of others trust that they would not be quoted or betrayed. See Hinnebusch, *Authoritarian Power and State Formation in Ba'thist Syria,* 121.

36. See Hinnebusch, *Authoritarian Power and State Formation in Ba'thist Syria,* 135.

37. See Heydemann, *Authoritarianism in Syria,* 22.

38. This claim is disputed by outspoken Syrian academics, most of whom believe that the Ba'th's standing was ameliorated by the UAR. Some argue that the UAR was ultimately a godsend to the Ba'th: "the effects of the UAR involve stemming the political development of Syria and setting the state for a takeover by the least popular party"; interview with Nasir Nasir, April 20, 1999. See Hinnebusch, *Authoritarian Power and State Formation in Ba'thist Syria,* 113.

39. See Hinnebusch, *Authoritarian Power and State Formation in Ba'thist Syria,* 114–15.

40. In line with this interpretation, former Ba'thists viewed the attachment of the radical Ba'thist elements to the party in instrumental terms but attributed the instrumentalism to the less ideologically inclined members of the secret committee, including Asad. See Hinnebusch, *Authoritarian Power and State Formation in Ba'thist Syria,* 115.

41. For the most sound information about the Military Committee, including the controversy over when it was founded and whom it included (for example, Asad claims to have been a founding member, whereas Ahmad al-Mir states that he joined a year later, in 1960), see Batatu, *Syria's Peasantry, the Descendants of Its Lesser Rural Notables, and Their Politics,* 144–45; and see 146–49 for a comprehensive list of members and background information. This list is significant because these members came to form the Regional Command of the Ba'th that effectively ruled Syria in the 1960s and beyond.

42. See Hinnebusch, *Authoritarian Power and State Formation in Ba'thist Syria,* 116.

43. Ibid., 117.

44. See Heydemann, *Authoritarianism in Syria,* 12; and Hinnebusch, *Authoritarian Power and State Formation in Ba'thist Syria,* 118.

45. The urban base of the Islamists limited their appeal to the newly mobilized and urbanized segments of Syrian society and to the ascending educated middle classes, many of whom were not even Sunni. The Communists had for long been suffering from the stigma of being subordinate to the Soviet Union, especially because of their support for the partition of Palestine, which followed a Soviet line. Finally, despite what many analysts have presented as arguments for the limited appeal of the SSNP (for example, their secularist, anti-Islamic stance and their minority-dominated leadership—as though the Ba'th were not), it would be safer to assume that the very ideology of the SSNP—reviving Greater Syria—did not immediately appeal to the larger segments of the lay population, whether devout Muslims and Christians or atheists. Instead, their cadres were, and remained, limited but always intense and fervent, especially among intellectuals prior to 1967.

46. See Hinnebusch, *Authoritarian Power and State Formation in Ba'thist Syria*, 122–23.

47. Ibid., 85.

48. See Rabinovitch, *Syria Under the Ba'th*, for a detailed account of Ba'thist internecine conflicts between 1963 and 1966.

49. See Hinnebusch, *Authoritarian Power and State Formation in Ba'thist Syria*, 133–35.

50. Ibid., 135.

51. According to Hinnebusch, "every major successful party faction has either been led or championed by an officer-politician. In the end, when disputes could not be resolved in party institutions, the resort to competitive military mobilization proved decisive and the coalition which commanded superior force prevailed: this was so in 1966 and would prove so again in 1970." See Hinnebusch, *Authoritarian Power and State Formation in Ba'thist Syria*, 132.

52. See Hinnebusch, *Authoritarian Power and State Formation in Ba'thist Syria*, 132.

53. Ibid., 134.

54. According to those in top ranks in the military, early on Asad felt that "the path the regime was taking is not going to last." Interview with a retired Syrian general living in the United States, September 30, 1999.

55. The new Ba'th's ideological underpinnings were laid out by a group of old Ba'thists and former Communists (including Jamal al-Atasi, Ilyas Murqus, and Yasin al-Hafiz) who retooled the amorphous ideological canon of the founders so as to avoid its strategic as well as ideological pitfalls: "[W]riting in *al-Ba'th*, [this group] criticized traditional Ba'thism for its emphasis on individual freedom and opposition to class struggle and called for an opening to Marxism and a stress on popular mass organization; these writers were important because their work expressed the ideological mutation going on in the party bases and laid the foundations for the radicalization of Ba'thist ideology after 1963." See Hinnebusch, *Authoritarian Power and State Formation in Ba'thist Syria*, 114. On the Ba'th's political and ideological underpinnings, see also Jabbur, *al-Fikr al-Siyasi al-Mu'asir fi Suriya* [Contemporary political thought in Syria], 375–76; and Safadi, *Hizb al-Ba'th* [The Ba'th party], 155–61.

56. See Hinnebusch, *Authoritarian Power and State Formation in Ba'thist Syria*, 137.

57. Ibid., 138.

58. Arif Dalila and other outspoken critics of the regime affirm that the personalities surrounding Asad at the time were among the most careerist and the least committed ideologically to the precepts of socialism. Interview, April 5, 1999. This view is also shared by army officials who saw their status diminish with the arrival to power of a number of "corrupt opportunists." Asad, though not absolved, is acknowledged to be of a different stock, largely because he was both a systematic leader and less interested in personal material and financial gain, as his lifestyle indicated. Interview with a former Syrian army general, Washington DC, September 30, 1999.

59. See Hinnebusch, *Authoritarian Power and State Formation in Ba'thist Syria*, 141.

60. This figure refers to the proportion of the economically active population. See Longuenesse, "Class Nature of the State in Syria"; and Hinnebusch, *Authoritarian Power and State Formation in Ba'thist Syria*, 142.

61. Notably, in the mid- to late 1970s, and by contrast, it is the middle classes' fortunes that expanded, as a reflection of the regime's changing priorities. See Perthes, *Political Economy of Syria Under Asad*, Fig. 3.2 on 118, and 119–20.

62. See Hinnebusch, *Authoritarian Power and State Formation in Ba'thist Syria*, 142.

63. See Khoury, *Syria and the French Mandate*.

64. According to former public sector officials who since then have opposed the regime, Asad was bent on controlling the party and avoiding a "regression into the socialism of the 1960s" (*al-awda ila ishtiraakiyyat al-sittinaat*), which he considered untenable in Syria. Interviews with former officials in the Central Bank of Syria, Damascus, October 7, 1998. Also see Riad al-Turk's famous two-part critique of the regime in *al-Hayat*, August 9 and 10, 2001. Al-Turk was imprisoned on September 1, 2001, presumably for writing these pieces that stirred a larger debate in civil society circles, on Al-Jazeera satellite television station, and in the Arab press.

65. See Hinnebusch, *Authoritarian Power and State Formation in Ba'thist Syria*, 122.

66. Although Batatu acknowledges the "minority-oriented policy pursued by the French from 1921 to 1945," he does not place the cause for the preponderance of the 'Alawis squarely on such policy. Rather, he cites a "more significant factor" to be "the depressed economic conditions of the 'Alawis" and the *badal* [financial substitute] which most urban Sunnis could pay to be exempted from military service while rural 'Alawis were drafted. However, while this accounts for the swelling of 'Alawis in the rank-and-file positions, it was "ultimately . . . the rise of the 'Alawis to dominance in the officer corps that assured their decisive control of the armed forces." Whereas the Sunni officers were "hopelessly divided in political, regional, and class terms," 'Alawi officers were not, in most of these respects, as most were from a largely similar station of peasant extraction. That fact, more than any other, accounted for their cohesion. See Batatu, *Syria's Peasantry, the Descendants of Its Lesser Rural Notables, and Their Politics*, 158–59.

67. See Hinnebusch, *Authoritarian Power and State Formation in Ba'thist Syria*, 64.

68. Notable here is that "with every purge, the Sunnis in the officer corps decreased in number and significance" by virtue of their divided stances and the alliances many of them had formed with ardent, or sometimes ostensible, opponents of the emerging new Ba'th. For these reasons, most of the Druze and rural Sunni officers were purged in 1966 and 1968, respectively, along with some of their 'Alawi partners, in both instances. See Batatu, *Syria's Peasantry, the Descendants of Its Lesser Rural Notables, and Their Politics*, 159.

69. This famous reshuffle was not a quiet or underhanded affair; according to army officials at the time, it was overt and justified by the regime: "[T]hose who sympathize with Nasir or non-Ba'thist ideas, are not going to be useful in the coming stage. . . . [T]hey will

bring about another coup." Interview with a retired Syrian general, September 30, 1999. See Hinnebusch, *Authoritarian Power and State Formation in Ba'thist Syria*, 120.

70. See Hinnebusch, *Authoritarian Power and State Formation in Ba'thist Syria*, 122.

71. See Batatu, *Syria's Peasantry, the Descendants of Its Lesser Rural Notables, and Their Politics*, 173.

72. See Hinnebusch, *Authoritarian Power and State Formation in Ba'thist Syria*, 126.

73. See Perthes, *Political Economy of Syria Under Asad*, Ch. 2.

74. See Hinnebusch, *Authoritarian Power and State Formation in Ba'thist Syria*, 154.

75. See Ayubi, *Overstating the Arab State*, 27.

76. Hinnebusch writes, "In effecting a more egalitarian distribution of resources in society, notably one in favor of the deprived rural periphery, the Ba'th hoped to win the masses to its side, while expanded state control over economic life would in practice make them more dependent on the new state"; see Hinnebusch, *Authoritarian Power and State Formation in Ba'thist Syria*, 127.

77. Much of the recent literature on state-business relations attempts to distinguish between differentially (un)productive kinds of rent-seeking. Relevant to this study is the tracing of that kind of rent-seeking behavior that proliferates in an environment of mutual state-business vulnerability, with a state bureaucracy that lacks administrative autonomy and a highly dependent but capital-rich business community. Under such conditions, rent-seeking becomes a vehicle that further weakens and fragments the economic bureaucracy, irrespective of political economic orientation, without increasing productivity and employment and, therefore, without providing any added value to the economy. See Alexeev and Leitzel, "Collusion and Rent-Seeking"; and Reynolds, "Political Economy of Interdependence in the Americas." See also, for a quick reference, Richards and Waterbury, *Political Economy*, Box 2.2 on "Economic Rent," 17.

78. See Haddad, "Change and Stasis in Syria"; and Central Bureau of Statistics, "National Accounts," in *Statistical Abstract 1998*. For 2005 figures, see Central Bureau of Statistics, "National Accounts," in *Statistical Abstract 2007*.

79. See Hinnebusch, *Authoritarian Power and State Formation in Ba'thist Syria*, 141.

Chapter 3

Portions of this chapter have been adapted from Bassam S. A. Haddad, "Enduring Legacies: The Politics of Private Sector Development in Syria," in *Demystifying Syria*, edited by Fred Lawson (London: London Middle East Institute, SOAS, 2009).

Epigraphs

Muhammad Ghassan al-Qalla': Interview, Damascus, December 10, 1998. Al-Qalla' is part of one of the more frugal and conservative families with ties to the old bourgeoisie of Damascus.

Ma'moun Tabba': Interview, May 30, 1999. Tabba' is part of a prominent family that belongs to the old bourgeoisie.

Riad Saif: Interview, Damascus, June 8, 1999. Saif's comments came in the context of an interview on the nature of selective relations between the regime and private businessmen that grow at the expense of the private sector proper. Saif is among the independents who accumulated wealth in the textiles sector in the 1980s, but with business operation roots in the 1970s. Saif considers himself a social democrat.

Ratib Badr al-Din al-Shallah: Interview, Damascus, May 9, 1999. Many independent analysts consider al-Shallah as (socially) among the most powerful men in Syria. He assumed the presidency of the Damascus Chamber of Commerce in 1992 after the resignation of his father, Badr al-Din al-Shallah. It is significant that Badr al-Din al-Shallah's funeral in 1999 was one befitting a head of state, if only because nearly all the officials in the most sensitive positions attended the funeral at the traditional quarter of Hay al-Midan in Damascus. Such indicators carry significant social weight in the context of Syrian politics and reflect the continuing strategic alliance between the top Damascene bourgeoisie and the regime.

Abdul Rahman al-'Attar: Interview, Damascus, May 9, 1999. Al-'Attar is a Syrian businessman.

Nabil Sukkar: Interview, Damascus, July 23, 2008. Sukkar runs one of the most efficient business consultancy firms in Syria.

1. See Benhassine, "From Privilege to Competition."

2. See Moore, *Doing Business in the Middle East*; Keshavarzian, *Bazaar and State in Iran*; Cammett, "Business-Government Relations and Industrial Change"; and various reports by John Sfakianakis at the Saudi British Bank (SABB).

3. Many Syria analysts of the contemporary period have discussed the private sector in a problematic manner, precisely because the private sector was taken at face value. With the possible exception of some of Perthes's indirect writing on the subject and Joseph Bahout's study on the Syrian business community, contemporary Syria analysts have rarely deconstructed this category to reflect realities on the ground. Some analysts divide the private sector along categorical lines that are not politically or economically salient in practice (for example, by sectoral division, commercial versus industrial division, old versus new bourgeoisie, exporters versus everyone else, those integrated into the national market versus those whose business activity bypasses the intricacies of this market). Although each such division carries a grain of practical salience, none are sufficient to explain the behavior of actors that are found in these categories. The absence of fruitful field research opportunities, even during the less restrictive Bashar al-Asad era, continues to be the single most significant obstacle to examining the complexities and subtleties of Syria's private sector, and the behavior, preferences, and mentality of actors within it.

4. Perhaps the best example of such partnerships can be gleaned from the dismal results of Investment Law No. 10 of 1991 and the numerous presidential decrees that directly
preceded the law. See Abdul Nour, "al-Qita' al-Khas fi Thill al-Himaya" [The private sector in the shadow of protection]; and Hinnebusch, "Democratization in the Middle East."

5. The difference here speaks to the kind of economic development the regime pursued, one marked by a severely controlled pattern of economic growth that prevents
the emergence of powerful industrial social forces. Alternatively, industrial deepening
would have required more far-sighted economic planning that subordinates political
imperatives, as well as a more open political and economic system that does not hinder
ingenuity and other price-setting mechanisms. For a comparative account of the Syrian
case in this regard, see Waldner, *State Building and Late Development*; for a comparative
account on the requirements and challenges of industrial deepening drawn from cases
in Latin America, see O'Donnell, *Modernization and Bureaucratic Authoritarianism*.

6. Though official statistics do not exist on class distribution in Syria, independent
analysts and economists who work on demographic distribution, urbanization, and
labor concur with the figures presented by Perthes's account, which remains the best
rough estimate for class distribution. See Perthes, *Political Economy of Syria Under Asad*,
Table 3.2, 118. Economists interviewed on this topic include Rizqallah Hilan, Arif Dalila,
Sa'id Nabulsi, Nabil Marzouq, and Nasir Nasir.

7. The trio of 'Uthman al-'A'idi, Sa'ib Nahhas, and Abdul Rahman al-'Attar are often
referred to as the first batch of the new private bourgeoisie in Syria. However, several
other individuals have surpassed their reputation and their wealth, including relatives of
the Asad, Makhlouf, Shalish, and other politically prominent families.

8. The wealthiest individuals, groups, and families in Syria are usually involved in
commerce, service, and manufacturing sectors, in both exports and imports. The Sanqar family is an example. A family of three enterprising brothers, they are involved in
the importation of luxury cars, own restaurants, and provide the local market with various agricultural products. The Sa'ib Nahhas group is perhaps the epitome of business
diversification in Syria, spanning nearly all sectors, including commerce, agriculture,
industry, transportation, and tourism. Whereas Nahhas declined personal interviews,
the records of his businesses are made public through a variety of brochures published
by his office in Damascus.

9. These exemptions and privileges are discussed in the chapters on the political
dynamics of economic liberalization (Ch. 5) and on fiscal policy change (Ch. 6).

10. This refers to the three business tycoons the Syrian regime engaged in the 1970s,
including 'Uthman al-'A'idi, Sa'ib Nahhas, and Abdul Rahman al-'Attar.

11. *Al-Hayat*, March 21, 2002.

12. Some individuals in this category have officially left the political scene but remain intimately involved in political decision-making and processes of allocating economic surplus and resources. Prominent among such individuals is Muhammad al-

Khuly, former president Hafiz al-Asad's brother-in-law, and other members of the Asad family, particularly his own brothers and their offspring.

13. See BBC News, "Timeline: Syria."

14. It is reported that Maher al-Asad, Bashar's brother, who occupies increasingly important roles within the military, shot his brother-in-law, Asif Shawkat, during a dispute over how to proceed after Asad's death in June 2000. Although a well-known incident among most observers, this episode was never written about in the Syrian press. Author's interviews, July–August 2001, Damascus.

15. This occurs primarily in the automotive sales sector, where members of this stratum, usually the younger generation, are attempting to take over the car dealership businesses of a host of private sector actors. Often, they enter into temporary partnerships that end up buying out private partners, as with the Sang Yong dealership that was previously owned by MP Ma'moun al-Homsi. Not incidentally, al-Homsi was arrested on dubious charges after initiating a hunger strike on August 8, 2001, and charged with inciting sectarian strife. See *al-Hayat*, August 8 and 10, 2001, 1; and Haddad, "Business as Usual in Syria?"

16. Most prominently in this respect, the customs officers in charge of traffic across the Lebanese borders since 1976, as well as those in similar positions along the Syrian-Turkish borders in the early 1980s, have found themselves in positions that allow them to accumulate untold wealth—as well as free products—simply by accepting "gifts" as compensation for turning a blind eye to cross-border shipments. Indeed, some of the fiercest administrative struggles within the military concern the occupation of such posts at the end of the incumbents' terms. This applies to the high-level generals and usually their own officer crews who move around with them. Such wholesale team changes have made corruption at land borders far more efficient and far less likely to be cracked down on. To illustrate the point further, see Dalila, "'Ajz al-Muwaazanah al-'Aamah wa Subul Mu'aalajatuhu" [The general budget deficit and ways for its treatment], in which he outlines the "lost income" of the Syrian government, income that goes right back to Syrian officials and paraofficials (for example, relatives of the top regime leadership who wield power through such ties or through quasi-official appointments by their kin).

17. It is no surprise that generals like Ghazi Kan'an and Shafiq Fayyad have literally created islands of wealth and power as a result of Syria's involvement in Lebanon and of their commanding army and intelligence positions there. Such high-level generals do not, and cannot, operate by themselves. They are assisted by both horizontal and vertical networks that share an interest in promoting semilegal and illegal avenues of accumulating wealth and securing positions.

18. See Hinnebusch, *Authoritarian Power and State Formation in Ba'thist Syria*; and "Democratization in the Middle East."

19. This term refers to competition between two parties where one party is heavily supported by the state. The outcome of such "competition" is invariably favorable to the state.

20. The best-informed work on the economics of Syria's private commercial and industrial sectors in the 1980s so far is Perthes, "Syrian Private Industrial and Commercial Sectors and the State."

21. See Leca, "Democratization in the Arab World."

22. See Hinnebusch, "Globalization and Generational Change."

23. This can be contrasted with the conditional and performance-oriented privileges characteristic of state intervention in East Asia and, to a lesser extent, in some Arab states, including Tunisia.

24. For more details on the nature of investments by the private sector in the early 1990s, including the protection of private manufacturing firms, see Abdul Nour, "al-Qita' al-Khas fi Thill al-Himaya" [The private sector in the shadow of protection].

25. Clearly, there are no official statistics documenting such figures, but the dominance of the oil, telecom, and other strategic industries by what can be called the state bourgeoisie or state-affiliated individuals is public knowledge in Syria.

26. The case of Rami Makhlouf, a cousin of the president who is considered to be the wealthiest man in Syria, is common-speak in the country.

27. For the best-informed account and nuanced narrative of private sector growth during that period, consult Perthes, "Emergence and Transformation of a Statist Economy," Ch. 2 in *Political Economy of Syria Under Asad.*

28. See Polling, "What Future for the Private Sector?"

29. For the most part, the dramatic increase in private sector assets and in the economy as a whole in the early 1990s is credited to the consumption boom that was made possible by the official liberalization measures under Hafiz al-Asad's "Economic Pluralism" strategy, which allowed private businesses to enter hitherto restricted sectors.

30. Private sector investments increased by 62 percent between 1991 and 1994, amounting to over 60 percent of gross investment in both 1992 and 1993, with economic implications following suit in the commerce, agriculture, service, construction, and transportation sectors, but less so in the manufacturing sector. However, beginning in 1995, private investment in Syria began a steep descent. Whereas between 1992 and 1995, private investment averaged roughly 16 percent of GDP, average private sector investment dropped to just under 9 percent between 1996 and 2000. Private sector imports and exports also increased significantly after 1991: by 1992 the amount of imports doubled and continued to increase until 1996, and by 1994 exports had risen by 85 percent and continued to rise until 1995, when Syria's consumption bubble burst, causing a decline in investments necessary for export-oriented ventures. See Abdul Nour, "al-Qita' al-Khas fi Thill al-Himaya" [The private sector in the shadow of protection], 338.

31. It is also notable that the distribution of ownership between public and private sectors in Syria in general camouflages the fact that the Syrian state controls far more of the most strategic and high-value sectors of the economy, including oil and gas.

32. Critical economists in Syria advance the argument that the deterioration of the

public sector was not entirely an accident. The evidence put forth is not uncompelling: various public sector firms were losing business to emerging private firms or, in fact, to semilegal operations owned by powerful members of the state bourgeoisie who often worked in the same business domain. Examples abound, including the decline of public sector firms that manufacture cigarettes (for example, Gota) and refrigerators (for example, Barada), both replaced by privately procured versions of the same products.

33. Most external analysis predicts that Syrian oil reserves will be exhausted in the late 2020s or early 2030s. See, for instance, International Monetary Fund, "Syrian Arab Republic: Article IV Consultation—Staff Report 2005," 4. Also, the Syrian weekly *al-Iqtisadiyyah* reported in a December 2001 article ('Izz al-Din Juni, "Oil, the Lifeblood of Development and Industrialization in Syria: World Prices Substantially Influence Oil Exports," 27, 30) that oil rents, constituting more than 60 percent of Syria's foreign exchange and supporting most public sector investments, are likely to dry up, as the oil wells do, by 2010–15.

34. Interviews with former public sector workers who abandoned state employment for jobs in the private sector or abroad in the late 1970s and early 1980s, Damascus, 1998–2001. These former "employees" were radical Ba'thists in their youth in the early 1960s and were disillusioned when the regime cast the party aside before, during, and after the Corrective Movement took place in 1970. These individuals, including those from whom the quotes were derived, are to remain anonymous.

35. The twelve years after the Corrective Movement were largely consumed by war—1973 with Israel, 1976–82 with the Islamists, 1976 with various factions in Lebanon, 1982 with Israel—and thus internal social alliances were fluid and ad hoc. Social forces did not really begin to coalesce until the end of that period, when ironically, Syrian civil society was dealt a decisive blow. Interview with an economics professor working as editor of a Syria-based Palestinian publication sponsored by the public sector, Damascus, April 20, 1999. Also, see Hinnebusch, "State and Civil Society in Syria."

36. Others are either not known to "researchers" not doing fieldwork or are in places that are too sensitive for them to be a researcher's subject of discussion. See articles on Syria's private sector and business community in Kienle, *Contemporary Syria.*

37. Interviews with individual businessmen in the Chambers of Commerce who are beholden to regime officials through joint businesses started under Investment Law No. 10 of 1991. It is not that these businessmen are all equally beholden to the regime or their partners therein: some sincerely dislike their partners but appreciate prosperity far more—not to mention their reputations, which they must protect by paying lip service to private sector independence.

38. Ironically, or perhaps not, Tahsin al-Safadi (referred to by members of the old bourgeoisie as al-Haj Tahsin al-Safadi, a sign of respect derived from his social position and from his pilgrimage to Mecca) was a true representative of the private sector, on the authority of traders who did business at the time and whom I interviewed. Thus, the

Chambers were more representative in the 1970s, when they were virtually powerless, and nonrepresentative at the time of this writing or since 1989, when they played a more significant role in aggregating interests, albeit selectively. Interview with Nizar Qabbani, a notable textiles merchant in al-Hariqa (a business quarter adjacent to the traditional al-Hamidieh *suq*), Damascus, April 28, 1999.

39. Interview with Mahmoud Salameh, a former government bureaucrat who coordinated relations between the public industrial sector, the private sector, and labor. He was a driving force behind the public sector reform project al-Idara bil-ahdaf (goals-oriented management) initiated in 1998, which gave public sector managers in the textiles industry (on a trial basis) more decisional leverage and autonomy vis-à-vis Prime Ministry agencies that traditionally scrutinize and interfere with public sector firms. See Salameh, "al-Idara bil-ahdaf" [Goals-oriented management].

40. Business actors become threatening to authoritarian regimes when they are able to achieve collective action at the level of the entire private sector or when their increasing bargaining power allows them to guide economic policy-making—leaving state officials bereft of one major component in reproducing the state's power.

41. Although this is characteristic of most authoritarian regimes, certainly those in the Arab world, the Syrian regime's zero-sum perception of state-business relations produces more risk-averse approaches that are more harmful to the health of the economy.

42. The People's Council was largely ceremonial and ineffective at the time, deliberating on local and politically nonsensitive matters.

43. Interview with Nizar Qabbani, Damascus, April 28, 1999. Also see Batatu, "Syria's Muslim Brethren"; and *Syria's Peasantry, the Descendants of Its Lesser Rural Notables, and Their Politics*.

44. Interview with Nizar Qabbani, a trader in textiles in the traditionally conservative al-Hariq quarter, who belongs to a family of the old bourgeoisie; Damascus, April 28, 1999.

45. Interview with Manar Jallad, a textiles trader from the prominent al-Jallad family, with firm roots in the traditional bourgeoisie; Damascus, April 7, 1999.

46. Interview with Nabil al-Jajeh, industrialist and board member in the Damascus Chamber of Industry, Damascus, May 31, 1999.

47. Interview with Riad Saif, Damascus, June 8, 1999.

48. Interview with Rizqallah Hilan, Damascus, March 15, 1999.

49. Interview with Haitham Midani, vice president of the Damascus Chamber of Industry, Damascus, May 12, 1999.

50. Interviews with Arif Dalila and a former official at the Commercial Bank of Syria, Damascus, April 12, 1999.

51. Interview with Riad Saif, Damascus, June 8, 1999.

52. See Perthes, *Political Economy of Syria Under Asad*, 211.

53. Interviews with Ratib Shallah and Abdul Rahman al-'Attar, both of whom have

sat on Guidance Committee meetings (Shallah in his official capacity, al-'Attar as a delegate from the Chamber of Commerce in Damascus). The president of the Syrian Union of Chambers of Commerce, Shallah says that the meetings are "irregular" in frequency, giving credence to its reactionary role, especially since the early 1990s. According to Shallah, the power of the Guidance Committee grew after 1986, and continued to grow in the 1990s, but the failure of the peace process slowed it down, as it did other reforms; Damascus, May 9, 1999. Al-'Attar, a businessman considered to be one of the symbols of regime-business partnerships in the 1970s, states that the Guidance Committee had a role in developing the private sector but that the private sector's role remains consultative; Damascus, May 9, 1999.

54. In contrast to the account above, Perthes accords more weight to the general economic role of the Guidance Committee. Though this research reveals the more particularist dimensions of the Guidance Committee, it still recognizes a residual general role, but not to the extent that Perthes observes:

> [The Guidance Committee] is a place for private-sector interests and demands to be officially injected into the process of governmental policy formation, as well as a corporatist body where private-sector and union representatives can bargain for their demands with government, party, and each other.

It is notable that since the early to mid-1990s, when Perthes's statements were made, the hopes were far higher for this institution, even among skeptics in the private sector. Nevertheless, it is unclear how labor unions "bargained," what they bargained for, and what benefits they ever received from the Guidance Committee after 1985, when the unions' powers were severely undermined by new laws. However, since the mid-1990s, the Guidance Committee has been viewed in a far more negative light because of the absence of any significant change in the economy by way of reforms. In fact, the role of the institution altogether has been reduced in favor of the earlier, more personalistic methods of distributing rents, as seen in 2000 and 2001 in the case of cellular telephone deals and free-trade zone expansion schemes that were won by relatives of the regime's top echelons. See Perthes, *Political Economy of Syria Under Asad*, 210–11.

55. The expression "corridor policies" refers to deals made in private between officials and businessmen.

56. Interview with Khalid Abdul Nour, economist and academic adviser for the Aleppo Chamber of Industry, Aleppo, April 2, 1999.

57. This state of affairs continued until 2005, when it was addressed at the Ba'th's tenth Regional Command Conference along with a plethora of other economic issues. For a summary of this state of affairs in the 1990s, see the 1995 report on private sector manufacturing firms, which shows a vast disproportion in the distribution of private sector firms across the country, the provinces of Damascus and Aleppo getting the lion's share of 61 percent; see Central Bureau of Statistics, *Nata'ij Bahth al-Istiqsaa' al-Sina'I*

fi-l Qitaaʿ al-Khaas li-ʿAam 1995 [Statistical research results of private sector industry for the year 1995].

58. At the turn of the century, the Syrian Central Bureau of Statistics revealed a shrinkage of private sector firms. See *al-Hayat*, March 23, 2001. Compare with Abdul-Nour, "Dawr al-Ajhiza al-Hukumiyyah fi Thill Aaliyaat al-Suq" [The role of governmental agencies in the shadow of market mechanisms], 190.

59. *Al-Hayat*, March 23, 2001.

60. Throughout the course of the 1990s, the number of private sector firms increased 245 percent and the volume of domestic investments increased 492 percent; *al-Hayat*, March 23, 2001.

61. Interview with Riad Saif, Damascus, December 12, 1998.

Chapter 4

1. On economic or policy networks, or alternatively on distributional coalitions, see, for instance, Buck, "Networks of Governance and Privatization"; and Schamis, "Distributional Coalitions and the Politics of Economic Reform in Latin America."

2. See, for instance, Lorenz, "Neither Friends nor Strangers"; and Schmitter and Streeck, "Community, Market, State and Associations?"

3. For an introduction to network analysis, see Knoke and Kuklinski, "Network Analysis"; Dimaggio, "Nadel's Paradox Revisited"; and Emirbayer and Goodwin, "Network Analysis, Culture, and the Problem of Agency."

4. See Note 1 and other citations throughout this chapter. For one of the more focused books on the topic in reference to the Middle East, see Heydemann, *Networks of Privilege*; and Keshavarzian, *Bazaar and State in Iran*.

5. Signs of economic stagnation beginning in the mid-1990s include an overall drop in production; a rise in unemployment to unprecedented levels; the shrinking of foreign investments; a drop in real wages, purchasing power, and aggregate demand; the shutting of some enterprises established under Law No. 10; and finally, the stockpiling of goods in factories and at retail stores. See Central Bureau of Statistics, "National Accounts," in *Statistical Abstract 1998*. For more information on indicators regarding Syria's economic stagnation in the late 1990s, see Economist Intelligence Unit, *Syria: Country Profile 1998, 1999,* and *2000*.

6. To be sure, economic networks did not cause economic decline but did exacerbate inefficiency in an economy with declining productivity since the early 1980s, despite numeric growth in the late 1980s. For more on the causes of economic decline in the 1980s and 1990s and on the artificial growth in the late 1980s, see Haddad, "Political Dynamics of Economic Liberalization in Populist-Authoritarian Regimes."

7. Such networks exist in normal or nontransitional periods and usually do survive such periods. What is peculiar, though, is the fact that in transitional or reform periods, the conditions for rent-seeking—blurry or contradictory laws and regulations—

increase the power of discretion given to middle- and lower-range policy-makers and regulators while the domain of economic activity expands considerably; the proliferation of new and bigger contracts with foreign companies; the further weakening of institutions and agencies that monitor and adjudicate, because of their incapacity to keep pace with or track of rapid and nontransparent reregulation, or by virtue of their muting by the powers-that-be.

8. In 1989–90, Egypt's shadow economy was roughly 68 percent of GDP. Russia's shadow economy grew dramatically in the 1990s from 14.7 percent of GDP in 1989 to over 40 percent in 1995. See Schneider, "Dimensions of the Shadow Economy"; Schneider and Enste, *Shadow Economy*, 29–38; and Dreher and Schneider, "Corruption and the Shadow Economy."

9. See Henry and Springborg, "Bully Praetorian Republics"; Soliman, "Egypt's Political Economy"; and Ray Bush, "Economic Crisis and the Politics of Economic Reform in Egypt."

10. See Hinnebusch, "Democratization in the Middle East."

11. See Heydemann, *Authoritarianism in Syria*, 85.

12. See Marsh and Smith, "Understanding Policy Networks," 421.

13. See Batatu, *Syria's Peasantry, the Descendants of Its Lesser Rural Notables and Their Politics*, 208.

14. See Perthes, *Political Economy of Syria Under Asad*, 49–53.

15. For more on generic criteria regarding the reliability of network partners, see Dimaggio, "Nadel's Paradox Revisited."

16. This occurred in the 1970s through various election and selection processes that benefited individuals primarily from rural backgrounds, but increasingly from 'Alawi backgrounds as the decade drew to a close. In many ways, such rural, secular, and sectarian favoritism—always a means not an end in Syrian politics hitherto—had fueled the growing urban-Sunni, petite bourgeoisie dissatisfaction with the regime. For more information on the regional, socioeconomic, communal, and sectarian causes for the confrontation between the state and the Islamists between the late 1970s and 1982, see Hinnebusch, *Authoritarian Power and State Formation in Ba'thist Syria*, Ch. 9.

17. These factors include the relative insulation of Syria from external economic actors; the sectoral distribution and organization of the business community, which is not conducive to collective action; the structure of state revenue, which includes large sums of capital inflow from rent; the lack of administrative autonomy/coherence of state institutions; the socially narrow nature of the leadership; and finally, the balance of social forces that include an extremist opposition feared by both the regime and big business.

18. Networks, almost by definition, do not have a figurehead or leader of sorts. They are usually loose, though the degree of decentralization can differ from one context or sector to another.

19. Economist Intelligence Unit, "Syria Country Report," 1991–2009.

20. See Economist Intelligence Unit, *Syria: Country Profile 2000*. For investment figures, see Central Bureau of Statistics, *Statistical Abstract 2000*, "National Accounts."

21. See Heydemann, "Taxation Without Representation."

22. Omar Sanqar is one such individual—among countless others, who shall remain anonymous—who has connections with the old bourgeoisie. As the succession crisis intensified, they became more eager, temporarily, to distance themselves from the regime.

23. See Al-Bab, "Economic Reform in the Arab World." The president's cousin, Rami Makhlouf, is widely known to be the recipient of such favoritism—so much so that he is said to own or partly own one-quarter of the non-oil Syrian economy. See US Department of Treasury, "Rami Makhluf Designated for Benefiting from Syrian Corruption."

24. See Perthes, "Syria: Difficult Inheritance," 87; Haddad, "Business as Usual in Syria?"; and "Change and Stasis in Syria."

25. See Haddad, "Syria's Curious Dilemma."

26. See Hinnebusch, "Democratization in the Middle East," 161.

27. Details of causes for this détente are discussed in the preceding chapter.

28. For a detailed account of the policies that were carried out, see Perthes, "First Infitah," 50–53.

29. Interviews with economists Hussein al-Shari', Damascus, April 14, 1999; Arif Dalila, Damascus, April 5, 1999; and Khalid Abdul Nour, Aleppo, February 4, 1999.

30. Interview with a former official at the Commercial Bank of Syria, Damascus, March 8, 1999.

31. See Batatu's useful breakdown of the four tiers of power in Syria: "The Four Levels of Asad's Power Structure and Their Basic Characteristics," in *Syria's Peasantry, the Descendants of Its Lesser Rural Notables, and Their Politics*, 206–7.

32. See Perthes, *Political Economy of Syria Under Asad*, 31.

33. Interview with a former official at the Commercial Bank of Syria who attended meetings between public sector officials and Saudi investors and donors in both Saudi Arabia and Damascus in 1973–75; Damascus, March 8, 1999.

34. Interviews with a retired Syrian engineer, Hama, August 2001.

35. For instance, a sugar factory was established in the Deir al-Zor province, an area with extremely high temperatures, a factor that leads to reducing the sweetness of sugar. Cement factories and oil refineries were established in the coastal city of Banias and in Homs, respectively: these projects caused much pollution near tourist resorts and heavily populated areas (respectively). Nearby forests and olive trees were laid waste because of the petrochemicals and dust released into the air from these refineries and factories; interview with Hussein al-Shari', Damascus, April 14, 1999.

36. See Perthes, *Political Economy of Syria Under Asad*, 50–53.

37. Material drawn from various author's interviews with historians and economists, including Riz'allah Hilan, 'Arif Dalila, Sa'id Nabulsi, Khalid Abdul Nour, and others who shall remain anonymous. August 1998 to June 1999, Damascus.

38. The smuggling through the Turkish border began in 1980 against the backdrop of the military coup there and petered out in 1983. Smuggling over the Turkish border involved primarily Aleppan traffickers in the north, whereas smuggling through the Lebanese borders involved traffickers everywhere in Syria but primarily those based in metropolitan areas (Damascus, Aleppo, Latakia, Homs, Hama, Tartous, Banias, Raqa, Hasaka, Deir al-Zor). Interviews with Arif Dalila, Damascus, April 5, 1999; and Nasir Nasir, Damascus, April 20, 1999.

39. According to the French *L'Evenement*, which is perhaps the only non-Arabic publication that examined the Rif'at empire in detail, under the pretext of Syrian intervention, "Lebanon became the major element in various forms of trafficking. . . . [S]muggled products—including drugs and luxury cars—were transported toward Lebanese ports and the special markets of Damascus in convoys of military vehicles belonging to the 569th army division, and sometimes, even by chopper"; in *L'Evenement*, March 11–17, 1993 (translated from French, here and below).

40. According to the French *L'Evenement*, "He [Rif'at] is considered to be the richest man in Damascus (American sources evaluated his fortune at 100 million dollars; ten years later, the estimation would be multiplied by 10!). Members of his close guard, the mukhabarrat, are the ones who 'hold' the black market of smuggled cigarettes and cars." These depictions were echoed in Damascus for more than a dozen years before Rif'at was relieved of his duties by the president; in *L'Evenement*, March 11–17, 1993.

41. See Hinnebusch, *Authoritarian Power and State Formation in Ba'thist Syria*, Ch. 5, on the construction of a Leninist state.

42. See Hinnebusch, "Democratization in the Middle East," 158.

43. Independent Syrian intellectuals insist that the Ba'th of the mid-1970s still retained principled Ba'thist elements that lent whatever ideological and administrative unity the state exhibited at the time. The claim is put forth comparatively: throughout the late 1990s and beyond, most Syrians viewed the Ba'th as an empty shell ideologically, while administrative disunity was the order of the day even for lay observers.

44. See Batatu, *Syria's Peasantry, the Descendants of Its Lesser Rural Notables, and Their Politics*, 215; and interview with Arif Dalila, Damascus, April 5, 2001.

45. Interview with a Syrian intellectual, who will remain anonymous.

46. See the elaborate charts on the social composition of the Regional Command of the Ba'th party in Batatu, *Syria's Peasantry, the Descendants of Its Lesser Rural Notables, and Their Politics*, Appendix, 332–53.

47. According to the French *L'Evenement* (March 11–17, 1993),

the brother of the Syrian president exerted a predominant influence on the north of Bekaa where the defense forces of the 569th division were deployed, at the time placed under his command. They assured the control of the production zones and, with the help of the Christian militias, the transportation of drugs to the Lebanese ports of

Tripoli, Beirut, and Jounieh, where they were sent to their destination in Europe and the United States.

48. Mainly those stationed in Lebanon.

49. Interview with Arif Dalila, April 5, 1999.

50. Sons and relatives of the core elite were heavily involved in such networks and accumulated fortunes during this period.

51. Interview with Ghassan al-Qalla', Damascus, December 10, 1998. Also see Perthes, *Political Economy of Syria Under Asad,* 60.

52. Interview with textile industrialist and parliamentarian, Riad Saif, Damascus, December 12, 1998.

53. Interview with Ghassan al-Qalla', Damascus, December 10, 1998.

54. Interview with textile industrialist and parliamentarian Riad Saif, Damascus, December 12, 1998.

55. According to Syrian economists, including Arif Dalila and Nabil Samman, Law No. 10 allowed the rentiers to "whiten" their wealth (*tabyid al-tharawaat*).

56. See Robinson, "Elite Cohesion, Regime Succession and Political Instability in Syria"; and Gambill, "Syria After Lebanon."

57. For instance, it is widely reported that among numerous others, the following relationships obtained during the third period: business mogul Sa'ib Nahhas (auto and mixed sector agribusiness) and 'Izz al-Din Nasir, president of GFTU (General Federation of Trade Unions); Muhammad Hamsho (Buraq Itisallat, public telephones) and sons of former chief of staff Ali Aslan; Badi' Fallaha and Muhammad Naseef. The list goes on and is not always verifiable because of the informality of these partnerships, especially in the 1990s.

58. The characteristics and contours of the last era (2005 on) are discussed in Chapter 5 of this book.

59. See Williamson, "Calculativeness, Trust, and Economic Organization." In short, calculative trust refers to short-term, project-bound trust.

60. Mahmood al-Zo'bi (prime minister, 1987–2000) and Muhammad Mustapha Miro (prime minister, 2000–2003) were active members of such informal relations and played a significant role in furthering the interest of dozens of businessmen in the 1990s and early 2000s. Author's interviews with Syrian businessmen quoted throughout this book, with their specific identity withheld in this particular context; Damascus and Aleppo, 1998–2004.

61. Interviews with the former deputy prime minister for economic affairs Abdallah al-Dardari, Damascus, July 25, 2007; and with prominent and well-respected businessman Haytham Joud, Damascus, July 24, 2007.

62. The telecommunications sector is one prominent example, but Makhlouf's economic empire stretches well beyond that sector to include transportation, technology, and tourism. See US Department of Treasury, "Rami Makhluf Designated for

Benefiting from Syrian Corruption"; Gambill, "Dossier: Rami Makhlouf"; and Landis, "Rami Makhlouf Stiffs Mercedes." Also see Wright, "Sanctions on Businessman Target Syria's Inner Sanctum"; and *Wall Street Journal*, "Syrian Tycoon Bristles at US Sanctions Against Him," March 26, 2008.

63. Interview with al-'Attar, Damascus, May 9, 1999.

64. This conceptualization captures the common denominator among various schools of thought on the emergence of institutions. The difference rests on the actual purpose. More pertinent to this study is the sociopolitical factor that motivated the concerned elites. That does not mean that transaction costs were not considered, as the new institutional economists would claim. Simply, transaction costs are determined on the basis of a more sociological and historical calculation that involves a number of social, economic, and political factors. These factors have been the subject of preceding chapters. Thus, an eclectic approach that combines historical, sociological, and rational choice institutionalism serves this study best. As will be made more apparent later, the task is to discern when the logic of consequences dominates behavior (the basis of rational choice new institutionalism) and when the logic of appropriateness dominates behavior (the basis of historical and sociological new institutionalism). See Ostrom, "Rational Choice Theory and Institutional Analysis"; and Hall and Taylor, "Political Science and the Three Institutionalisms." For transaction cost institutionalism, see North, *Institutions, Institutional Change and Economic Performance*.

65. Actual economic reforms, which began in 1986, preceded their officially proclaimed variety in Syria. Economic reform as an official policy—defined by a minimal acknowledgment by the government of the need to liberalize the economic system—was not pronounced until 1991, when the government rejuvenated what came to be known as "economic pluralism" (*al-ta'addudiyya al-iqtisadiyya*). This term, used extensively in official statements by Hafiz al-Asad upon his assumption of power in 1970, refers primarily to the actualization of the complementary formula that brings together the public, private, and mixed sectors in the service of the "national economy" (*al-iqtisad al-watani*).

66. A more detailed discussion of private sector institutions and their role is presented in Chapter 3.

67. Here is an abridged list of businessmen who served on the board of prominent Chambers in Damascus and Aleppo in the late 1990s. Note that this is a cross section of Chambers' members, not a list of privileged state-business networks. *Damascus Chamber of Commerce*: Burhan al-Deen al-Ashqar, Basheer al-Bardan, Muhammad al-Khattab, 'Arfan Darkal, Muhammad Yihya Darweesh, Hussain al-Zo'bi, Sami' 'Abbas, Muhammad 'Isam Qashlan, Haneen Namr, Basheer Hazza'. *Aleppo Chamber of Commerce*: Muhammad Saleh al-Mallah, Mustafa al-Shaikh Ahmad, Hasan Zaido, Muhammad Mansour, Basheer al-Naser, Qarahbit Jamjian, Fawzi Mustafa, Muhammad Adeeb Badenjki, George Halouji, Malik Rahmoun, Nadir 'Ajam, Muhammad Mahrouseh, 'Ad-

nan Mousa Agha, Muhammad Majd al-Deen Dabbagh, Rasheed Kayyali, Ahmad Suhad Jabbara, Mahmoud 'Uday, Ahmad Thurayya Ka'dan, Khaldoun Azraq. *Damascus Chamber of Industry*: Yihya al-Hindi, Zaid al-Hariri, Hassan al-Nouri, 'Adel Hasanain, Sayyah Abu Sha'r, Muhammad Ratib Saif, Ibrahim al-Nahhas, Jamal al-Deen Qinbriyyeh, Muhammad Nabil al-Jajeh, Omar al-Sairawan, Hussain al-Zo'bi, Ali Kamel Sulayman, 'Issa Daoud, Bassam al-Masri. The external connections and relationships of some of these individuals will remain undisclosed, as they were interviewed by the author and shared information—about themselves and one another—in confidence.

68. Labor representatives have since 1985 become little more than mouthpieces for the government. Interview with Dr. Nabil Marzouq, an academic consultant at the GFTU, Damascus, April 21, 1999.

69. This view is very much shared across the board among Syrian businessmen. Few, however, are willing to go on record with such depictions. Ihsan Sanqar has said as much in his parliamentary commentaries and proposals. Interview with Ihsan Sanqar, Damascus, December 29, 1998.

70. Business members from the Chambers of Commerce and Industry who are "not in favor," or are outside the crony networks, do occasionally attend and make requests, but such requests are limited and usually insignificant. When I asked a prominent member in an Aleppo Chamber, who had sat in some of the meetings, about the progress of the Guidance Committee's role since 1991, he replied, "Yes, a year ago 'we' permitted the export of donkeys to Kuwait." Interview, Aleppo, March 4, 1999.

71. Mahmoud al-Zo'bi was accused of corruption and later committed suicide, in the spring of 2000. See the weekly *al-Wasat* no. 437, June 12–18, 2000, 12.

72. Salim Yassin was also found to be involved in corruption and has been under house arrest since the end of the spring of 2000. See ibid.

73. Various informal interviews with former officials at the Industrial Bank and the Commercial Bank of Syria validate this commonly known fact; Damascus, March–April 1999. Although such partnerships are not always formal, that is, the names of officials do not always appear on contracts, their involvement in running businesses and securing accounts and foreign exchange is evident to bank personalities and to other business partners who know well who is behind various exemptions and protected products.

74. As noted in the source cited in Note 70, both men were placed under house arrest when their economic ventures began to collide with political interests of the top rung of elites in early 2000. Contrary to official rhetoric, their arrest had much more to do with the then-impending succession crisis.

75. Interview with Ihsan Sanqar, Damascus, December 29, 1998.

76. Parliament member and prominent industrialist Riad Saif is a prime example of such personalities.

77. Usually independent businessmen can accumulate only so much capital before they become subject to harassment or attempts at co-optation.

78. Interview with Nabil Sukkar, Damascus, August 11, 2009.

79. One prominent independent businessman notes the following when asked about new opportunities presented by new regulations in 1999: "I would not exploit such opportunities. I may accumulate financial capital on a deal or two, but I may lose respect among my peers"; interview with Ihsan Sanqar, Damascus, April 13, 1999.

80. Interview with Riad Saif, former board member at the Damascus Chamber of Industry and a two-term member of parliament since 1991. At the time of this writing, Saif had been sentenced to five years in prison because of his civil society activism and outspoken criticism of government policies (see *al-Hayat*, April 5, 2002); interview, Damascus, December 22, 1998.

81. See Kramer, "Trust and Distrust in Organizations."

82. See Farrell and Knight, "Trust, Institutions, and Institutional Evolution."

83. See Schneider and Maxfield, "Business, the State, and Economic Performance in Developing Countries," 7. The authors provide a review and a commentary about various arguments and theories on state-business relations. Furthermore, chapter 2, on theories of state-business relations, and Peter Evans's chapter (Evans, "State Structures, Government-Business Relations, and Economic Transformation") provide a theoretical framework that potentially guides research on the subject. Also, for a nuanced version of business-state relations, see Kim, "State and Business in the Developmental Process."

84. See Perthes, *Political Economy of Syria Under Adad*, Ch. 5, 203.

85. See Central Bureau of Statistics, "National Accounts," in *Statistical Abstract 1998*.

86. See Schneider and Maxfield, *Business and the State in Developing Countries*, 13.

87. Ibid., 12–15. For a detailed account regarding the effect of trust on cooperation, see Gambetta, *Trust*.

88. Williamson, "Calculativeness, Trust, and Economic Organization."

89. Intranetwork trust in Syria is a case in point. The same applies to similarly constituted networks in Egypt. See Sfakianakis, "Whales of the Nile."

90. As discussed elsewhere in this book, Investment Law No. 10 can be considered a "political" move that was intended to keep Syria apace with global changes in 1991. According to Ihsan Sanqar, "[Investment] Law #10 is political, designed to give the appearance that Syria is riding the global economic wave. It is not an economic law, neither is it rational"; interview, Damascus, December 29, 1998. But as will be discussed in the next chapter, Law No. 10 has a social basis: network members were pushing for the formalization of tax-exempted private sector ventures.

Chapter 5

1. Riad Saif, Syrian industrialist, parliament member, and board member in the Damascus Chamber of Industry, Goethe Institute Lecture Series, Damascus, April 4, 1999.

2. The contrast referred to here is not a result of expected causal connections between economic liberalization and structural economic reform. Rather, given the stark-

ness of the contrast, it points to a deviant case of liberalization without any structural reform, when viewed comparatively. Ostensibly comparable cases such as Egypt and Jordan have undergone economic liberalization followed by some form of limited structural economic reform (for example, banking, judiciary, labor-capital relations, market mechanisms). See Harrigan and El-Said, "Economic Liberalisation, Social Capital and Islamic Welfare Provision"; Saif and Shoucair, "Status-Quo Camouflaged."

3. "Economic pluralism" figured prominently in President Hafiz al-Asad's inauguration address in 1991 and served thereafter as a catalyst and shield for burgeoning private sector interests. It refers to a national economic development strategy affirming the complementary roles of the public, private, and mixed sectors.

4. For instance, either structural economic changes have not occurred (for example, vis-à-vis state-owned banks), or liberalization measures (for example, trade and investment liberalization, currency devaluation) have not been institutionalized. All the while, the existing legal framework, informed as it is by a central command economy, remains untouched. Additional laws and regulations after 1986 exacerbated contradictions.

5. "Liberalization" is associated with selective loosening of economic controls (including stabilization measures) and partial official state retreat from the economic sphere, while "reform" refers to levels of actual restructuring of economic institutions (for example, institutional mechanisms) and relations (such as law, labor/capital). The word *reform*, or *islaah*, does not appear anywhere in the official and most of the unofficial discourse in Syria. The reason is obvious for the regime: there is nothing essentially wrong with the way the Syrian economy works, and therefore *islaah* (to reform, to make sound, to fix) is unnecessary. Hence, we see the emphasis on "economic pluralism" (*al-ta'addudiyyah al-iqtisaadiyya*) in the official rhetoric after 1991.

6. For instance, that which explains the adoption of particular liberalization strategies may not always explain developmental outcomes. Particular liberalization/reform patterns and strategies are primarily a product of systemic and structural causes, whereas particular developmental outcomes vary more readily, and within short periods of time, with particular institutional arrangements and strategic factors. Ultimately, for explanatory purposes, the point is to avoid mixing levels of analysis (that is, systemic/structural, institutional, strategic).

7. See especially the work of Volker Perthes, Steven Heydemann, and Raymond Hinnebusch: Perthes, *Political Economy of Syria Under Asad*; "Look at Syria's Upper Class"; "Syrian Economy in the 1980's"; "Private Sector, Economic Liberalization and the Prospects of Democratization"; "Stages of Economic and Political Liberalization in Syria"; "Syria's Parliamentary Elections"; Heydemann, "Political Logic of Economic Rationality"; "Taxation Without Representation"; Hinnebusch, "State Formation in a Fragmented Society"; *Authoritarian Power and State Formation in Ba'thist Syria*; "State and Civil Society in Syria"; "Political Economy of Economic Liberalization in Syria."

8. After 1997, and throughout the first year of Bashar al-Asad's presidency, a selec-

tively tolerant atmosphere of openness about social and economic issues engendered broader and freer public discussion. This openness was buttressed by an anticorruption drive led by Bashar, prior to succeeding his father. A solid indicator is the yearly lecture series on economic issues organized by *al-Jam'iyyah al-Iqtisaadiyyah* (Economic Sciences Association—ESA), between February and May. Officially a nongovernmental organization, the ESA's yearly lecture series represents a microcosm of the debates that occur privately, both in the official and private realms. According to the ESA's secretary, the 1999 series attracted hundreds of lay persons, academics, businesspeople, and state officials, including the president of the Syrian Union of Chambers of Commerce and Industry. In February 2000 the same lecture series was attended by Bashar, who sat among the hundreds of citizens crowding the gigantic conference room in Damascus's Arab Cultural Center in Mezzeh. At the close of the first decade of the twenty-first century, the ESA and its publications continue to provide relatively critical studies on Syria's social and economic affairs.

9. An indicative manifestation of the opening in the media occurring at that time was a series of articles published in *al-Hayat* in May and June 1999, presenting contending views by academics, businesspeople, and government officials about Syria's economic stagnation, corruption, and political future. Spurred by two seminal investigative reports conducted by *al-Hayat*'s editor, Joseph Samaha, and reported on May 14–15, these articles represent a window on the latency of Syria's sociopolitical plurality, where business leaders and critics have begun calling for the establishment of representative parties outside the National Front. It is significant that while the regular censorship authorities initially prevented these articles from entering Syria, on higher orders the papers were sold everywhere on Syrian soil by May 17—hence, the deliberate nature of spurring debate, albeit a controlled debate. The dynamics behind allowing the dissemination of such information were seen as a manifestation of the split among the ruling elite on the issue of succession.

10. Most sources quoted herein emphasized the growth of the private sector in the early 1990s as a sign of sorts. However, it is no wonder that Perthes is more skeptical about the import of such figures, for his field research has been generally more exhaustive.

11. Central Bureau of Statistics, "National Accounts," in *Statistical Abstract 2007* (for years 1963–1998); International Monetary Fund, "Syrian Arab Republic: Statistical Appendix"; and International Monetary Fund, "2009 Article IV Consultation Report" (for years 1999–2009).

12. Central Bureau of Statistics, "National Accounts," in *Statistical Abstract 2007*.

13. For a comprehensive review of the development of the Syrian economy during this period, see al-Humush, *al-Iqtisaad al-Suri 'Ala Masharif al-Qarn al-Hadi wal-'Ishrin* [Syrian economy at the turn of the twenty-first century].

14. For a detailed examination of the crisis of 1986 and the regime's response, see Sukkar, "Crisis of 1986 and Syria's Plan for Reform."

15. It is unclear exactly how much foreign exchange reserves the country possessed at the time. However, the estimates fluctuate between an incredible $10 million to $400 million. Nabil Sukkar, a Syrian economist who had privileged access to official statistics at the time, set the figure at $357 million. See Sukkar, "Crisis of 1986 and Syria's Plan for Reform," 28.

16. Ibid., 32–36.

17. One way to understand the decline of authority of the five-year plans, as well as the Regional Command Conferences, is to contrast the content of successive five-year plans before 2005 and the resolutions of the eighth conference with the actual measures the government adopted in response to the 1986 crisis. While the Regional Command Conference and the five-year plan focused on the importance of the public sector's control and monopoly over imports and agricultural inputs, respectively, the adopted measures expanded the role of the private sector in foreign trade and industry and allowed it to encroach on the import and distribution monopoly of the public sector in various economic spheres. See the reports of the eighth Regional Command Conference (*Taqaarir wa Muqarraraat al-Mu'tamar al Qutri al-Thamin*) (Damascus, 1985) as compared with the actual measures described by Sukkar, "Crisis of 1986 and Syria's Plan for Reform," 32–36.

18. For further discussion of the 2005 Regional Command Conference, see Haddad, "Syria's Curious Dilemma."

19. See Sukkar's delineation of various suggested reform programs, both by more liberal economists, such as himself, and by the General Federation of the Workers' Syndicates (or Trade Unions), in "Crisis of 1986 and Syria's Plan for Reform," 28–30.

20. See Central Bureau of Statistics, "National Accounts," in *Statistical Abstract 1998*, 516–17, 523.

21. See, for instance, Lawson, "Private Capital and the State in Contemporary Syria."

22. It is important to factor in the effect of the consumer boom after Investment Law No. 10 allowed for the importation of various previously unavailable products. High rates of economic growth between 1991 and 1994 reflected this consumption drive, until wages declined relative to prices and soaring inflation took hold after 1994.

23. Signs of the stagnation that set in at the end of the 1990s were: an overall drop in production; a rise of unemployment to unprecedented levels; the shrinking of foreign investments; the drop in real wages, purchasing power, and aggregate demand; the shutting of some enterprises established under Law No. 10; and finally, the stockpiling of goods in factories and at retail stores. See Central Bureau of Statistics, "National Accounts," in *Statistical Abstract 1998*.

24. As discussed in Chapter 1, Syria's liberalization experience has been a regime affair that has not been determined or guided from abroad. This makes Syria, in the words of Perthes, a "laboratory case of sorts" because of the relative absence of external interference. See Perthes, *Political Economy of Syria Under Asad*, 203.

25. See Perthes, *Political Economy of Syria Under Asad*, 54.

26. Ibid., 55–56.

27. However, most of the large-scale joint-stock companies established under Decree No. 10 failed to promote exports and turned into "packaging" companies for agricultural products that flourished as a result of the government's doubling and tripling of prices for certain basic crops, encouraging farmers to produce incessantly. The three most significant such companies are owned by well-known businessmen, who by 1986 had begun to diversify their business ventures. In the mid- to late 1990s, the ten largest companies established under this law were irreversibly failing, not least because of their neglect of long-term production schemes.

28. By 1988, the list became quite considerable, and henceforth the Ministry of Industry and the Chambers of Industry began to publish, if inconsistently, special pamphlets delineating liberalized industrial sectors for manufactured goods.

29. See report and figures on Investment Law No. 10 in this chapter.

30. See World Bank, "Syrian Investment Climate Assessment," 48.

31. See Marshall, "Syria and the Financial Crisis."

32. See Oxford Analytica, "Syria: Unreformed Economy Suits Regime Stability," November 24, 2006; World Bank, "Syrian Investment Climate Assessment"; United Nations Development Programme, "First National Competitiveness Report of the Syrian Economy"; and so on.

33. See United Nations Development Programme, "First National Competitiveness Report of the Syrian Economy."

34. Most Syrian economists concur that "the most important reform decisions have been taken by the [Guidance] Committee"; see al-Humush, *al-Iqtisaad al-Suri 'Ala Masharif al-Qarn al-Hadi wal-'Ishrin* [The Syrian economy at the turn of the twenty-first century], 194.

35. See Perthes, *Political Economy of Syria Under Asad*, 54.

36. See Galdo, "Policies for Business in the Mediterranean Countries," 15.

37. See Syrian Investment Agency, "Important Points in Legislative Degree 8 / Investment Promotion."

38. According to Syrian businessmen working in the textiles trade (especially those discussed in Chapter 3), *hurriyyat al-tijara* (free trade) is another term for *tafseel*, that is, tailoring (of policies). When asked about the benefit to others who may want to take advantage of such measures, businesspeople point to the structure of internal trade and to those who dominate certain subsectors, such as Sabbagh and Sharabati, who had a monopoly over the jean thread in Aleppo. Usually, tailored policies are accompanied by natural or "protected" monopolies (protected by partners in the regime) over distribution. This leaves a small margin for competition, and thus the average consumer ends up paying the difference between the international market value and the local price. Free trade policies have therefore contributed to an upward redistribution of wealth. Vari-

ous interviews with businessmen working in the textiles trade, Damascus and Aleppo, September 1998 to June 1999.

39. See World Bank, "Syrian Investment Climate Assessment," 48.

40. This law was modified in 2001 by Legislative Decree No. 7 of 2000, but according to Syrian economists and businessmen alike, Decree No. 7 is too little, too late. See al-Raddawi, *al-Siyasaat al-Muhaffitha lil-Istithmaar fi Suriyya* [Policies that provide incentives for investment in Syria]. Compare the criticism (of Law No. 10 and its revision) leveled by al-Raddawi to the praise by Muhammad Saraqbi, the president of the Higher Council of Investment, presented at the same conference and under the same title.

41. See accompanying information on Investment Law No. 10 in Table 5.1.

42. Although enterprises established under Law No. 10 are exempt from Law No. 24, which prohibits dealing with foreign currency, investors remain vulnerable since they must procure more foreign exchange than the law permits (within the context of exemption) to run their businesses.

43. Interview with Hussein al-Shari', Damascus, April 14, 1999.

44. Interview with Riad Saif, December 12, 1999.

45. For a sectoral example of this kind of essentially nonproductive investment, see Hopfinger and Khadour, "Development of the Transportation Sector in Syria and the Actual Investment Policy." Also see Hopfinger and Khadour, "Investment Policies in Syria."

46. See Abdul Nour, "Ta'hil al-Qita' al-Sina'i" [Improving the industrial sector].

47. These individuals come from well-known families such as Nahhas, Sharabati, Makhlouf, Khaddam, Tlas, Shaleesh, 'Aqqad, Da'bul, Nasir, and 'Attar.

48. Interview with Ihsan Sanqar, Damascus, December 29, 1998.

49. This is a frequent source of debate between independent businessmen and "connected" businessmen. Interview with Manar Jallad, Damascus, April 7, 1999.

50. See Saif, "Cellular Telephone Contracts," a controversial paper presented by MP Riad Saif to the Syrian parliament on August 14, 2001. The paper exposes the scandal of the cellular telephone contracts between the government and individuals affiliated with the state but acting as private businessmen.

51. Of importance here is the near absence of official investment avenues for small and medium capital. Since the 1980s, but more conspicuously in the "liberalization" years of the early 1990s, this dearth led to a series of investment scandals known as the phenomenon of *jami'i al-amwaal* (literally, "money collectors/accumulators"), which was halted by Decree No. 8 in 1994. Essentially, these were informal investment avenues arranged by private individuals who rounded up more than 25 billion Syrian pounds only to flee the country, disappear, or default on returns or reimbursements to helpless investors, in most instances. High-ranking bureaucrats and academics make strong connections between this phenomenon and the liquidity crisis in the period after 1994–95. Interview, Damascus, June 1, 1999.

52. The list is long and complex (not all members of a given family are necessar-

ily involved) and includes these families: Kan'aan, Khalil, al-Tajir, Naseef, Suleiman, Huari, Hassan, Khawli, Fayyad, Tlas, Aslan, Abdul Nabi, Fayyad, Habib, al-Safi, Shihabi, Makhlouf, As'ad, Khaddam, Zu'bi, Akhtarini, Shaleesh, Zayyoud, Isma'il, Haidar, Nasir, Qaddoura.

53. See Perthes, "Syrian Private Industrial and Commercial Sectors and the State," 222.

54. See Dalila, "'Ajz al-Muwaazanah al-'Aamah wa Subul Mu'aalajatuhu" [The general budget deficit and ways for its treatment]. The paper was informally distributed, but not delivered.

55. Although such operations do not always involve large sums of capital, they do emanate from the same networks that secure other larger operations. More important, the power to press for such decisions—that is, reducing the quality of subsidized food—reveals deep-rooted connections to powerful decision-makers and their own networks. Carrying out such decisions could not possibly be limited to a small number of individuals. See Dalila, "General Budget Deficit and Ways for Its Treatment."

56. See al-Humush, *Syrian Economy at the Turn of the Twenty-First Century*, 18.

57. See Perthes, *Political Economy of Syria Under Asad*, 60.

58. See Dalila, "General Budget Deficit and Ways for Its Treatment."

59. This occurs in Syria for several reasons having to do with existing foreign exchange policies (which prevent a liberalized currency exchange and impose government-set exchange rates) and investment laws (which impose a particular balance of trade policy that aims at achieving parity between exports and imports within each private firm). Under Syria's relatively recent Investment Law No. 10, for instance, producers can only import products at a value equivalent to that which is exported. This gives producers an incentive to exaggerate exports so as to be allowed to import more products or factors of production. This explains the thriving black market foreign exchange industry, in which individuals sell their foreign exchange earned from exports (investors are allowed to keep 75% of their foreign exchange profits and have to exchange the remaining 25% at the government's rate of 46 Syrian pounds to the dollar). Generally, investors in the transport sector earning foreign exchange from shipping or transporting export goods are the ones who sell hard currency to importers. Exchange rates vary from the neighboring country rate of $50 to $55 or more, depending on such supply. Interview with Muhammad Ghassan al-Qalla', Damascus, December 10, 1998.

60. See Central Bureau of Statistics, "National Accounts," in *Statistical Abstract 1998*. These figures are repeated by disgruntled economists and former senior officers at the Commercial Bank of Syria whose positions were not served by the "under the table transactions." Author's interview, Damascus, March 8, 1999.

61. Whereas many Syrians and Syria observers point to corruption as being the principal culprit, I posit that we must seek answers elsewhere, in the constraints imposed on political actors by particular institutional legacies (which in the Syrian case are, in part, of these actors' own making).

62. In 2005 the notion of a Social Market Economy began, officially, to dilute the socialist pretense of the Syrian economy.

63. For a detailed study of the Syrian regime's populist legacy, see Heydemann, *Authoritarianism in Syria*; and Hinnebusch, *Authoritarian Power and State Formation in Ba'thist Syria*.

64. Such reasons include: the regime's narrowing social base, which has limited its maneuvering capacity, especially since the late 1970s; age-old Ba'thist suspicion of the traditional business community despite rapprochement by the state during the Asad era; the latent threat of a "radical" Islamist opposition, despite its seeming torpidity and disarray; and finally, the regime's hesitancy to irreversibly dilute its populist and distributive basis of legitimacy.

65. These networks include the regime elite drawn from the Ba'th party, the army, security services, top government officials, public sector managers, particular labor union leaders, and initially, dependent private sector individuals who rose to prominence through the surge of public sector investments after the 1973 oil boom and Arab aid. Private sector individuals who do not occupy a "political" position within the regime are considered junior partners within these networks, especially before 1994.

66. More specifically, the winners are the appointed and senior officials, the state bourgeoisie and their vertical clients, as well as the upper new bourgeoisie, especially its rentierist segment, and peasants working in subsidized crops (wheat, cereals, cotton). The losers are the petite bourgeoisie, salaried public sector workers, job seekers, and the less connected business sectors (medium-sized manufacturing firms relying on local primary resources).

67. Barriers to subsidized investment remained high as the minimum amount required under the new Investment Law No. 10 was ten million Syrian pounds. Another clear indication of circumscribing reform were domains within particular sectors that were decided in the licensing process by the Higher Council of Investments. Investors did not need to heed the letter of the law; they needed to find partners in officialdom and beyond who were willing to "go into business" with them by protecting them politically from other instruments of control, for example, subsequent licensing for various business transactions and protection against Law No. 24, which prohibits dealing in foreign currency.

68. See Sukkar, "Crisis of 1986 and Syria's Plan for Reform," 35–36. The maximum level of taxation dropped from 92 to 60 percent. See also al-'Imadi, "Economic and Investment Policies of Syria," 59. In 2003 a new tax law was passed that lowered the highest tax rates even further, to 35 percent. See Sadhna Shanker, "Syria's Reforms: An Overview," *Syria Comment*, November 24, 2004.

69. A notable example is the opposition in 1995 by three major business tycoons to the creation of a stock market for agricultural products. These tycoons ran the joint-sector agricultural establishments and were able to freely set the prices of such stocks at

a level higher than their market value. Interview with a former high-ranking official at the Commercial Bank of Syria, December 1998.

70. Interview with Khalid Abdul Nour, Aleppo, April 2, 1999.

71. See Haddad, "Change and Stasis in Syria."

72. Business leaders and critics have begun calling for the establishment of representative parties outside the National Front. See special report cited earlier by *al-Hayat*, May 14–15, 1999.

73. Although there was a degree of fanfare in the domestic and some foreign press about the intentions with which this government was formed—that is, "modernizing" Syria's economy—the ministries that have not changed hands tell another story. Most conspicuously with regard to the economy, the minister of finance and the minister of the economy and foreign trade, al-Mahayni and al-Imadi, respectively, retained their positions. Al-Mahayni's macroeconomic and fiscal financial policies have been largely responsible for Syria's macroeconomic problems, according to most local economists. He is seen as a catalyst for diverting resources from the public treasury to the corrupt and rent-seeking top rungs in the private sectors at the expense of collective beneficiaries through various selectively implemented taxation policies and measures.

74. Independent businessmen, especially in the industrial sector, affirm that it is the regime's strategy to keep the private sector, as a whole, from being able to do business in the open, or as the phrase goes, "under the sun." It must be "continuously cut down to size and dwarfed . . . forced to operate in a situation of collective violation and chaos so it can be uprooted at any given moment." Interview, June 8, 1999.

75. Interview by author with a resident advisor at the General Federation of Trade Unions, Damascus, April 20, 1999.

76. The more direct—but less readily ascertainable in official statistics—illustration of networks' influence on economic and fiscal decisions, if not policies, is the lending pattern of the Central Bank of Syria and its sectoral branches. See the following chapter for details on the networks' impact on fiscal policy change.

77. United Nations Development Programme, "First National Competitiveness Report of the Syrian Economy," 89.

78. Wages were raised again in 2008. See Kabbani, "Why Young Syrians Prefer Public Sector Jobs."

79. Public domestic investment declined from 105,215 million Syrian pounds (SP) in 1985 to 45,623 million SP in 1993, while private domestic investment rose from 53,337 million SP to 83,233 million SP during the same period. See Central Bureau of Statistics, "National Accounts," in *Statistical Abstract 1998*. Specifically, see 517, section "Expenditures on the Gross Domestic Product."

80. See block quote from Riad Saif in the introduction to this chapter.

81. See Sami Moubayed, "Syria Heralds Entrance of a Freer Press: Assad Authorizes New Media Law," *Daily Star*, September 24, 2001.

82. The pages of the economic weekly *al-Iqtisaadiyya*, for instance, were replete with stories and scandals involving formerly untouchable individuals. Launched on June 24, 2001, *al-Iqtisaadiyya* seeks to educate the Syrian reader as to how the Syrian economy really works; interview with the editor in chief, Waddah Abid-Rabbo, Damascus, August 2001.

83. Investment Law No. 10 of 1991 was the last major symbol of economic liberalization under Hafiz al-Asad, and it was not even modified and supplemented as required, and promised, until 2000 (by Legislative Decree No. 7).

84. A stark difference between projected yearly budgets and the government's actual balance of payments throughout the 1990s has led to a deteriorating state of economic affairs. Every year, the Ministry of Finance announces budget surpluses drawn from a 30 percent increase in tax collection over projected figures. What it fails to note, however, is that while government spending on public investment is being slashed by 25–40 percent, current spending on personal luxury commodities exceeds projected figures. See Dalila, "General Budget Deficit and Ways for Its Treatment."

85. Unpublished report obtained by the author from the Ministry of Industry. For similar figures on the grim state of the labor market in Syria, see Nabulsi, "Tasheeh al-Khalal fi Suq al-'Amaalah" [Correcting the problems of the labor market].

86. For instance, Investment Law No. 10 conflicts with Decree No. 24, which prohibits dealing in hard currency. This is one of the major obstacles that independent businesspeople vehemently complain about. Recently, however, a ministerial, and later a parliamentary, committee were set up to "study" the possibility of legal reforms to facilitate investment. See *al-Hayat*, July 21, 1999.

87. Central Bank of Syria, quarterly bulletins.

88. Economist Intelligence Unit, "Syria Country Report," 1998–2001.

89. According to unpublished government statistics on Syrian living standards in 1997–98, 90 percent of an average working individual's wage was required to cover 30 percent of basic living expenses; interview with a high-level official at the Ministry of Industry, Damascus, June 1, 1999. Comparatively, in 1985 just over 60 percent of the average wage covered most basic expenses.

90. See Perthes, "Syrian Private Industrial and Commercial Sectors and the State."

91. See Arab Socialist Ba'th Party, "Al-taqrir al-iqtisadi" [Economic report], 122.

92. Syria does not publish official unemployment statistics in its yearly *Statistical Abstract*, but outspoken economists estimated the levels of unemployment at 20–25 percent in June 1999, not including disguised employment and underemployment. These figures are based on official statistics on the distribution of the actual labor force relative to the growing population and returning migrant workers. For more information, see Nabulsi, "Correcting the Problems of the Labor Market." A report uncharacteristically commissioned by the government in 2001 revealed that unemployment is well over 20 percent; see *al-Hayat*, June 18, 2001.

93. Various formal and informal interviews with popular and independent businesspeople, outspoken members of parliament, and middle-level party functionaries, who were taken aback by the magnitude of the protest; Damascus, 1999–2007.

94. Once the factors of rising prices and exchange rate fluctuations are accounted for, the effect of the last wage increase for public sector workers in 1994 becomes, at best, annulled.

95. See al-Nayyal, Ali, and Oghali, "Al-Qita' Ghair al-Munadham" [The informal sector], 3, 7 (quoted from original paper).

96. Ibid.; see Table 4.2 in the original article.

97. See al-Nayyal, Ali, and Oghali, "Informal Sector."

98. Ibid., 7.

99. Ibid., 8. It is also significant that this sector attracts most female laborers entering the market.

100. Ibid., 14–15.

101. See Rana Isma'il, "Syria: Average Gross Domestic Product Growth Rate Has Not Reached 1% in 2000," al-Hayat, February 15, 2001.

102. See Central Bureau of Statistics, "National Accounts," in Statistical Abstract 1998, 526–27.

103. This diminishing institutional capacity has been widely acknowledged, even in the president's inaugural address: "Developing the state's agencies and institutions has become a persistent necessity and a national responsibility so that the gap between the others and us does not expand, and so that we can be efficient partners in various political and economic developments in the Arab nation and the world." President Hafiz al-Asad, inaugural address, March 13, 1999. The speech was distributed, not delivered, in the Syrian parliament.

104. For a penetrating examination of the bureaucratic incoherence and some of its outright contradictory objectives, see Abdul-Nour, "Role of Governmental Agencies in the Shadow of Market Mechanisms."

105. "Extrapolitical" here refers to problematic outcomes, usually of the unintended variety, that cannot be resolved politically, that is, by a political or administrative decision: for instance, the lack of a common bureaucratic identity, which itself is related to broader social processes. Rather, such problematic institutional outcomes can be changed only gradually and over the long run. It is therefore a matter of consistent public policy that is not within the regime's purview.

106. For instance, to the benefit of those who carry out or deal with the implementation process, including those for whom the policies are intended: for example, the tax officer and the taxpayer.

107. See, for instance, Tishreen, May 22, 1999, where six ministries provide, through their press staff, contradictory answers to the simple question of which agency or organizational body is supposed to monitor exports. Also, in more than one instance at

the Economic Sciences Association lectures, audience members would suggest that "we need to pick up our legal and regulatory framework and throw it in the trash"; 1999 Economic Sciences Association Lecture Series, Damascus, February–May 1999.

108. As the public sector began to give way to the private sector in the late 1980s, Syria's state capitalism or central command economy began to give way to an amorphous political economy marked by half-baked policies, regulations, and rhetoric.

109. For instance, the anticorruption drive led by heir-apparent Bashar al-Asad at the end of the 1990s reached a climax when the government cracked down on an illegal seaport run by Hafiz al-Asad's exiled brother, Rif'at. The point here is that Rif'at is no longer a significant player with officially anchored local allies, and still the move wreaked havoc. Most locally grounded businesses with an equivalent illegal or semilegal nature seem beyond reach at the moment on politically rational grounds.

Chapter 6

1. See Samar Izmishli, "Syria: The Amount of Tax Evasion Equals Three Times the Revenues, and Weakens the Capacity of the State to Spend on Health, Education, and Services," *al-Hayat*, March 26, 2001.

2. See the 1997 and 1998 reports of the Central Bureau of Statistics in Syria; and Dalila, "'Ajz al-Muwaazanah al-'Aamah wa Subul Mu'aalajatuhu" [The general budget deficit and ways for its treatment].

3. This has become a part of conventional knowledge in Syria to the point where most Syrians generally disregard the budget's contents. Economists, however, insist on pointing out the social and economic implications of such (deliberate) delinquency, in various public forums and, in the late 1990s, in the state-run press. The Economic Sciences Association's (ESA's) annual lectures are one site where prominent economists bring this issue to the fore. See the 1999 collection of ESA's Tuesday Lecture Series.

4. See Dalila, "General Budget Deficit and Ways for Its Treatment," 282.

5. Ibid., 284 (emphasis mine).

6. See Perthes, *Political Economy of Syria Under Asad*, 56. Perthes states that "from 1991, the government also began to calculate *certain* budgetary items and public-sector imports and exports on the basis of the neighboring countries' rate" (emphasis mine).

7. See Dalila, "General Budget Deficit and Ways for Its Treatment," 275.

8. Dalila cites five principal reasons that account for the unreliability of the budget: the budget adopts a lower exchange rate for the US dollar; the largest portion of the supply deficit is excluded from the budget; some revenues and expenditures are not accounted for in the budget; the budget does not refer to the revenues and expenditures of local administrations; and the budget ignores some crucial factors, such as dramatic drops in oil prices. See Dalila, "General Budget Deficit and Ways for Its Treatment," 289.

9. Ibid., 269.

10. Outspoken Syrian economists estimate that at the end of the 1990s nearly all the

national income "goes to the hands of five percent of the Syrian people," with a quickly declining middle class and widespread poverty on the horizon. For other statistics presented in this paper, see *al-Hayat*, October 1, 2000, 4.

11. See Central Bureau of Statistics, "National Accounts," in *Statistical Abstract 1998*, 526–27. Per capita NDP at factor cost dropped from 43,450 SP (Syrian pounds) in 1980 to 3,310 SP in 1997.

12. The Syrian government does not release such statistics, but independent Syrian economists estimate that average Syrians are making much less today than they did in the 1960s when NDP was even lower. This has been recorded in various interviews conducted by the author in 1998–2000. According to the 1997 budget alone, for instance, if we calculate the difference between increased extraction measures and expected fiscal revenues (that generally target lower-income salaried workers) and decreased government spending, we find that the living standards of the general population have dropped by 15 percent in one year. See Dalila, "General Budget Deficit and Ways for Its Treatment," 284.

13. It is notable that the government could do so only if decision-makers were confident that there exists an alternative on the supply end—that is, the very same economic networks that supplied the Syrian domestic markets with consumer goods that the government was unable to provide or unwilling to subsidize in the early 1980s when a severe shortage economy took hold.

14. See Dalila, "General Budget Deficit and Ways for Its Treatment," 278.

15. See Dalila, "al-Qita' al-'Am fi Suriya" [The public sector in Syria].

16. See Dalila, "General Budget Deficit and Ways for Its Treatment," 278.

17. Economist Intelligence Unit, "Syria Country Report: Political Outlook for 2009–10" (London: The Economist Intelligence Unit Limited, 2008).

18. Dalila, "General Budget Deficit and Ways for Its Treatment," 279.

19. Ibid.

20. This includes the belated collection of taxes from delinquent sources. By the time these accounts were paid, inflation had gobbled up the initial real value of taxes due. Ibid., 284.

21. There are several key sources for "nominal" budget surpluses. One major structuring source is the fact that investment budgets are not executed until the sixth or seventh month into the respective year. Another serious source is that by administrative orders, the budget leaves out most figures under the category of supply deficits, and at the same time inflates the category of "other revenues," which are in essence numeric price differentials that reflect the rise in inflation rates (that is, inflation here can be considered a form of indirect taxes on the majority of the population). Ibid.

22. See Dalila, "Syria's Economic Troubles," an article in the Communist Party publication *al-Sha'b*.

23. Investment Law No. 10 of 1991 allowed for both legal and illegal maneuvering around tax laws by virtue of the generous tax exemptions that it provided as well as

other distinctions that were henceforth abused by the majority of investors. In 2006, as the government coffers began drying up along with projections of future oil revenue, the government decided to end the tax exemptions associated with investment projects under Investment Law No. 10. See "Tax Policy: The Significance of Tax Exemptions" later in this chapter for more detail.

24. See Landis, "Lebanon and the Syrian Economy."

25. See Dalila, "General Budget Deficit and Ways for Its Treatment," 281.

26. See Khaddour, "Tax and Customs Exemption Policy."

27. One way to understand the decline of authority of the five-year plans, as well as of the Regional Conferences before 2005, is to contrast the content of the last five-year plan in the 1980s and the resolutions of the eighth conference with the actual measures that the government adopted in response to the 1986 crisis. While the Regional Command Conference and that five-year plan focused on the importance of the public sector's control and monopoly over imports and agricultural inputs, respectively, the measures adopted expanded the role of the private sector in foreign trade and industry and allowed it to encroach on the import and distribution monopoly of the public sector in various economic spheres. See the reports of the eighth Regional Command Conference (Taqarir wa Muqarrarat al-Mu'tamar al-Qutri al-Thamin) (Damascus, Arab Socialist Ba'th Party, 1985) as compared with the actual measures described in Sukkar, "Crisis of 1986 and Syria's Plan for Reform," 32–36.

28. Most critically, state-owned banks do not enjoy any significant measure of autonomy to conduct banking functions, nor does the central bank have available to it the traditional banking policy tools that are intended to direct savings and investments; interview with Dr. Amr Lutfi at the Faculty of Economics, Aleppo University, Aleppo, February 1999. See also articles on the state of the Syrian banking system in the ESA's 1999 Lecture Series. Even after private banking emerged and the Syrian pound was unpegged from the dollar, being pegged instead to the IMF's Special Drawing Rights basket (allowing for a managed float), and even after the exchange rate was unified, the Central Bank of Syria still lacks crucial monetary instruments for regulating fiscal policy. For a full discussion, see Burns and Myerscough, "Change Within Stability."

29. See Dalila, "General Budget Deficit and Ways for Its Treatment," 285.

30. Interview with a high-level official at the Industrial Bank in Damascus, May 1999. The names of these individuals are well known to the interested Syrian public, and they include such tycoons as Sa'ib Nahhas and the recently disfavored Anwar al-'Aqqad, both of whom borrowed money to invest in projects under Law No. 10 of 1991. It is noteworthy that despite the large amounts borrowed by more than ten prominent businessmen (each amounting to more than 100 million SP, and some more than 200 million SP), they are borrowed at interest rates lower than those at which public sector workers borrow from the Public Lending Bank to cover their basic living expenses. The latter loans are collected "to the last drop."

31. The operating mechanism for implementing such lending practices varies from a letter (unrelated to policy) from a top cabinet official to a simple telephone call. In fact, if there is a system of checks and balances, it works in a more detrimental direction. According to a number of employees (mostly former ones) in the commercial, agricultural, and industrial banks, permission to grant a loan with no collateral to a particular business partner is sometimes rivaled by a similar loan grant to another partner. As one former employee put it, "they say, 'this way, we are equal.'" These individuals shall remain unnamed.

32. See the Central Bank of Syria report of 1998 for a more "muffled" version of these figures. The cited figures were obtained in an interview with a former official at the Commercial Bank of Syria, Damascus, April 1999. Another strikingly similar set of figures was obtained in an interview with an academic who has access to "ministerial papers" that broke down central bank figures on lending patterns; Damascus, June 1990. These individuals are to remain anonymous.

33. Interview with former employee at the Commercial Bank of Syria. Also see Dalila, "General Budget Deficit and Ways for Its Treatment," 286.

34. In 2003 the law was reformed, and in 2006 private currency exchanges were licensed.

35. Two of the most extensive hard currency black market networks—that is, networks of individuals who have a political cover for providing foreign exchange to satisfy domestic demands—are run out of Latakia and Aleppo, and are partners in some of the most powerful economic networks in Syria. These networks, both business and black market ones, have an interest in perpetuating the hard currency shortage, as the latter benefit directly from speculative exchange deals, and the former get a better exchange rate than the less (or un-) connected businessmen.

36. See Dalila, "General Budget Deficit and Ways for Its Treatment," 287.

37. A number of banks in Lebanon, beginning in the early 1990s, conducted a substantial portion of their business with Syrian investors who are free to travel back and forth for their banking needs; interviews with two assistant bank managers in Beirut, February–April 1999. The names of the banks were requested to be undisclosed. Lebanese bank employees and consultants have begun to provide "special" services to Syrian investors by driving across the border, collecting deposits, and returning to Lebanon to credit their respective accounts. As a participant-observer, the author has been on one such trip, in which a Lebanese bank employee meeting informally with traders in the traditional Suq al-Hamidiyyah of Damascus conducted such a transaction. Two important facts stand out: first, nearly all of such Syrian "depositors" do not document such transactions—that is, no papers are signed by either party, for fear of reprisal—and second, bank employees who shuttle back and forth carry special passes (*khatt 'askari*, or military line) that allow them to bypass heavy traffic and meticulous searching (often excavating) at the border. Such passes are handed out only by official permission from the Syrian government or those who influence the respective agency.

38. Interview with a Syrian businessman residing in Dubai, who was on one of six yearly visits to see his family in Damascus; June 2000.

39. See Economist Intelligence Unit, "Syria Country Report," October 1996, 8.

40. "Heated Debate over the Social Market Economy," *Al-Thawra*, February 28, 2007, cited in Raphaeli, "Syria's Fragile Economy."

41. Interview with an official at the Department of Industry, Damascus, April 1999. The same method by which some of the money is deposited in foreign accounts was described by a former bureaucrat at the Commercial Bank of Syria (see interview documentation in the notes above).

42. See Dalila, "General Budget Deficit and Ways for Its Treatment," 289.

43. See Central Bureau of Statistics, "National Accounts," in *Statistical Abstracts 1997 and 1998.*

44. See Perthes, *Political Economy of Syria Under Asad,* 58.

45. See Hopfinger and Khaddour, "Investment Policies in Syria."

46. The source of indirect taxes in Syria is the dramatically rising inflation that severely affected most middle- and lower-income Syrians in the early to mid-1990s. The source of this rapidly rising inflation was largely a result of inflationary spending that was meant to cover the cost of rising subsidized prices. Those prices, for items such as wheat, were administratively hiked, as discussed earlier, to "encourage agricultural production" and render public sector institutions profitable.

47. See Dalila, "General Budget Deficit and Ways for Its Treatment," 289.

48. Most new ventures were launched under Investment Law No. 10 of 1991. See Perthes, *Political Economy of Syria Under Asad,* 60–61.

49. See Dalila, "General Budget Deficit and Ways for Its Treatment," 289.

50. International Monetary Fund, "Syrian Arab Republic: Statistical Appendix," 2005 and 2009; and Central Bureau of Statistics, "National Accounts," in *Statistical Abstract 2007.*

51. For an updated account, see al-Jlailati, "al-Niththam al-Daribi al-Suri wa-ittijahaat islahihi" [The Syrian tax system and avenues for its reform].

52. See al-Jlailati, "Syrian Tax System and Avenues for Its Reform."

53. See Khaddour, "Tax and Customs Exemption Policy," 94.

54. Ibid.

55. See summary of Investment Law No. 10 in Chapter 5, Table 5.1.

56. Beneficiaries of exemptions, most often part of powerful public-private economic networks, use(d) their import privilege to satisfy the local market. Moreover, the goods and services provided by projects that benefit from these exemptions are provided at relatively high costs and prices, rendering them nonconducive to exports—an essential part of the conditions of any project under Investment Law No. 10.

57. A notable example is the opposition in 1995 of three major business tycoons to the creation of a stock market for agricultural products. These tycoons ran the joint sec-

tor agricultural establishments and were able to freely set the prices of such stocks at a level higher than their market value; interview with a former official at the Commercial Bank of Syria, December 1998.

58. See Khaddour, "Tax and Customs Exemption Policy," 108–9.

59. Interview with an Aleppan economist who occasionally sat in on Guidance Committee meetings as a consultant for one of the Chambers of Industry; Aleppo, February 1999. According to him, many of the explicit decisions at the meetings seem superficial, but certain "requests" are put on the discussion table to "encourage us to invest," if not attract Arab or even foreign money. Such requests are not explicitly decided upon in reference to those who made the requests—trade unions and party representatives attending would not have this kind of responsiveness!—but they subsequently end up being quite responsive to particular individuals' needs.

60. See the empirical record above, which shows how exemptions were abused for purposes not related to exempted investment. The contradictory legal environment in Syria (let alone the notorious category of verbal decrees and decisions issued, and reversed, regularly by the minister of the economy and foreign trade and through the prime minister's office) makes virtually all major business transactions both legal and illegal at the same time.

61. See Khaddour, "al-Athaar al-Iqtisadiyyah li-Thahirat al-Fasad al-Idari" [The economic effects of the phenomenon of administrative corruption].

62. See Chapter 3, particularly the institutional configuration of the new Ba'th regime under Hafiz al-Asad.

63. For instance, the constitution states that no tax is to be imposed or exempted without undergoing a legal process, which in most cases involves ratification by the legislature; however, several tax exemptions have been decreed by politicians, including Decision No. 186 (1985) issued by the prime minister to exempt all investors in first- and second-class tourism projects from all kinds of taxes, customs, and municipal and financial duties. See Khaddour, "Tax and Customs Exemption Policy."

64. For various figures on both customs duties and direct tax revenue, see statistics that follow in this paragraph, which are drawn from Khaddour, "Tax and Customs Exemption Policy," 87–114; and Dalila, "General Budget Deficit and Ways for Its Treatment."

65. See Khaddour, "Tax and Customs Exemption Policy," 103.

66. See Dalila, "Issues in the General Budget," a column in *al-Hayat*, March 2001.

67. See Landis, "Lebanon and the Syrian Economy."

68. In ESA symposia, what are called the "new bourgeoisie" are often referred to as "criminals, robbing the public." More outspoken critics such as Dalila do not shy away from openly associating them with "partners" in the government. Author's notes from ESA's 1999 Conference Series, al-Markaz al-'Arabi al-Thaqafi, Damascus, February–May 1999.

69. The state's institutional capacity with regard to economic issues at the end

of the 1980s became dismal, leading to various problems including fragmentation of policy-making and contradictory regulations. 1999 ESA Lecture Series, Damascus, February–May 1999. For more information, see Chapter 5 in this volume.

70. The unwillingness of the regime refers here to the fact that in the 1990s, regime officials themselves were benefiting from both a lopsided tax "system" and their ability "legally" to maximize rent under existing conditions.

71. See Chapter 5 of this book.

Conclusion

The epigraphs in this chapter are from an interview with Abdallah al-Dardari, former deputy prime minister for economic affairs, Damascus, July 25, 2007.

1. This book did not explicitly address regional and international factors, but not because they are irrelevant. Rather, on the one hand, their impact was largely overridden by internal dynamics, and on the other, the effects of regional and international factors did not impinge on the particular argument herein, namely, the economic and developmental impact of privileged networks.

2. See Knoke and Yang, *Social Network Analysis*, 8–9.

3. This view has long been held by Syria analysts. According to Perthes, "[a]s a rule we can say that economic policy-making, compared to matters of high policy such as security and foreign affairs, is a broader, more complex process that involves a relatively high number and large spectrum of institutional and individual participants"; see Perthes, *Political Economy of Syria Under Asad*, 207.

4. See Gibson, "Social Networks, Civil Society, and the Prospects for Consolidating Russia's Democratic Transition."

5. See Kienle, "Reconciling Privilege and Reform," 81–296.

6. See Marsh and Smith, "Understanding Policy Networks."

7. Ibid., 9–10.

8. Ibid. Marsh and Smith discuss the agricultural policy network in Britain since the 1930s. In the case of late-developing countries, certainly in Syria, speaking of networks often refers to networks that operate across most if not all policy areas. The example above, and others, abound in the case of advanced capitalist countries; policy networks are often differentiated by sector.

9. See Marsh and Smith, "Understanding Policy Networks," 11.

10. Interview with Abdallah al-Dardari, deputy prime minister for economic affairs, Damascus, July 25, 2007.

BIBLIOGRAPHY

Abdul-Nour, Ayman. "Dawr al-ajhiza al-hukumiyyah fi thill aaliyaat al-suq" [The role of governmental agencies in the shadow of market mechanisms]. Paper no. 5, presented to the annual conference of the Economic Sciences Association, Damascus, Syria, March 16, 1999.

Abdul Nour, Khalid. "al-Qita' al-Khas fi Thill al-Himaya" [The private sector in the shadow of protection]. Paper no. 13, presented to the annual conference of the Economic Sciences Association, Damascus, Syria, April 25, 2000.

Abdul Nour, Khalid. "Ta'hil al-Qita' al-Sina'i" [Improving the industrial sector]. Paper no. 6, presented to the annual conference of the Economic Sciences Association, Damascus, Syria, March 23, 1999.

Alexeev, Michael, and Jim Leitzel. "Collusion and Rent-Seeking." *Public Choice* 69 (1991).

Alston, Lee J., Thrainn Eggertsson, and Douglass C. North, eds. *Empirical Studies in Institutional Change.* New York: Cambridge University Press, 1996.

American Embassy in Damascus. "1998 Annual Report on the Syrian Economy." Damascus: 1998.

Amsden, Alice. *Asia's Next Giant: South Korea and Late Industrialization.* New York: Oxford University Press, 1989.

Arab Business Council of the World Economic Forum. "Economic Reform Priorities in the Arab World: A Private Sector Perspective." 2004. http://bmena.state.gov/rls /55664.htm (accessed August 2009).

Arab Socialist Ba'th Party. "Al-taqrir al-iqtisadi" [Economic report]. Regional Command, reports and resolutions of the 6th Regional Conference. Damascus, April 5–15, 1975. Damascus: Arab Socialist Ba'th Party, 1976.

Arab Socialist Ba'th Party. "Al-taqrir al-iqtisadi" [Economic report]. Regional Command, reports and resolutions of the 8th Regional Conference. Damascus, January 1985. Damascus: Arab Socialist Ba'th Party, 1985.

Ayubi, Nazih. *Overstating the Arab State.* London: I. B. Tauris, 1995.

Al-Bab. "Economic Reform in the Arab World." http://www.al-bab.com/arab/background /economic_reform.htm (accessed August 4, 2010).

Bahout, Joseph. *Les Entrepreneurs syriens: Economie, affaires et politique.* Beirut: Cermoc, 1994.

Banck, Geert A. "Network Analysis and Social Theory: Some Remarks." In *Network Analysis: Studies in Human Interaction.* Edited by Jeremy Boissevain and J. Clyde Mitchell. The Hague: Mouton, 1973.

Barkey, Henri J., ed. *The Politics of Economic Change in the Middle East.* New York: St. Martin's Press, 1992.

Batatu, Hanna. "Some Observations on the Social Roots of Syria's Ruling Military Group and the Causes for Its Dominance." *Middle East Journal* 35 (1981).

Batatu, Hanna. "Syria's Muslim Brethren." *MERIP* no. 110 (November–December 1982): 12–20.

Batatu, Hanna. *Syria's Peasantry, the Descendants of Its Lesser Rural Notables, and Their Politics.* Princeton, NJ: Princeton University Press, 1999.

Bates, Robert H., and Anne O. Krueger, eds. *Political and Economic Interactions in Economic Policy Reform.* London: Blackwell, 1993.

Bates, Robert H., et al. *Analytic Narratives.* Princeton, NJ: Princeton University Press, 1998.

BBC News. "Timeline: Syria." December 27, 2001. http://news.bbc.co.uk/hi/english/world/middle_east.

Beblawi, Hazim, and Giacomo Luciani, eds. *The Rentier State.* London: Croom Helm, 1987.

Bellin, Eva. "The Politics of Profit in Tunisia: Utility of the Rentier Paradigm?" *World Development* 22, no. 3 (1994): 427–36.

Bellin, Eva. "Tunisian Industrialists and the State." In *Tunisia: The Political Economy of Reform.* Edited by William Zartman. Boulder, CO: Lynne Rienner, 1991.

Benhassine, Najy. *From Privilege to Competition: Unlocking the Private-Led Growth in the Middle East and North Africa.* Washington, DC: World Bank, 2009.

Bhagwati, Jagdish. "Directly Unproductive Profit-Seeking (DUP) Activities." *Journal of Political Economy* 90 (October 1982): 988–1002.

Bianchi, Robert. "Businessmen's Associations in Egypt and Turkey." *Annals* 482 (1985): 147–54.

Brass, Daniel J., and David Krackhards. "Intraorganizational Networks, the Micro Side." In *Advances in Social Networks Analysis, Research in the Social and Behavioral Sciences.* Edited by Joseph Galaskiewicz and Stanley Wasserman, 207–27. London: Sage, 1994.

British Petroleum. "Statistical Review of World Energy." London: British Petroleum, June 2009.

Brumberg, Daniel. "Authoritarian Legacies and Reform Strategies in the Arab World." In *Political Liberalization and Democratization in the Arab World.* Edited by Rex Brynen, Bahgat Korany, and Paul Noble. Boulder, CO: Lynne Rienner, 1995.

Brynen, Rex, Bahgat Korany, and Paul Noble, eds. *Political Liberalization and Democratization in the Arab World*, vol. 1. Boulder, CO: Lynne Rienner, 1995.

Bu'Ali, Yasin. "Mawqi' al-tabaqa al-'amila fi al-mujtama' al-suri" [The position of the working class in Syrian society]. *Dirasat 'arabiyya* [Arab studies] 7 (October 1971): 7–29.

Buck, Andrew W. "Networks of Governance and Privatization: A View from Provincial Russia." *Political Power and Social Theory*. Edited by Diane E. Davis. Stamford, CT: JAI Press, 1999.

Bugra, Ayse. *State and Business in Modern Turkey: A Comparative Study*. Albany: State University of New York Press, 1994.

Burns, Russ, and Rhea Myerscough. "Change Within Stability: The Politics of Financial Sector Reform in Syria." Working paper, George Washington Institute for Middle East Studies, 2009. www.gwu.edu/~imes (accessed September 2009).

Burt, Ronald S., and Michael J. Minor, eds. *Applied Network Analysis: A Methodological Introduction*. London: Sage, 1983.

Bush, Ray. *Economic Crisis and the Politics of Economic Reform in Egypt*. Boulder, CO: Westview Press, 1999.

Callaghy, Thomas. "Lost Between State and Market: The Politics of Economic Adjustment in Ghana, Zambia, and Nigeria." In *Economic Crisis and Policy Choice: The Politics of Adjustment in the Third World*. Edited by Joan M. Nelson, 257–319. Princeton, NJ: Princeton University Press, 1990.

Cammett, Melani. "Business-Government Relations and Industrial Change: The Politics of 'Clustering' in Morocco and Tunisia." *World Development* 35, no. 11 (2007).

Central Bank of Syria. "Gross Domestic Product at Market Prices by Sector." *Quarterly Bulletin* (1997–2008).

Central Bank of Syria. "Indicators of Foreign Trade." *Quarterly Bulletin* (1975–2008).

Central Bank of Syria. "Main Syrian Exports." *Quarterly Bulletin* (1975–2008).

Central Bureau of Statistics. *Nata'ij Bahth al-Istiqsaa' al-Sina'I fi-l Qitaa' al-Khaas li-'Aam 1995* [Statistical research results of private sector industry for the year 1995]. Damascus: Central Bureau of Statistics, 1998, 4–5.

Central Bureau of Statistics. "National Accounts." In *Statistical Abstract 1998*. Damascus: Central Bureau of Statistics, 1998, Ch. 16, 503–63.

Central Bureau of Statistics. "National Accounts." In *Statistical Abstract 2007*. Damascus: Central Bureau of Statistics, 2007, Ch. 16, Table 16/38, 565.

Central Bureau of Statistics. *Statistical Abstract* [yearly]. Damascus: Central Bureau of Statistics, 1990–2000.

Chaudhry, Kiren. "Economic Liberalization and the Lineages of the Rentier State." *Comparative Politics* 27 (October 1994).

Chaudhry, Kiren. "The Middle East and the Political Economy of Development." *Items* 41 (June–September 1994).

Chaudhry, Kiren. "The Myths of the Market and the Common History of Late Developers." *Politics and Society* 21 (September 1993).

Chaudhry, Kiren. *The Price of Wealth: Economies and Institutions in the Middle East.* Ithaca, NY: Cornell University Press, 1997.

Choueiri, Youssef M., ed. *State and Society in Syria and Lebanon.* New York: St. Martin's Press, 1993.

Coleman, James S. "Social Capital in the Creation of Human Capital." *American Journal of Sociology* 94, Supplement: Organizations and Institutions: Sociological and Economic Approaches to the Analysis of Social Structure (1988).

Cook, Karen S., and J. M. Whitmeyer. "Two Approaches to Social Structure: Exchange Theory and Network Analysis." *Annual Review of Sociology* 18 (1992).

Cornard, Jocelyne. *L'Entrepreneur et l'état en Syrie.* Paris: L'Harmattan, 1994.

Dalila, Arif. "'Ajz al-Muwaazanah al-'Aamah wa Subul Mu'aalajatuhu" [The general budget deficit and ways for its treatment]. Paper no. 9, presented to the annual conference of the Economic Sciences Association, Damascus, Syria, April 20, 1999.

Dalila, Arif. "al-Qita' al-'Am fi Suriya: min al-Himaya ila al-Munafasa" [The public sector in Syria: from protection to competition]. Paper no. 14, presented to the annual conference of the Economic Sciences Association, Damascus, Syria, May 2, 2000.

Dalila, Arif. "al-Qita' Al'am wa Dawrahu fi al-Tanmiya" [The public sector and its role in development]. Paper no. 3, presented to the annual conference of the Economic Sciences Association, Damascus, Syria, 1986.

Dalila, Arif. "al-Ray' al-Markazi ka Mu'ashir Naw'I Murakkab li Wad'iyyat al-Takhalluf w-al Taba'iyya al-Mu'asira" [Centralized rent as a constructed qualitative indicator for dependency and reactionary position]. In *A Research in Political Economy.* Beirut: Dar al-Tali'a, 1982, Ch. 4.

Dalila, Arif. *A Research in Political Economy.* Beirut: Dar al-Tali'a, 1982.

Dalila, Arif. "Syria's Economic Troubles." In *Al-Sha'b.* Damascus: Syrian Communist Party, March 1999.

Dillman, Bradford L. *State and Private Sector in Algeria: The Politics of Rent-Seeking and Failed Development.* Boulder, CO: Westview Press, 2000.

Dimaggio, Paul. "Nadel's Paradox Revisited: Relational and Cultural Aspects of Organizational Structure." In *Networks and Organizations: Structure, Form, and Action.* Edited by Robert G. Eccles, and Nitin Nohria, 118–42. Boston: Harvard Business School Press, 1992.

Dreher, Axel, and Friedrich Schneider. "Corruption and the Shadow Economy: An Empirical Analysis." *Public Choice* 144, nos. 1–2 (2010).

Eccles, Robert G., and Nitin Nohria, eds. *Networks and Organizations: Structure, Form and Action.* Boston: Harvard Business School Press, 1992.

Economic Sciences Association. *Al-Jam'iyyah al-Iqtisaadiyyah* [yearly volumes of conference series]. Damascus: Economic Sciences Association, 1986, 1989–2001.

Economic Sciences Association. Tuesday lectures on topic of economic reform. Damascus: Economic Sciences Association, 1991–2008.

Economist Intelligence Unit. *Syria: Country Profile* [yearly volumes]. London: The Economist Intelligence Unit Limited, 1993, 1994, 1998, 1999, 2000, 2001.

Economist Intelligence Unit. "Syria Country Report" [yearly reports]. London: The Economist Intelligence Unit Limited, 1991–2009.

Economist Intelligence Unit. "Syria Country Report: Political Outlook for 2009–10." London: The Economist Intelligence Unit Limited, 2008.

Egbert, Henrik. "Business Success Through Social Networks? A Comment on Social Networks and Business Success." *American Journal of Economics and Sociology* 68, no. 3 (July 2009).

Ehteshami, Anoushirivan, and Raymond A. Hinnebusch. *Syria and Iran: Middle Powers in a Penetrated Regional System.* London: Routledge & Kegan Paul, 1997.

Elster, Jon, et al. *Institutional Design in Post-Communist Societies: Rebuilding the Ship at Sea.* Cambridge, UK: Cambridge University Press, 1998.

Emirbayer, Mustafa, and Jeff Goodwin. "Network Analysis, Culture, and the Problem of Agency." *American Journal of Sociology* 99, no. 6 (1994): 1411–54.

Euro-Med Partnership. "Syrian Arab Republic: Strategy Paper 2007–2013." http://ec.europa.eu/world/enp/pdf/country/enpi_csp_nip_syria_en.pdf.

Euromediterranean Network of Investment Promotion Agencies. "Building the New Syrian Investment Agency." 2007. http://www.animaweb.org/uploads/bases/document/Ani_TechAssist_BuildingSyrianInvest_15-5-07.pdf (accessed October 2009).

Evans, Peter. *Embedded Autonomy: States and Industrial Transformation.* Princeton, NJ: Princeton University Press, 1995.

Evans, Peter. "The State as Problem and Solution: Predation, Embedded Autonomy, and Structural Change." In *The Politics of Economic Adjustment.* Edited by Stephen Haggard and Robert Kaufman. Princeton, NJ: Princeton University Press, 1992.

Evans, Peter. "State Structures, Government-Business Relations, and Economic Transformation." In *Business and the State in Developing Countries.* Edited by Sylvia Maxfield and Ben Ross Schneider. Ithaca (NY) and London: Cornell University Press, 1997.

Farrell, Henry, and Jack Knight. "Trust, Institutions, and Institutional Evolution: Industrial Districts and the Social Capital Hypothesis." Unpublished paper, 2001.

Farsoun, Samih K., and Christina Zacharia. "Class, Economic Change, and Political Liberalization in the Arab World." In *Political Liberalization and Democratization in the Arab World.* Edited by Rex Brynen, Bahgat Korany, and Paul Noble, 261–80. Boulder, CO: Lynne Rienner, 1995.

Fukuyama, Francis. *Trust.* New York: Free Press, 1995.

Galaskievicz, Joseph, and Mark S. Mizruchi. "Networks of Interorganizational Relations." In *Advances in Social Networks Analysis: Research in the Behavioral Sciences.* Edited by Joseph Galaskiewicz and Stanley Wasserman, 230–53. London: Sage, 1994.

Galdo, Anna. "Policies for Business in the Mediterranean Countries: The Syrian Arab Republic." Centre for Administrative Innovation in the Euro-Mediterranean Region, 2006. http://unpan1.un.org/intradoc/groups/public/documents/caimed/unpano18700 .pdf (accessed May 2009).

Gambetta, Diego, ed. *Trust: Making and Breaking Cooperative Relations.* Cambridge, UK: Blackwell, 1988.

Gambill, Gary C., ed. "Dossier: Rami Makhlouf." *Mideast Monitor* 1, no. 3 (January–March 2008). http://www.mideastmonitor.org/issues/0801/0801_8.htm.

Gambill, Gary C. "Syria After Lebanon: Hooked on Lebanon." *Middle East Quarterly* 12, no. 4 (Fall 2005).

Geddes, Barbara. "Challenging the Conventional Wisdom." In *Fragile Coalitions: The Politics of Economic Adjustment.* Edited by Joan Nelson. Washington, DC: Overseas Development Council, 1989.

Geddes, Barbara. "Challenging the Conventional Wisdom." *Journal of Democracy* 5, no. 4 (October 1994).

Geddes, Barbara. "The Heart of the Matter? Public Enterprise and the Adjustment Process." In *The Politics of Economic Adjustment.* Edited by Stephen Haggard and Robert Kaufman. Princeton, NJ: Princeton University Press, 1992.

Gerschenkron, Alexander. *Economic Backwardness in Historical Perspective.* Cambridge, MA: Belknap Press of Harvard University Press, 1962.

Gibson, James L. "Social Networks, Civil Society, and the Prospects for Consolidating Russia's Democratic Transition." *American Journal of Political Science* 45, no. 1 (January 2001): 51–69.

Giugle, Marcelo M., and Hamed Mubarak, eds. *Private Sector Development in Egypt.* Cairo: American University Press, 1996.

Goldsmith, Arthur A. "Africa's Overgrown State Reconsidered: Bureaucracy and Economic Growth." *World Politics* 51 (July 1999): 520–46.

Granovetter, Mark. "Economic Action and Social Structure: The Problem of Embeddedness." *American Journal of Sociology* 91, no. 3 (1985): 481–510.

Granovetter, Mark. "Problems of Explanation in Economic Sociology." In *Networks and Organizations: Structure, Form, and Action.* Edited by Robert G. Eccles and Nitin Nohria, 25–56. Boston: Harvard Business School Press, 1992.

Granovetter, Mark, and Richard Swedberg. "Introduction." In *The Sociology of Economic Life.* Edited by Mark Granovetter and Richard Swedberg. Boulder, CO: Westview Press, 1992.

Haddad, Bassam. "Business as Usual in Syria?" *MERIP* Press Information Note 68, September 7, 2001.

Haddad, Bassam. "Change and Stasis in Syria: One Step Forward . . ." *MERIP* no. 213 (Winter 1999).

Haddad, Bassam. "The Formation and Development of Economic Networks in Syria:

Implications for Economic and Fiscal Reforms, 1986–2000." In *Networks of Privilege: The Politics of Economic Reform in the Middle East.* Edited by Steven Heydemann. New York: Palgrave–St. Martin's Press, 2004.

Haddad, Bassam. "The Political Dynamics of Economic Liberalization in Populist-Authoritarian Regimes: Administrative Disintegration, Social Polarization, and Economic Stagnation in Syria, 1986–2000." Conference paper, First Mediterranean Social and Political Research Meeting, European University Institute, Florence, Italy, March 2000.

Haddad, Bassam. "Syria's Curious Dilemma." *Middle East Report* 236 (2005).

Haggard, Stephen. *Pathways from the Periphery: The Politics of Growth in the Newly Industrializing Countries.* Ithaca, NY: Cornell University Press, 1990.

Haggard, Stephen, and Robert Kaufman, eds. *The Political Economy of Democratic Transitions.* Princeton, NJ: Princeton University Press, 1995.

Haggard, Stephen, and Robert Kaufman, eds. *The Politics of Economic Adjustment.* Princeton, NJ: Princeton University Press, 1992.

Hall, Peter A., and Rosemary C. R. Taylor. "Political Science and the Three Institutionalisms." *Political Studies* 44 (1996): 936–57.

Halpern, Manfred. *The Politics of Social Change in the Middle East and North Africa.* Princeton, NJ: Princeton University Press, 1963.

Hamilton, Gary G. *Asian Business Networks.* Berlin and New York: Walter de Gruyter, 1996.

Hardin, Russsell. *Collective Action.* Baltimore: Johns Hopkins University Press, 1982.

Harik, Iliya. "Privatization: The Issue, the Prospects and the Fears." In *Privatization and Liberalization in the Middle East.* Edited by Denis Sullivan and Iliya Harik. Bloomington: Indiana University Press, 1992.

Harrigan, Jane T., and Hamid El-Said. *Economic Liberalisation, Social Capital and Islamic Welfare Provision.* New York: Palgrave Macmillan, 2009.

Hellman, Joel S. "Winners Take All: The Politics of Partial Reform in Postcommunist Transitions." *World Politics* 50 (January 1998).

Henry, Clement M., and Robert Springborg. "Bully Praetorian Republics." In *Globalization and the Politics of Development in the Middle East.* Cambridge, UK: Cambridge University Press, 2007, Ch. 5.

Heydemann, Steven. *Authoritarianism in Syria: Institutions and Social Conflict 1946–1970.* Ithaca, NY: Cornell University Press, 1999.

Heydemann, Steven, ed. *Networks of Privilege in the Middle East: The Politics of Economic Reform Revisited.* New York: Palgrave Macmillan, 2004.

Heydemann, Steven. "The Political Logic of Economic Rationality: Selective Stabilization in Syria." In *The Politics of Economic Stabilization Programs in the Middle East.* Edited by Henri J. Barkey. New York: St. Martin's Press, 1992.

Heydemann, Steven. "Taxation Without Representation." In *Rules and Rights in the Mid-*

dle East. Edited by Ellis Goldberg, Joel Migdal, and Resat Kasaba. Seattle: University of Washington Press, 1993.

Heydemann, Steven. "Upgrading Authoritarianism in the Arab World." Analysis paper no. 13. Washington, DC: Saban Center on Middle East Policy, October 2007.

Hinnebusch, Raymond A. *Authoritarian Power and State Formation in Ba'thist Syria.* Boulder, CO: Westview Press, 1990.

Hinnebusch, Raymond A. "Democratization in the Middle East: The Evidence from the Syrian Case." In *Political and Economic Liberalization: Dynamics and Linkages in Comparative Perspective.* Edited by Gerd Nonneman. Boulder, CO: Lynne Rienner, 1996.

Hinnebusch, Raymond A. "Globalization and Generational Change: Syrian Foreign Policy Between Regional Conflict and European Partnership." *Review of International Affairs* 3, no. 2 (Winter 2003).

Hinnebusch, Raymond A. "Political Economy of Economic Liberalization in Syria." *International Journal of Middle East Studies* 27, no. 3 (May 1995).

Hinnebusch, Raymond A. "State and Civil Society in Syria." In *Civil Society in the Middle East.* Edited by Richard Norton. Leiden, Netherlands: E. J. Brill, 1995.

Hinnebusch, Raymond A. "State Formation in a Fragmented Society." *Arab Studies Quarterly* 4 (1982).

Hirschman, Albert O. *Exit, Voice, and Loyalty: Responses to Decline in Firms, Organizations, and States.* Cambridge, MA: Harvard University Press, 1970.

Hopfinger, Hans, and Rislan Khadour. "Development of the Transportation Sector in Syria and the Actual Investment Policy." *Middle Eastern Studies* 35, no. 3 (July 1999): 64–71.

Hopfinger, Hans, and Rislan Khadour, eds. "Investment Policies in Syria" [Siyasaat al-Istithmaar fi Suriyah]. Procedures of the First Syrian-German Forum in Cooperation with the Faculty of Economy, Damascus University, 1997.

Hudson, Michael C. "Democratization and the Problem of Legitimacy in Middle East Politics." *Middle East Studies Association Bulletin* 22, no. 2 (1987).

Hudson, Michael C. *Middle East Dilemma: The Politics and Economics of Arab Integration.* New York: Columbia University Press, 1999.

al-Humush, Munir. *al-Iqtisaad al-Suri 'Ala Masharif al-Qarn al-Hadi wal-'Ishrin* [The Syrian economy at the turn of the twenty-first century]. Damascus: Mashriq Maghrib Printing House, 1997.

Ihyaa', Lijaan. "al-Mujtama' al-Madani," *al-Watha'iq al-Sadira 'an al-Hay'a al-Ta'sisiyya* [documents released by the Central Committee]. Damascus, April 14, 2000.

al-'Imadi, Muhammad. "The Economic and Investment Policies of Syria." In *Investment Policies in Syria.* Edited by Hans Hopfinger and Rislan Khadour. University of Damascus and Central Institute for Regional Research, University of Erlangen-Nuremberg, 1997.

International Monetary Fund. "Syrian Arab Republic: Article IV Consultation—Staff

Report" [yearly]. IMF Country Report no. 05/356. 2005, 2009. http://www.imf.org /external/pubs/ft/scr/2005/cr05356.pdf (accessed May 2009).

International Monetary Fund. "Syrian Arab Republic: Statistical Appendix." October 2005. http://imf.org/external/pubs/ft/scr/2005/cr05355.pdf (accessed May 2009).

International Monetary Fund. "Syrian Arab Republic: Statistical Appendix." IMF Country Report No. 09/56. February 2009.

Jabbur, George. *al-Fikr al-siyasi al-mu'asir fi suriya* [Contemporary political thought in Syria]. London: Riad al-Rayyis, 1987.

Jackman, Robert W., and Ross A. Miller. "A Renaissance of Political Culture?" *American Journal of Political Science* 40, no. 3 (1996): 632–59.

al-Jlailati, Muhammad. "al-Niththam al-Daribi al-Suri wa-ittijahaat islahihi" [The Syrian tax system and avenues for its reform]. Paper no. 7, presented to the annual conference of the Economic Sciences Association, Damascus, Syria, March 2, 1999.

Johnson, Chalmers. *MITI and the Japanese Miracle: The Growth of Industrial Policy, 1925–1975.* Stanford, CA: Stanford University Press, 1982.

Johnson, Chalmers. "Political Institutions and Economic Performance: The Government-Business Relationship in Japan, South Korea, and Taiwan." In *The Political Economy of the New Asian Industrialism.* Edited by Frederic C. Deyo, 136–64. Ithaca, NY: Cornell University Press, 1987.

Kabbani, Nader. "Why Young Syrians Prefer Public Sector Jobs." *Middle East Youth Initiative Policy Outlook,* March 2009. http://www.dsg.ae/LinkClick.aspx?link=MEYI +Policy+Outlook+2+English.pdf&tabid=308&mid=826&language=en-US (accessed August, 2009).

Kattaa, Maha, and Sattouf Alcheik Hussein. "Gender and Workers' Rights in the Informal Economy of Syria." Unpublished conference paper presented at Gender and Rights in the Informal Economies of Arab States, International Labor Organization/ Center of Arab Women for Training and Research, Tunis, Tunisia, July 15–17, 2008.

Kaufman, Robert, and Stephen Haggard, ed. *The Political Economy of Democratic Transitions.* Princeton, NJ: Princeton University Press, 1995.

Keshavarzian, Arang. *Bazaar and State in Iran: The Politics of the Tehran Marketplace.* Cambridge, UK: Cambridge University Press, 2007.

Khaddour, Rislan. "al-Athaar al-Iqtisadiyyah li-Thahirat al-Fasad al-Idari" [The economic effects of the phenomenon of administrative corruption]. Paper no. 2, presented to the annual conference of the Economic Sciences Association, Damascus, Syria, February 23, 1999.

Khaddour, Rislan. "Tax and Customs Exemption Policy." *Buhuuth Iqtisaadiyyah 'Arabiyyah,* June 1996.

al-Khouri, Riad. "Syria's Economy Opens to Regional Opportunities, Syrians Account for About $6 Billion of Deposits in Lebanese Banks Alone." *Daily Star,* September 6, 2001.

Khoury, Philip. *Syria and the French Mandate: The Politics of Arab Nationalism, 1920–1945.* Princeton, NJ: Princeton University Press, 1987.

Kienle, Eberhard. "Reconciling Privilege and Reform: Fiscal Policy in Egypt, 1991–2000." In *Networks of Privilege: The Politics of Economic Reform in the Middle East.* Edited by Steven Heydemann. New York: Palgrave–St. Martin's Press, 2004.

Kienle, Eberhard. "The Return of Politics? Scenarios for Syria's Second Infitah." In *Contemporary Syria: Liberalization Between Cold War and Cold Peace.* Edited by Eberhard Kienle. London: British Academic Press, 1994.

Kim, Eun Mee. "State and Business in the Developmental Process." In *Big Business, Strong State: Collusion and Conflict in South Korean Development, 1960–1990.* Albany: State University of New York Press, 1997, Ch. 7.

Knight, Jack. "The Bases of Cooperation: Social Norms and the Rule of Law." *Journal of Institutional and Theoretical Economics* 54, no. 4 (1998).

Knight, Jack. *Institutions and Social Conflict.* Cambridge, UK: Cambridge University Press, 1992.

Knight, Jack. "Models, Interpretations and Theories: Constructing Explanations of Institutional Emergence and Change." In *Explaining Social Institutions.* Edited by Jack Knight and Itai Sened. Ann Arbor: University of Michigan Press, 1995.

Knight, Jack, and Itai Sened, eds. *Explaining Social Institutions.* Ann Arbor: University of Michigan Press, 1995.

Knoke, David. *Changing Organizations: Business Networks in the New Political Economy.* Boulder, CO: Westview Press, 2001.

Knoke, David, and James H. Kuklinski. "Network Analysis: Basic Concepts." In *Markets, Hierarchies, and Networks: The Coordination of Social Life.* Edited by Graham Thompson, Jennifer Frances, Rosalind Levacic, and Jeremy Mitchell, 173–82. London: Sage, 1991.

Knoke, David, and Song Yang. *Social Network Analysis.* Thousand Oaks, CA: Sage, 2008.

Knowles, Warwick. *Jordan Since 1989: A Political Economy.* London: I. B. Tauris, 2005.

Kramer, Roderick M. "Trust and Distrust in Organizations: Emerging Perspectives, Enduring Questions." *Annual Review of Psychology* 50 (February 1999).

Krause, Lawrence B., and Kim Kihwan. *Liberalization in the Process of Economic Development.* Berkeley: University of California Press, 1996.

Krueger, Anne O. *Political Economy of Policy Reform in Developing Countries.* Cambridge, MA: MIT Press, 1993.

Krueger, Anne. "The Political Economy of the Rent-Seeking Society," *American Economic Review* 64 (June 1974).

Laclau, Ernesto, and Chantal Mouffe. *Hegemony and Socialist Strategy.* London: New Left Books, 1985.

Landis, Joshua. "Lebanon and the Syrian Economy." SyriaComment blog. June 8, 2004.

http://faculty-staff.ou.edu/L/Joshua.M.Landis-1/syriablog/2004/06/lebanon-and -syrian-economy.htm (accessed July 31, 2010).

Landis, Joshua. "Rami Makhlouf Stiffs Mercedes." SyriaComment blog. June 26, 2004. http://faculty-staff.ou.edu/L/Joshua.M.Landis-1/syriablog/2004/06/rami-makhlouf -stiffs-mercedes.htm (accessed July 31, 2010).

Lawson, Fred. "External Versus Internal Pressures for Liberalization in Syria and Iraq." *Journal of Arab Affairs* 11 (1992).

Lawson, Fred. "Private Capital and the State in Contemporary Syria." *MERIP* 27, no. 203 (Spring 1997).

Leca, Jean. "Democratization in the Arab World: Uncertainty, Vulnerability and Legitimacy. A Tentative Conceptualization and Some Hypotheses." In *Democracy Without Democrats: The Renewal of Politics in the Muslim World.* Edited by Ghassan Salame. London: I. B. Tauris, 1994.

Leca, Jean. "Opposition in the Middle East and North Africa." *Government and Opposition* 32, no. 4 (1997): 557–77.

Levi, Margaret. "Social and Unsocial Capital: A Review Essay of Robert Putnam's *Making Democracy Work.*" *Politics and Society* 24, no. 1 (1996): 45–55.

Levi, Margaret. "A State of Trust." In *Trust and Governance.* Edited by Valerie Braithwaite and Margaret Levi, 77–101. New York: Russell Sage Foundation, 1998.

Lomnitz, Larissa Adler, and Diana Sheinbaum. "Trust, Social Networks and the Informal Economy: A Comparative Analysis." *Review of Sociology* 10, no. 1 (June 2004): 5–26.

Longuenesse, Elizabeth. "The Class Nature of the State in Syria." *MERIP Reports* 9, no. 4 (1979): 3–11.

Longuenesse, Elisabeth. "Labor in Syria." In *The Social History of Labor in the Middle East.* Edited by Ellis Jay Goldberg. Boulder, CO: Westview Press, 1996.

Longuenesse, Elisabeth. "The Syrian Working Class Today." *Middle East Report* 134 (July–August 1985).

Lorenz, Edward H. "Neither Friends nor Strangers: Informal Networks of Subcontracting in French Industry." In *Trust: Making and Breaking Cooperative Relations.* Edited by Diego Gambetta, 194–210. New York: Blackwell, 1988.

Lucas, John. "Politics of Business Associations in the Developing World." *Journal of Developing Areas* 32, no. 1 (Fall 1997).

Luciani, Giacomo. "Allocation vs. Production States: A Theoretical Framework." In *The Arab State.* Edited by Giacomo Luciani. Berkeley: University of California Press, 1990.

Luhmann, Niklas. *Trust and Power.* New York: John Wiley and Sons, 1979.

MacGaffey, Janet. *Entrepreneurs and Parasites: The Struggle for Indigenous Capitalism in Zaire.* Cambridge, UK: Cambridge University Press, 1987.

Macintyre, Andrew J., ed. *Business and Government in Industrializing Asia.* Ithaca, NY: Cornell University Press, 1994.

March, James G., and Johan P. Olsen. *Rediscovering Institutions: The Organizational Basis of Politics.* New York: Free Press, 1989.

Marsh, David, and Martin Smith. "Understanding Policy Networks: Towards a Dialectical Approach." *Political Studies* 48 (2001).

Marshall, Shana. "Syria and the Financial Crisis: Prospects for Reform." *Middle East Policy* 16, no. 2 (Summer 2009): 109.

Marzouq, Nabil. "al-Tanmiya wa al-'Ummal" [Development and labor]. Paper no. 17, presented to the annual conference of the Economic Sciences Association, Damascus, Syria, March 1998.

Migdal, Joel S. *Strong States and Weak Societies: State-Society Relations and Capabilities in the Third World.* Princeton, NJ: Princeton University Press, 1988.

Moore, Pete. *Doing Business in the Middle East: Politics and Economic Crisis in Jordan and Kuwait.* Cambridge, UK: Cambridge University Press, 2004.

Musacchio, Aldo, and Ian Read. "Bankers, Industrialists, and Their Cliques: Elite Networks in Mexico and Brazil During Early Industrialization." *Enterprise and Society* 8, no. 4 (December 2007): 842–80.

Nabulsi, Sa'id. "Tasheeh al-Khalal fi Suq al-'Amaalah" [Correcting the problems of the labor market]. Paper no. 6, presented to the annual conference of the Economic Sciences Association, Damascus, Syria, March 23, 1999.

al-Nayyal, Abdul Qadir, Ibrahim Ali, and 'Issam al-Sheikh Oghali. "Al-Qita' Ghair al-Munadham: al-Waqi' wa Mutatalibaat al-Indimaaj fi al-Iqtisaad al-Rasmi" [The informal sector: its state and the requirements for its integration into the formal sector]. Paper no. 11, presented to the annual conference of the Economic Sciences Association, Damascus, Syria, May 29, 1999.

Nelson, Joan, ed. *Fragile Coalitions: The Politics of Economic Adjustment.* Washington, DC: Overseas Development Council, 1989.

Niblock, Tim. "International and Domestic Factors." In *Economic and Political Liberalization in the Middle East.* Edited by Tim Niblock and Emma Murphy. London: British Academic Press, 1993.

Nonneman, Gerd, ed. *Political and Economic Liberalization: Dynamics and Linkages in Comparative Perspective.* Boulder, CO: Lynne Rienner, 1996.

North, Douglass C. *Institutions, Institutional Change and Economic Performance.* Cambridge, UK: Cambridge University Press, 1990.

O'Donnell, Guillermo. *Modernization and Bureaucratic Authoritarianism: Studies in South American Politics.* Institute of International Studies, University of California, Berkeley, 1973.

O'Donnell, Guillermo, and Philippe G. Schmitter, eds. *Transitions from Authoritarian Rule: Prospects for Democracy.* Baltimore: Johns Hopkins University Press, 1986.

Offe, Claus, and Helmut Wiesenthal. "Two Logics of Collective Action: Theoretical

Notes on Social Class and Organizational Form." *Political Power and Social Theory* 1 (1980): 67–115.

Office of the Prime Minister. "Nata'ij Bahth al-Istiqsaa' al-Sina'I fi-l Qitaa' al-Khaas li-'Aam 1995" [Statistical research results of private sector industry for the year 1995]. Damascus: Central Bureau of Statistics, 1998.

Olin Wright, Erik. *Class Counts: Comparative Studies in Class Analysis.* Cambridge, UK: Cambridge University Press, 1997.

Olson, Mancur. *The Logic of Collective Action: Public Goods and the Theory of Groups.* Cambridge, MA: Harvard University Press, 1971.

Olson, Mancur. *The Rise and Decline of Nations.* New Haven, CT: Yale University Press, 1982.

Olson, Mancur. "Why Poor Economic Policies Must Promote Corruption: Lessons from the East for All Countries." In *Institutions and Economic Organization in the Advanced Economies.* Edited by Mario Baldassarri, Luigi Paganetto, and Edmund S. Phelps, 9–51. New York: St. Martin's Press, 1998.

Ostrom, Elinor. "Rational Choice Theory and Institutional Analysis: Toward Complementarity." *American Political Science Review* 85, no. 1 (March 1991): 238–43.

Perthes, Volker, ed. *Arab Elites: Negotiating the Politics of Change.* Boulder, CO: Lynne Rienner, 2004.

Perthes, Volker. "Emergence and Transformation of a Statist Economy." In *The Political Economy of Syria Under Asad.* London: I. B. Tauris, 1995, Ch. 2.

Perthes, Volker. "The First *Infitah*: Liberalization in the Shadow of State-Led Growth." In *The Political Economy of Syria Under Asad.* London: I. B. Tauris, 1995.

Perthes, Volker. "A Look at Syria's Upper Class: The Bourgeoisie and the Ba'th." *MERIP* 21 (May–June 1991).

Perthes, Volker. *The Political Economy of Syria Under Asad.* London: I. B. Tauris, 1995.

Perthes, Volker. "The Private Sector, Economic Liberalization and the Prospects of Democratization: The Case of Syria and Some Other Arab Countries." In *Democracy Without Democrats? The Renewal of Politics in the Muslim World.* Edited by Ghassan Salamé. London: I. B. Tauris, 1994.

Perthes, Volker. "Stages of Economic and Political Liberalization in Syria." In *Contemporary Syria: Liberalization Between Cold War and Cold Peace.* Edited by Eberhard Kienle. New York: St. Martin's Press, 1994.

Perthes, Volker. "Syria: Difficult Inheritance." In *Arab Elites: Negotiating the Politics of Change.* Edited by Volker Perthes. Boulder, CO: Lynne Rienner, 2004, Ch. 4.

Perthes, Volker. "Syria Under Bashar al-Asad: Modernisation and the Limits of Change." International Institute for Strategic Studies, 2004.

Perthes, Volker. "The Syrian Economy in the 1980's." *Middle East Journal* 46 (1992).

Perthes, Volker. "The Syrian Private Industrial and Commercial Sectors and the State." *International Journal of Middle East Studies* 24, no. 2 (May 1992).

Perthes, Volker. "Syria's Parliamentary Elections: Remodeling Asad's Political Base." *MERIP* no. 174 (January–February 1992).

Pfeifer, Karen. "How Tunisia, Morocco, Jordan and Even Egypt Became IMF 'Success Stories' in the 1990s." *MERIP* no. 210 (Spring 1999): 23–27.

Pierson, Paul. "The Limits of Design: Explaining Institutional Origins and Change." *Governance* 13, no. 4 (2000): 475–99.

Polling, Sylvia. "Which Future for the Private Sector?" In *Contemporary Syria: Liberalization Between Cold War and Cold Peace*. Edited by Eberhard Kienle. London: British Academic Press, 1994.

Pool, David. "The Links Between Economic and Political Liberalization." In *Economic and Political Liberalization in the Middle East*. Edited by Tim Niblock and Emma Murphy. London: British Academic Press, 1993.

Powell, Walter W. "Neither Market nor Hierarchy: Network Forms of Organization." *Research in Organizational Behavior* 12 (1990): 295–336.

Powell, Walter W., and Paul Dimaggio, eds. *The New Institutionalism in Organizational Analysis*. Chicago: University of Chicago Press, 1991.

Pratt, Nicola. "Maintaining the Moral Economy: Egyptian State-Labor Relations in an Era of Economic Liberalization." *Arab Studies Journal* 8, no. 2; 9, no. 1 (Fall 2000/ Spring 2001).

Przeworski, Adam. *Democracy and the Market*. New York: Cambridge University Press, 1991.

Putnam, Robert. *Making Democracy Work: Civic Traditions in Modern Italy*. Princeton, NJ: Princeton University Press, 1993.

Rabinovitch, Itamar. *Syria Under the Ba'th, 1963–1966: The Army-Party Symbiosis*. Jerusalem: Israel University Press, 1972.

al-Raddawi, Taisir. "al-Siyasaat al-Muhaffitha lil-Istithmaar fi Suriyya" [Policies that provide incentives for investment in Syria]. Paper no. 10, presented to the annual conference of the Economic Sciences Association, Damascus, Syria, May 22, 2001.

Raphaeli, Nimrod. "Syria's Fragile Economy." *MERIA* 11, no. 2 (June 2007): 42. http://meria.idc.ac.il/journal/2007/issue2/jv11no2a4.html (accessed October 6, 2009).

Reynolds, Clark. "The Political Economy of Interdependence in the Americas." *Asian Journal of Economics and Social Studies* 11, no. 1 (1992).

Richards, Alan. "Economic Pressures for Accountable Governance in the Middle East and North Africa." In *Civil Society in the Middle East*. Edited by Augustus Richard Norton. Vol. 1. New York: E. J. Brill, 1995.

Richards, Alan. "Ten Years of Infitah: Class, Rent, and Policy Stasis in Egypt." *Journal of Development Studies* 20 (July 1984): 323–38.

Richards, Alan, and John Waterbury. "Contradictions of State-Led Growth." In *A Political Economy of the Middle East*. Boulder, CO: Westview Press, 1996, Ch. 8.

Richards, Alan, and John Waterbury. "The Emergence of the Public Sector." In *A Political Economy of the Middle East.* Boulder, CO: Westview Press, 1996, Ch. 7.

Richards, Alan, and John Waterbury. *A Political Economy of the Middle East.* Boulder, CO: Westview Press, 1996.

Richer, Frank-Jurgen. *Business Networks in Asia Promises Doubts and Perspectives.* Westport, CT: Quorum Books, 1999.

Robinson, Glenn E. "Elite Cohesion, Regime Succession and Political Instability in Syria." *Middle East Policy* 5, no. 4 (January 1998).

Robinson, Richard. "Authoritarian States, Capital-Owning Classes, and the Politics of Newly Industrializing Countries: The Case of Indonesia." *World Politics* 41 (1988): 52–74.

Rodrik, Dani. "The Limits of Trade Reform in Developing Countries." *Journal of Economic Perspectives* 6, no. 1 (Winter 1992): 87–105.

Ross, Michael L. "The Political Economy of the Resource Curse." *World Politics* 51 (January 1999): 297–322.

Rothe, Dawn. "Iraq and Halliburton." In *State-Corporate Crime: Wrongdoing at the Intersection of Business and Government.* Edited by Raymond J. Michalowski and Ronald C. Kramer. New Brunswick, NJ: Rutgers University Press, 2006.

Rueschemyer, Dietrich, and Louis Putterman. *State and Market in Development: Synergy or Rivalry?* Boulder, CO: Lynne Rienner, 1992.

Sadowski, Yahya. "Cadres, Guns and Money. The Eighth Regional Congress of the Syrian Ba'th." *MERIP* 15 (July–August 1985).

Sadowski, Yahya. *Political Vegetables: Businessman and Bureaucrat in the Development of Egyptian Agriculture.* Washington, DC: Brookings Institution Press, 1991.

Safadi, Muta'. *Hizb al-Ba'th: Ma'saat al-Mawlid, Ma'saat al-Nihaya* [The Ba'th party: the tragedy of birth, the tragedy of the end]. Beirut: Dar al-Adab, 1964.

Sager, Abdulaziz. "The Private Sector in the Arab World: Road Map Towards Reform." December 10, 2007. www.Arab-Reform.net (accessed September 23, 2008).

Saif, Ibrahim, and Farah Choucair. "Status-Quo Camouflaged: Economic and Social Transformation in Egypt and Jordan." *Middle East Law and Governance* (May 2010).

Saif, Riad. "The Cellular Telephone Contracts" [*Safqat 'Uqud al-Khilyawi*]. Paper presented to the Syrian Parliament, Damascus, August 14, 2001.

Saif, Riad. "al-Tasdir bayna il-Hilm wa-l-Waqi'" [Exports: between dream and reality]. Paper no. 13, presented to the annual conference of the Economic Sciences Association, Damascus, Syria, May 13, 1999.

Salameh, Mahmoud. "al-Idara bil-Ahdaf: ila Ayn?" [Goals-oriented management: where to?]. Paper no. 3, presented to the annual conference of the Economic Sciences Association, Damascus, Syria, February 1, 2000.

Schamis, Hector E. "Distributional Coalitions and the Politics of Economic Reform in Latin America." *World Politics* 51 (January 1999): 236–68.

Schmitter, Philippe C., and Wolfgang Streeck. "Community, Market, State and Associations? The Prospective Contribution of Interest Governance to Social Order." In *Markets, Hierarchies, and Networks: The Coordination of Social Life.* Edited by Graham Thompson, Jennifer Frances, Rosalind Levacic, and Jeremy Mitchell, 227–41. London: Sage, 1991.

Schneider, Ben Ross. "Big Business and the Politics of Economic Reform: Confidence and Concertation in Brazil and Mexico." In *Business and the State in Developing Countries.* Edited by Ben Ross Schneider and Sylvia Maxfield. Ithaca (NY) and London: Cornell University Press, 1997, Ch. 7.

Schneider, Ben Ross. *Business Politics and the State in Twentieth-Century Latin America.* Cambridge, UK: Cambridge University Press, 2004.

Schneider, Ben Ross, and Sylvia Maxfield, eds. *Business and the State in Developing Countries.* Ithaca (NY) and London: Cornell University Press, 1997.

Schneider, Ben Ross, and Sylvia Maxfield. "Business, the State, and Economic Performance in Developing Countries." In *Business and the State in Developing Countries.* Edited by Ben Ross Schneider and Sylvia Maxfield. Ithaca (NY) and London: Cornell University Press, 1997, Ch. 1, Part I.

Schneider, Friedrich. "Dimensions of the Shadow Economy." *Independent Review* 5, no. 1 (2000).

Schneider, Friedrich, and Dominik Enste. *The Shadow Economy: An International Survey.* Cambridge, UK: Cambridge University Press, 2002.

Schwab, Klaus, ed. *The Global Competitiveness Report 2009–2010.* Geneva: World Economic Forum, 2009.

Scott, John. *Social Network Analysis.* London: Sage, 1991.

Seale, Patrick. *Asad: The Struggle for the Middle East.* London: I. B. Tauris, 1988.

Sfakianakis, John. "Whales of the Nile: Networks, Businessmen and Bureaucrats During the Era of Privatization in Egypt." In *Networks of Privilege: The Politics of Economic Reform in the Middle East.* Edited by Steven Heydemann, 77–101. New York: Palgrave–St. Martin's Press, 2004.

Shafer, Michael D. *Winners and Losers: How Sectors Shape the Developmental Prospects of States.* Ithaca, NY: Cornell University Press, 1994.

al-Shallah, Badr al-Din. *Lil-Tarikh wa-l-Thikra, Badr al-Din al-Shallah, Qissat Juhd wa 'Umur* [For history and memory: Badr al-Din al-Shallah, a story of effort and life]. 2nd ed. Damascus: Alif Baa' al-Adeeb Press, 1995.

Shepsle, Kenneth A. "The Political Economy of State Reform—Political to the Core." Working paper archive, University of Michigan, June 10, 1998. http://www.isr.umich .edu/cps/pewpa/1998.htm (accessed October 2009).

Silva, Eduardo. "Business Elites, the State, and Economic Change in Chile." In *Business and the State in Developing Countries.* Edited by Sylvia Maxfield and Ben Ross Schneider. Ithaca (NY) and London: Cornell University Press, 1997.

Silva, Eduardo. "Capitalist Coalitions, the State, and Neoliberal Economic Restructuring in Chile, 1973–1988." *World Politics* 45 (July 1993): 526–59.

Simon, David. "Development Reconsidered: New Directions in Development Thinking." *Geografiska Annaler, Serier B, Human Geography* 79, no. 4 (1997).

Skocpol, Theda. "Bringing the State Back In: Strategies of Analysis in Current Research." In *Bringing the State Back In*. Edited by Theda Skocpol, Peter Evans, and Dietrich Rueschemeyer. New York: Cambridge University Press, 1985.

Skocpol, Theda. "Why I Am a Historical Institutionalist." *Polity* 28, no. 1 (Fall 1995): 106.

Snyder, Richard. "After Neoliberalism: The Politics of Reregulation in Mexico." *World Politics* 51 (January 1999): 173–204.

Soliman, Samer. "Egypt's Political Economy: Unholy Coalition Between Bureaucracy and Business." *Islam Online*, November 13, 2008. http://www.islamonline.net/serv let/Satellite?c=Article_C&cid=1226471419306&pagename=Zone-English-Muslim _Affairs%2FMAELayout (accessed March 2010).

Stallings, Barbara. "International Influence on Economic Policy." In *The Politics of Economic Adjustment International Constraints, Distributive Conflicts and the State*. Edited by Stephen Haggard and Robert R. Kaufman. Princeton, NJ: Princeton University Press, 1992.

State Planning Commission. "10th Five Year Plan." Damascus: State Planning Commission, 2006. www.planning.gov.sy/files/file/FypChapter1En.pdf (accessed October 13, 2009).

Steinberger, Peter J. "Public and Private." *Political Studies* 47, no. 2 (June 1999).

Steinmo, Sven, Kathleen Thelen, and Frank Longstreth. *Structuring Politics: Historical Institutionalism in Comparative Analysis*. Cambridge, UK: Cambridge University Press, 1992.

Sturzenegger, Federico, and Mariano Tommasi, eds. *The Political Economy of Reform*. Cambridge, MA: MIT Press, 1998.

Sukkar, Nabil. "The Crisis of 1986 and Syria's Plan for Reform." In *Contemporary Syria: Liberalization Between Cold War and Cold Peace*. Edited by Eberhard Kienle. London: British Academic Press, 1994.

Sullivan, Denis, and Ilia Harik, eds. *Privatization and Liberalization in the Middle East*. Bloomington: Indiana University Press, 1992.

Syrian Enterprise and Business Center. "Syria's GDP Rose by 7% in 2008." June 1, 2009. http://www.sebcsyria.com/web2008/art.php?art_id=1680 (accessed October 2009).

Syrian Investment Agency. "Important Points in Legislative Degree 8 / Investment Promotion." http://www.syriainvestmentmap.org/english/8&9.htm (accessed August 13, 2009).

Tabler, Andrew. "The High Road to Damascus: Engaging Syria's Private Sector." *Stanley Foundation Policy Analysis Brief*, August 2007, 3. http://www.stanleyfoundation.org /publications/pab/Tabler_PAB_807.pdf (accessed October 2009).

Tapscott, Don, and David Ticoll. *The Naked Corporation: How the Age of Transparency Will Revolutionize Business.* New York: Free Press, 2003.

Thompson, Graham, Jennifer Frances, Rosalind Levacic, and Jeremy Mitchell, eds. *Markets, Hierarchies, and Networks: The Coordination of Social Life.* London: Sage, 1991.

Tignor, Robert L. *State, Private Enterprise, and Economic Change in Egypt, 1918–1952.* Princeton, NJ: Princeton University Press, 1984, 246–52.

United Nations Conference on Trade and Development. "World Investment Report 2009: Transnational Corporations, Agricultural Production and Development." New York and Geneva: United Nations, 2009.

United Nations Development Programme. "The First National Competitiveness Report of the Syrian Economy." 2007, p. 89. http://www.undp.org.sy/files/Competitiveness %20Report %20.pdf (accessed September 23, 2009).

United Nations Development Programme. "al-Taqrir al-Watani al-Istishraafi al-Asaasi al-Awwal li-Mashrou' Sourya 2025" [The first basic prospective national report for the Syria 2025 Project]. United Nations Development Programme, Syria, 2008.

US Department of Treasury. "Rami Makhluf Designated for Benefiting from Syrian Corruption." *Press Room.* February 21, 2008. http://www.ustreas.gov/press/releases /hp834.htm.

Van Dam, Nikolaos. *The Struggle for Power in Syria: Sectarianism, Regionalism, and Tribalism in Politics, 1961–1980.* London: Croom Helm, 1981.

Vitalis, Robert. "Imagining Capitalists: Ideologies of Class and Client in Egyptian Political Economy." *al-Jadal* 1 (1991): 54–83.

Vitalis, Robert. "On the Theory and Practice of Compradors: The Role of 'Abbud Pasha in the Egyptian Political Economy." *International Journal of Middle East Studies* 22 (1990): 291–315.

Vitalis, Robert. *When Capitalists Collide: Business Conflict and the End of Empire in Egypt.* Berkeley: University of California Press, 1999.

Wade, Robert. "East Asia's Economic Success: Conflicting Perspectives, Partial Insights, Shaky Evidence." *World Politics* 44 (January 1992): 270–320.

Wade, Robert. *Governing the Market: Economic Theory and the Role of Government in East Asian Industrialization.* Princeton, NJ: Princeton University Press, 1990.

Waldner, David. *State Building and Late Development.* Ithaca, NY: Cornell University Press, 1999.

Wallerstein, Immanuel. "The Bourgeois(ie) as Concept and Reality." *New Left Review* 167 (January–February 1988): 91–106.

Wasserman, Stanley, and Katherin Faust. *Social Network Analysis: Methods and Applications.* Cambridge, UK: Cambridge University Press, 1994.

Wasserman, Stanley, and Joseph Galaskiewicz, eds. *Advances in Social Network Analysis: Research in the Social and Behavioral Sciences.* Thousand Oaks, CA: Sage, 1994.

Waterbury, John. "Coalition Management." In *Fragile Coalitions: The Politics of Eco-*

nomic Adjustment. Edited by Joan Nelson. Washington, DC: Overseas Development Council, 1989.

Waterbury, John. *The Egypt of Nasser and Sadat: The Political Economy of Two Regimes.* Princeton, NJ: Princeton University Press, 1983.

Waterbury, John. "The Heart of the Matter? Public Enterprise and the Adjustment Process." In *The Politics of Economic Adjustment.* Edited by Stephen Haggard and Robert Kaufman. Washington, DC: Overseas Development Council, 1989.

Waterbury, John. "The Political Management of Economic Adjustment and Reform." In *Fragile Coalitions: The Politics of Economic Adjustment.* Edited by Joan Nelson. Washington, DC: Overseas Development Council, 1989.

Waterbury, John. "The Private Sector: Out of the Shadows." In *The Egypt of Nasser and Sadat: The Political Economy of Two Regimes.* Princeton, NJ: Princeton University Press, 1983, Ch. 8.

Waterbury, John. "The State Bourgeoisie and Its Allies." In *The Egypt of Nasser and Sadat: The Political Economy of Two Regimes.* Princeton, NJ: Princeton University Press, 1983.

Waterbury, John. "Twilight of the State Bourgeoisie." *International Journal of Middle East Studies* 23 (1991).

Wedeen, Lisa. *Ambiguities of Domination: Politics, Rhetoric, and Symbols in Contemporary Syria.* Chicago: University of Chicago Press, 1999.

Wellman, Barry, and S. D. Berkowitz, eds. *Social Structures: A Network Approach.* Cambridge, UK: Cambridge University Press, 1988.

Williams, Robert. "Editorial: The New Politics of Corruption." *Third World Quarterly* 20, no. 3 (1999): 487–89.

Williamson, Oliver E. "Calculativeness, Trust, and Economic Organization." *Journal of Law and Economics* 36 (1993): 453–86.

Williamson, Oliver E. *Markets and Hierarchies: Analysis and Antitrust Implications.* New York: Free Press, 1975.

Williamson, Oliver E. *The Mechanisms of Governance.* New York: Oxford University Press, 1996.

World Bank. "Syrian Investment Climate Assessment: Unlocking the Potential of the Private Sector." Rep. 36673. In *Private Sector, Financial Sector and Infrastructure Group, Middle East and North Africa Region,* Syria, 2005, 22–23.

Wright, Robin. "Sanctions on Businessman Target Syria's Inner Sanctum, U.S. Action Alleges Corruption." *Washington Post,* February 22, 2008, World section. http://www.washingtonpost.com/wpdyn/content/article/2008/02/21/AR2008022102839.html.

Wurzel, Ulrich. "Patterns of Resistance." In *Networks of Privilege: The Politics of Economic Reform in the Middle East.* Edited by Steven Heydemann. New York: Palgrave–St. Martin's Press, 2004.

Zaalouk, Malak. *Power, Class, and Foreign Capital in Egypt: The Rise of the New Bourgeoisie.* London: Zed Press, 1989.

Zaman, Constantin. "Quantifying the Excess Supply of Labor in the Syrian Economy." *Social Science Research Network* (January 2007): 8. http://ssrn.com/abstract=959967 (accessed September 23, 2009).

Zorob, Anja. "An Agreement Surrounded by Uncertainty." *Syria Today*, March 2009. http://www.syria-today.com/index.php?option=com_content&view=article&id=608:an-agreement-surrounded-by-uncertainty&catid=75:business-features&Itemid=49 (accessed March 2009).

al-Zuhairi, Bashir. "Ta'hil al-Nithaam al-Masrifi fi Suriyya li-Talbiyat Ihtiyajaat al-Tanmiya al-Iqtisaadiyya" [Improving the banking system in Syria to satisfy the needs of economic development]. Paper no. 3, presented to the annual conference of the Economic Sciences Association, Damascus, Syria, March 2, 1999.

Zukin, Sharon, and Paul DiMaggio, eds. *Structures of Capital: The Social Organization of the Economy.* Cambridge, UK: Cambridge University Press, 1990.

INDEX

Italic page numbers indicate figures or tables.

Stanford Studies in Middle Eastern and Islamic Societies and Cultures

Joel Beinin, *Stanford University*

Juan R. I. Cole, *University of Michigan*

Editorial Board

Asef Bayat, *University of Illinois at Urbana-Champaign*

Marilyn Booth, *University of Edinburgh*

Laurie Brand, *University of Southern California*

Saba Mahmood, *University of California, Berkeley*

Timothy Mitchell, *New York University*

Karen Pfeifer, *Smith College*

Rebecca L. Stein, *Duke University*

Noah Coburn, *Bazaar Politics: Conflict, Violence, and Political Relationships in an Afghan Market Town*
2011

Laura Bier, *Revolutionary Womanhood: Feminisms, Modernity, and the State in Nasser's Egypt*
2011

Joel Beinin and Frédéric Vairel, editors, *Social Movements, Mobilization, and Contestation in the Middle East and North Africa*
2011

Samer Soliman, *The Autumn of Dictatorship: Fiscal Crisis and Political Change in Egypt under Mubarak*
2011

Rochelle A. Davis, *Palestinian Village Histories: Geographies of the Displaced*
2010

Haggai Ram, *Iranophobia: The Logic of an Israeli Obsession*
2009

John Chalcraft, *The Invisible Cage: Syrian Migrant Workers in Lebanon*
2008

Rhoda Kanaaneh, *Surrounded: Palestinian Soldiers in the Israeli Military*
2008

Asef Bayat, *Making Islam Democratic: Social Movements and the Post-Islamist Turn*
2007

Robert Vitalis, *America's Kingdom: Mythmaking on the Saudi Oil Frontier*
2006

Jessica Winegar, *Creative Reckonings: The Politics of Art and Culture in Contemporary Egypt*
2006

Joel Beinin and Rebecca L. Stein, editors, *The Struggle for Sovereignty: Palestine and Israel, 1993–2005*
2006

CPSIA information can be obtained
at www.ICGtesting.com
Printed in the USA
LVOW10s2158040517

533267LV00002B/453/P

9 780804 785068